The Development of
WEST INDIES CRICKET

Soon we must take a side
or be left in the rubble

In a divided world that don't need islands no more,
Are we doomed for ever to be at somebody's mercy?

Little keys can open up mighty doors
Rally round the West Indies now and for ever.

David Rudder: "Rally Round the West Indies"

The Development of
WEST INDIES CRICKET

Volume 1
The Age of Nationalism

Hilary McD Beckles

The

PRESS
University of the West Indies
Barbados • Jamaica • Trinidad and Tobago

Pluto Press
London • Sterling, Virginia

The Press University of the West Indies
1A Aqueduct Flats Mona
Kingston 7 Jamaica
ISBN 976–640–064–4 (The Press UWI)

Published simultaneously in England by
Pluto Press
345 Archway Road
London N6 5AA England
ISBN 0–7453–1467–8 (hb Pluto Press)
ISBN 0–7453–1462–7 (pb Pluto Press)

Printed in England

02 01 00 99 98   5 4 3 2 1

CATALOGUING IN PUBLICATION DATA (UWI)

Beckles, Hilary McD., 1955–
The development of West Indies cricket / Hilary McD. Beckles.

v. cm.
Contents: v. 1. The age of nationalism – v. 2. The age of globalization
Includes bibliographical references and index.
ISBN 976-640-064-4 (v. 1)
ISBN 976-640-065-2 (v. 2)

1. Cricket – West Indies – History. 2. Cricket – West Indies – Social aspects.3. Cricket players – West
Indies. 4. Cricket managers – West Indies. 5. Cricket captains – West Indies. 6. Nationalism and
sports. I. Title. II. Title: The Age of Nationalism. III. Title: The Age of Globalization.

GV928W47 B53 1998   796.35'865 dc-20

Set in 9.5 on 14 pt Georgia with Fritz headlines
Book design and composition Jenni R. Anderson
Cover design Robert Harris
Cover photo used with the kind permission of the Nation Publishing Company, Barbados

The photographs used in this book are from the author's personal collection except
otherwise acknowledged

For
My friend and comrade Michael 'Joshua' Manley
who "stood firm" and did the best he could for his time

To
George Challenor, Learie Constantine, George Headley, Frank Worrell,
Gary Sobers, Rohan Kanhai, Clive Lloyd and Viv Richards
who revolutionized our cricket culture

In celebration of
Toussaint L'Ouverture, Bussa, Fedon, Sam Sharpe, Samuel Jackman Prescod, Nanny,
Paul Bogle, Marcus Garvey, C.L.R. James, Fidel Castro, Franz Fanon, José Martí,
Clement Payne, Bob Marley, Eric Williams, George Lamming, Rex Nettleford, Walter
Rodney, Kamau Brathwaite, Elsa Goveia, Alister McIntyre, Maurice Bishop
Dame Nita Barrow, Lucille Mair, Orlando Patterson, Mighty Gabby,
David Rudder, George Beckford, Austin Clarke
and all the others . . .

Contents

List of Illustrations and Tables

Tables

Preface

For me, the matter was settled in 1965. I sat in the Schoolboys' Stand at Kensington Oval and watched the Aussies pile up a massive 650 for 6 declared in the fourth Test. When Bob Simpson's off-stump was ripped out of the ground by a Wes Hall in-swinger for 201 my heart stood still for 'an hour' because, it seemed, I had anticipated the event. The West Indies' response of 573 was unacceptable – Kanhai's 129 and Nurse's 201 notwithstanding – and I wished terribly for my own piece of the action in defence of West Indies honour. Sobers scored what was a mere 55 in the first innings, but when he drove McKenzie down the wicket for four the shot etched a mark on my memory, and I knew then precisely where I was heading.

The following year, I set out from Rock Hall, the village of my birth, in the deep, rural parish of St Andrew in Barbados, to enter secondary school, two months before the epic drama of the country's attainment of national independence. Among my first educational discoveries, despite the maze that followed exposure to Virgil's Latin prose, was the realization that like me all boys of my generation had but one dream – to be a Gary Sobers, a Wes Hall, a Conrad Hunte, a Rohan Kanhai, a Lance Gibbs, or a Jackie Hendricks. My strategic response to peer competition was that if I did enough of all things in the game something would certainly develop. Everton Weekes was our coach, and Wes Hall my hero, and everything I thought was going well – and to plan.

At age 16, the instability of my new dispensation transformed the concreteness of my core concept. My world was turned upside down in 1971 on a cold, snowy Saturday morning at the Edgbaston Test ground in Warwickshire, England. I was still in secondary school but in the city of Birmingham where I had migrated three years earlier to join my parents after ten years of loving exile with grandparents – a typical West Indian working class experience. By this time I was considered a nippy little pacer, reasonably safe in the slips, and a useful number four with the bat for the Warwickshire County Schoolboys team. The morning in question, Derrief Taylor, my coach, a former Jamaican/West Indies player, came over to me in the indoor school and asked that I take a turn to face Lance Gibbs who had been giving Rohan Kanhai a workout in the nets.

What a nightmare! Gibbs' first three balls banged into the metal off-stump as I tried to caress the flighted off-breaks through the extra-cover position. I did everything correctly. I was confident, my feet moved, eyes tracked the drift, but the ball did mysterious, magical things. The noise behind me was unbearable. One moment the ball was there, then it was not, and I was stroking air as if conducting an orchestra.

My father was as cool as all tailors are. He received my unnerving story like a stoic. Well, he said, you better finish the 'A' Levels and go off to university and find some other useful *thing* to do with your future. While the household pondered the meaning of the financial loss of the investment it had made in my cricket gear, I decided, almost tearfully, that for me the rational, commonsense path was in the direction indicated by my 'old man'. And so I did; I trundled off to Hull University and emerged six years later as an apprentice professional historian. Lance Gibbs is now a friend, but I have not forgiven him, and I have told him so a million times. Each time he grins and pats me on the back.

When I met Viv Richards a few years later, and we became comrades, little did he know that I had exorcized my desire to be a West Indies cricketer through the soothing therapy of observing close up his exploits in Test and county cricket. He was magnificent; the most destructive batsman I ever saw. Respectful of opposing arguments, I concluded then in 1980 that he was the best batsman against all types of bowling; I still believe this, and so does Imran Khan – he said so.

I took up my pen instead, and began what, hopefully, will be a lifelong project of researching, writing and teaching the history of West Indies cricket. In 1992, I introduced a course in West Indies cricket history, from 1820 to the present, at the University of the West Indies (UWI), and established the Centre for Cricket Research (CCR) two years later. The CCR has arranged public lectures in honour of Sir Gary and Viv, and organizes the annual Sir Frank Worrell Memorial Lecture. Through the UWI, the CCR is seeking to develop and maintain a close conversation with West Indies cricket at all levels.

Every single run counts; this is the philosophy that guides the thinking and programmes of the CCR. In 1995, we conceived and developed with the West

Indies Cricket Board (WICB) the Vice Chancellor's XI match which is played annually against all touring Test teams. The project has been a great success, starting with the clash against New Zealand at Sabina Park in 1995. One objective of the game is to raise scholarship money for the Sir Frank Worrell Student Fund; another is to strengthen the bond between sport and education, between the UWI and WICB – the two oldest regional institutions committed to the process of West Indian sociopolitical integration.

In all of this, I have come to realize the extent of my hopeless addiction to West Indies cricket culture, expressed in many ways, but most obviously in my following the West Indies team to distant parts of the world. But, that is how it is. Over the years, I have been encouraged and 'spoilt' in my passions by several persons. This writing and research project has exposed me to many supportive minds. Joey Carew, Alloy Lequay, Gerry Gomez, Peter Short, Arnold McIntyre, Willie Rodriguez, Rangy Nanan, Rex Fennell, Maurice Foster, Michael Holding, Tony Becca, Pat Rousseau, Baldwin Mootoo, Tony Marshall, Wes Hall, Joseph 'Reds' Perreira, Gary Sobers, Everton Weekes, Rawle Branker, Andy Roberts, Vaneisa Baksh, Tim Hector, and many others have been supportive and kind.

I must pay special tribute to the patience, encouragement and support of my wife, Mary, who single parented our children while I researched and wrote this text. The writing of this book drew upon the skills and patience of other persons who were called upon to assist with a range of production issues. Grace Franklin and Camileta Neblett, my secretaries, did what was asked of them, and more, much more. To them I am deeply indebted. Sandra Taylor assisted with the typing, and Tony Cozier was harassed with requests for information; I thank them for their support. Special thanks go also to Mervyn 'Pee Wee' Wong who read the manuscript and checked the statistics.

Conversations with Michael Manley, Woodville Marshall, Tim Hector, Wes Hall, Joey Carew and David Holford offered insights into a range of complex issues. The scholarship of C.L.R. James, Keith Sandiford, Michael Manley, Tony Cozier, Brian Stoddart, Frank Birbalsingh, Mike Marqusee and Christine Cummings has helped to shape the contours, if not the contents, of my thinking, and I am very appreciative.

I have not set out to write a book that deals directly with players' careers or their statistical expressions. My concern is with the political meaning and the social process of cricket culture beyond the boundary. In effect, I wish to extend the debate on cricket, national society, and nationalism initiated by C.L.R. James into the age of globalization. I have taken quite a liberty indeed, but it has been a journey to self-discovery and heightened awareness of the 'future in the present'.

The decision to publish the text in two volumes came as a result of several critical comments. The point was made forcefully that two analytically distinct discourses are represented, and should be separated for comfortable engagement. While Volume 1 deals chronologically with aspects of the social history of cricket culture, paying close attention to the empirical evidence, Volume 2 departs aggressively into conceptual discussions and theoretical projections. The nature of these departures cannot be divorced from the social history; rather, they justify the importance of the historical evidence as an organized body of knowledge that works to offer insights into the future.

I am aware that some readers may find parts of the text rather judgmental of the future, and certainly too critical of the present. Others might find it rather gloomy within the context of the status quo. But as an historian my role is to discern future trends from past and present patterns. Ultimately, my simple wish is that the provoked reader may continue the assessment having added at least a single run to the score.

I love this game; and so do my two sons, Rodney and Biko. Ambitions can never be inherited, and so my desire for them is that they find a way in the years ahead to add and extract the maximum from an association with it. The cricket culture of their time is conceived here as shaped by the 'third paradigm' – the age of globalization. The 'third rising' in West Indies cricket is the mandate of their generation. I hope that they will be able to give their best for their time.

University of the West Indies
Cave Hill, Barbados

Introduction

For Rex Nettleford cricket culture is the vehicle on which West Indians journeyed deepest into modernity. It is a perspective that raises important questions about what they have made of Enlightenment idealism. If the West, as C.L.R. James has argued, was invented in the space that is now called the Caribbean, then what its inhabitants have done with cricket within western discourse should speak to its social history as 'modernity in action'. It is a splendidly provoking narrative that invokes a range of objective interpretations. Biographies represent signposts along the way, and it is through them that we come to learn about cricket as historical process.

Modernity in action is an efficient conceptual conflation of the endless energies generated by a thousand cricket journeys that converge on the place now described as national freedom. The story of each phase of history points to the spirit of emergence, of liberation, and cultural creativity of West Indian people. The cricketer in the colonial context, resisting ideological hegemony, represents these forces, and more. He confirms at once the instability and viability of the social order, and with each contest validates the necessity of conflict in securing the future and consolidating the present. These are not contradictory currents. Rather, they call for a recognition of cricket culture as a contested terrain on which possible futures were identified as discernible products of social progress. The journey to a West Indian modernity, then, is charted in the countless moments and movements which we know to typify the culture that is cricket.

There are no great stories; only great moments and storytellers. The one that runs through the valley of this text greatly disfigured my young mind and broke an important friendship. A close school friend told it with a tone of unreal detachment and a definitely disturbing air of indifference. We were in fifth grade in a secondary school in Birmingham, England, where the children of West Indian immigrants, and marginalized natives, were thrown together – off the streets to acquire in the semi-formal setting the 'basic minimum'. I had asked him to accompany me to Egbaston to watch the match between England and a Rest of the World team. Recently arrived from Barbados, it was an opportunity for me to examine Gary Sobers in action, one more time but in a foreign place. Would he leave behind his Caribbean style and wear a stiff upper lip? Would these people here know what it was that he represented back home leading the whole world against the former owners of most of it? I was anxious and conveyed this state in all my expression as the bus curled its way through the suburbs towards the ground.

None of this anxiety made an impression on my companion. You see, he didn't understand. In fact, he couldn't understand, because his circumstance was altogether quite different. But we were together, or so it seemed. I was a Barbadian immigrant of two years' vintage, but he, much to his immigrant parents' surprise, and dismay, was born hurriedly on local land. For him, his story was a meaningless tale that spoke of the perversity and irrationality of a Caribbean peasant who did not know how to conduct himself in a metropole. He distanced himself from the tale because for a reason he could not understand, his father and himself were poles apart in the metropole.

His father, you see, had kept the framed photograph on the mantlepiece above the fireplace for 20 years. It was 1970, and he had watched his father wipe and smile at it all his life and had assumed that it was a picture taken on his wedding day. Dressed in a black tuxedo – fully loaded with hat, gloves, and cane – his father looked out over his drawing room as aristocrats survey inherited or stolen land. There was a certain elevation of the chin, a flaring of the nostrils, and the gulping of fresh air. Two days before the game he managed somehow to ask his father why his mother wasn't a part of the photograph, and why he smiled at it with such satisfaction despite his seemingly unhappy marriage. His father had been driving the buses of the West Midlands Transport Board from his arrival in England, and had no intention of following any other profession. That morning he was running late, so to speak, and had indicated to an anxious son that he would explain on his return from work in the early evening.

It wasn't a wedding photograph at all, and his mother had walked out on her husband for a week over the entire matter. Well, his father said, that portrait resting there, represents the greatest, most fulfilling day of my life. It was taken the day after the West Indies defeated England at Lord's in 1950 – 29 June 1950 to be exact – and by 326 runs. "Winning the series 3–1, the first time we beat them wasn't the big thing. It was Lord's, son – going in to their own backyard and taking their chickens out of the coop and frying them on the front lawn. For me son, the empire collapse right there; not Churchill or Wellington could bring it back. Shackles were gone, and we were free at last because the chickens were out of the coop."

The following day, 30 June, his father had rented the tuxedo, fully loaded, and had worn it to work to drive the West Midland Transport Board's bus through the streets of Birmingham. The photograph was taken by a professional photographer, a passenger on the bus, who requested that the driver pull up his bus in front of his premises in order to seize the moment. Twenty copies were made, 19 of which were posted to friends back home (one of which appeared in the *Barbados Advocate News* to the embarrassment of family). The rental was £2.10s out of the week's salary, and that is why his wife had left him for the week, and took every opportunity to turn the picture down.

My friend, on hearing the story, closed ranks with his mother (a Nigerian) and broke with his father and, by extension, with me, his good friend. Certainly, I could not consort with someone who 'read' his father as 'mad' at the seminal moment of his deliverance. Nothing was said about this matter for the remainder of the school term, but I knew that we would part company, and that he wouldn't understand. The movement from colonialism to nationhood is a journey that has been told in many a text, but none for me as clearly as in the bus driver's photograph.

Popular writers of cricket have succeeded in establishing a literary hegemony that emphasizes the exciting, flamboyant, aggressive, artful and energetic aspects of West Indies' styles and methods. This text, however, does none of these things. Rather, it seeks to analyse the historical evolution of the social features and ideological expressions of the region's cricket by indicating its specific colonial and anticolonial cultural imperatives. It takes as its point of departure the central paradigm around which an impressive body of recent literature revolves. That is, the debate which seeks to explore the extent to which West Indies cricket has strengthened the reproductive capacity of a colonized mentality or has functioned as an ideological weapon of a subversive, anticolonial, creole nationalism.

In seeking out the central ideological pulse of West Indies cricket culture, the question is asked: what did the imported/imposed Victorian cricket ethic do to or for West Indians, and what in turn did these ethnic groups do to or for it? Answers address the specific forms of cricket domestication by colonials, and indicate that whites and blacks established their own different traditions within the indigenization process. The hegemonic tradition was that of the white, élite, planter–merchant communities that expressed a distinctive subservient ideological stance in relation to empire, and was fully committed to the importance of white supremacy attitudes within it. The initially subordinate black tradition emitted all the cultural characteristics of an alienated, marginalized subtype seeking to establish itself in the little space made available to it. Both indigenous forms developed simultaneously, but were kept apart by the potency of an officially enforced social policy of racial segregation.

West Indies cricket, then, like all other aspects of sociocultural life, eventually displayed the consequences of a racially fractured nationalism that threatened the movement towards nationhood in the era of dying English colonialism. Not every one agrees with this view. It has been suggested, for example, that by the end of the nineteenth century when cricket became the region's leading expression of popular culture, its inner logic, methods, moral codes and aesthetics, were no longer shaped by the political ideologies of ethnic relations. The truth of the matter, however, is that by this time cricket, unlike any other form of community interaction, reflected the deepest ideological thoughts of colonials, and suggested the conflicting nature of ethnic and class interests. This meant, of course, that from its early days cricket in the West Indies functioned as an agency of colonial oppression and at the same time provided an area in which the socially oppressed majority ventilated endemic, antisystemic attitudes and ideals.

Dialectical analysis best explains the dichotomous development of the social culture of West Indies cricket. The élite colonial community saw in cricket a zone of exclusive cultural activity consistent with its social and ideological outlook. Blacks, Asians, and other oppressed ethnic minorities – the Chinese in particular – in turn saw this space as one on which they could gradually encroach without incurring severe penalties, but at the same time promote actions of a powerful symbolic nature designed to further the cause of the democratic revolution initiated by antislavery legislation.

West Indies cricket, therefore, was born, raised and socialized within the fiery cauldron of colonial oppression and social protest In its mature form it is essentially an ideological and politicized species and knows no world better than that of liberation struggle. No one has written about this process with as much intellectual rigour and literary sophistication as C.L.R. James. That is why he was able to disguise effectively his masterful examination of West Indies cricket culture as a semi-autobiography and political history of the modern region. Several distinguished scholars have engaged C.L.R. James's work in the past decade. The research of Keith Sandiford and Brian Stoddart deserves special mention. In many respects, this text is a response to this body of sound and provocative scholarship. The issues of creolization, cultural domestication and the emergence of popular culture bind together the diversity of these works. When, how, and why cricket culture found its way into the West Indies is debated in such a way as to disclose its ideological luggage and chart the path of its precise mission.

The imported brand of Victorian cricket was transformed into a vehicle of the nascent democratizing nationalist order. The infusion into its core values of a range of subaltern expressions and expectations resulted in the 'carnivalization' of crowd responses, which in turn became a barometer of political consciousness and a promoter of antisystemic ideology. The text offers a sociological comment on the process whereby cricket was creolized, politicized and ritualized within the context of the region's radical anticolonial tradition.

Ethnicity and mass politics provided the social and ideological mechanics of Caribbean race relations and determined the manner in which the cricket culture, already a carrier of imperialistic attitudes and values about 'natives', was further transformed by ideologies found 'beyond the boundary'. Cricket was both a mirror and an arena that allowed ethnic groups to display, defend and define differences and similarities within the format of civic respectability and nonviolent protest. I have tried to reflect the ethnic differences that divided West Indian nationalism, in spite of a concerted rhetorical effort to promote a nonracial meritocracy. Also, I have tried to examine how nationalism and liberation found popular expression within the social praxis of cricket, and therefore secured for itself a prominent place in the making and design of the modern society. That cricket constitutes the first and most popular forum in which West Indies human resources were brought together for regional development remains a powerful historical fact filled with significance for the future. James's classic explanation of how the struggle for popular leadership under Frank Worrell in 1958–59 was organized demonstrates with clarity the political seductiveness of the game within the democratic ethos. That debate is a useful place to begin an explanation of why, within these small nation states, cricket culture transcends institutional politics in the process of nationalist self-perceptions.

I also explore, in an archaeological sort of way, the cultural materials embedded within the cricket world that, when excavated by sensitive artists, yield fascinating sources for the creative imagination. In the West Indies the term 'cricket' is, perhaps, more appropriate than 'metaphor' – certainly in terms of the influence of the game upon language, popular art and literature. In this context C.L.R. James stands as a monument to the 'intellectualization' of popular culture. James, however, had overstated the impact of the Graeco-Roman literary and theatrical tradition upon West Indies cricket; here, I went in search of its African and Asian social cosmology by examining the nature of the 'crowd' and its relationship to the literary and performing arts.

A concept of West Indian history, therefore, seems the appropriate place to begin a search for the internal motion and ideological meaning of the cricket culture. Here we assert, with reference to a notion of what is the *essence*, that no matter how many times and how many ways we toss the coin of West Indian history, more often than not it comes down on the side of resistance rather than accommodation. The implication of this view is clear, certainly with respect to the issue of popular consciousness and political action. It says, principally, that though the experiences of West Indian people have been shaped by the need to come to terms with powerful hegemonic, colonial and imperialist structures and ideas, their essential response has been one of antisystemic resistances. Whether it was during the period of the Amerindian-European encounter, or the subsequent slavery epoch, the majority of West Indian inhabitants have sought to define their own existence in terms of an appropriation of space that could be autonomously manipulated in the building of discrete realities of freedom. Cricket, then, became enmeshed in all these considerations, and represents an ideological and cultural terrain on which this very intensive battle is fought. This is precisely why we can confirm that the cricket history of the region is but a mirror within which its modern social undertakings can be examined and assessed.

List of Abbreviations

ANC	African National Congress
Av.	Average
BBC	British Broadcasting Corporation
BCA	Barbados Cricket Association
BEGF	British Empire Games Federation
BOP	*Boy's Own Paper*
CANA	Caribbean News Agency
CC	Cricket Club
CCR	Centre for Cricket Research
CWCF	Caribbean Women's Cricket Conference
ICC	International Cricket Conference
IWCC	International Women's Cricket Council
JCBC	Jamaica Cricket Board of Control
JWCA	Jamaica Women's Cricket Association
KSAC	Kingston and St Andrew Corporation
MCC	Marylebone Cricket club
QRC	Queen's Royal College
SACCB	South African Coloured Cricket Board
SACU	South African Cricket Union
UWI	University of the West Indies
WICB	West Indies Cricket Board
WICBC	West Indies Cricket Board of Control

1

West Indian Embrace of Englishness

Garrisons and Slave Plantations

There was nothing spectacular or surprising about the journey of English cricket culture to the 'sugar colonies' of the West Indies at the end of the eighteenth century. Defeating Napoleon's West India project required the deployment of thousands of 'gentlemen' officers and their troops about the islands. These soldiers entertained themselves with bats and leather balls within garrisons while taking respite from hurling cannon balls at the French. It all developed in the heat of war as representatives of conflicting nationalisms fought bloody battles in pursuit of the national interest.

The West Indies, long a main theatre of globalized conflict and rivalry, embraced cricket with a combative intensity that speaks to its military origins. Commandants welcomed the game, and with their cousins on the plantations, built an ethnic wall around it. Wars between the English and French soon gave way to cricket battles between English colonists and their imperial protectors. After defeating the French in 1815, both groups set out to exclude 'their' Africans, and mixed race subordinates, from the game that seemed to fascinate them all. Cricket became the centre of a postslavery culture war that saw ethnic contests in a most sophisticated civil form.

Undoubtedly, the introduction of cricket within the nineteenth century West Indian world is reflective of much of what was taking place within the British imperial sphere.[1] The West Indian colonies constituted a specific territorial space that had been on the receiving end of transatlantic cultural inputs for over three centuries. The nature of this exchange was determined by the colonial nexus that placed European cultural expressions in a dominant relation to other forms. The Africanization of things English, however, was also a feature of the process known as West Indianization. The creole formation within which nineteenth century cultural institutions emerged and evolved, therefore, was determined by intense forces of cross-cultural and intercultural fertilization. In this sense, then, the social making of West Indies cricket is a history shaped by dialectical processes of conflict and co-option.

In addition, importance should be attached to the sense of spatial ordering and cultural movement intrinsic to the periphery-centre paradigm that informs world-system theory. If, however, such a construct can explain the presence of cricket within the culture zone of plantation West Indies, doubt must be raised about its further usefulness in assessing the specifications of its internal logic and value system. The plantation society paradigm, on the other hand, departs from here and provides an incisive conceptual instrument in the search of sociological insights.

Distinguished cricket historians, such as the late C.L.R. James, Brian Stoddart, Frank Birbalsingh and Keith Sandiford, have established that imperial cricket culture arrived laden with coded philosophical messages conducive to the furtherance of empire building.[2] In addition, they have indicated that the nineteenth century witnessed the début of mass sport as part of the leisure culture of the work oriented plantation ethos. From these perspectives it is possible to argue that cricket was introduced into the West Indies and projected in particular ways because it represented the latest and principal form of imperial cultural technology. World-systems theory indicates that it was essentially an agent of empire sent into the field as a politicized cultural protector of England's share of the spoils of global capitalism. From this perspective its mission was to consolidate the view that 'high' culture emanated only from the centre from whence the ideology of white supremacy came.

Given the contents of its mission statement, the success of cricket over the duration of the century was remarkably swift. It penetrated first the insecure and dependent cultural world of the propertied white creole élite who embraced it as a celebration of the tight, unbroken bond between themselves and their metropolitan 'cousins'. For this élite it served all intended purposes; particularly, it assisted in the social elevation of its members above 'uncivilized' indigenes who lacked proper access to, or an informed appreciation of, things 'English'. By mid century it was clear that cricket was at once an instrument of imperial cultural authority as well as a weapon of class and race domination within a plantation civilization that still clung to the fabric of a dying slavery ethos.

There is nothing particularly phenomenal about this process. The white West Indian colonial community was a dependent one that looked towards the imperial centre as the source for all normative values and institutional edifices. From the seventeenth century it had been weaned upon an increasingly unconvincing cultural diet of imported 'Englishness' that required sanction by the colonial state in order to ensure its legitimacy. Cultural dependency, of course, came hand in hand with mercantile economic dependency which ultimately blunted the edge of the nascent eighteenth century creole proto-nationalism that offered, at best, a token gesture of support to American political and cultural revolutionary independence.

Cricket, then, imported into most West Indian territories by the beginning of the nineteenth century, and carrying the 'made in England' hallmark, was marketed and consumed as a refined élite product in much the same way as was 'high church' Anglicanism, which also explains in part the kinship-like bond that was forged between them. Within the recipient plantation world, cricket helped to reaffirm existing race/class divisions of labour while at the same time it reassured supporters of empire that the central purpose of colonies in the industrial age was to consume with satisfaction things English. It was not relevant from the colonizers' viewpoint that such an unashamed level of mindless consumption would provide ideological evidence of colonial philistinism. Cricket, for them, fitted well into the existing scheme of things. Ships went out from the colonies carrying material products and vessels returned partly filled with cultural products, the value of which was such that one need look no further for evidence of the unequal exchange endemic to the nineteenth century capitalist world system.

An Institution of High Culture

Within this framework the colonial élite moved swiftly to canonize organized cricket within its definition of what constituted advanced culture. The earliest pioneers of the game intimated that it was part of the cultural tradition of the English gentry, and that the corresponding colonial class merely inherited what was logically theirs by right of ancestry. Cricket by the mid nineteenth century, had become part of the colonial élite's chest of 'customs' – the ultimate and most concrete status social and cultural activity could acquire within a given formation.

In the promotion and legitimization of cricket as an institution of high culture, and in the process integrating it within the wider system of imperial oppression, the colonial élite also succeeded in establishing a cultural sphere within which the antisystemic resistance of disenfranchised blacks would be assured. The logical progression of this conflict created the circumstances within which the exclusive activity of the élite was appropriated subsequently by subordinate social groups. The downward social mobility of cricket into

3

the villages of workers was guaranteed as long as the élite ascribed to it the normative values of respectability and honour, since the frantic search for betterment by this 'semi-free' population involved the attainment of these social goals. As the West Indian colonial élite basked unashamedly in imperial cultural mimicry, therefore, it also established a framework of oppositional behaviour for its subjected and dishonoured minions.

It was only a matter of time before the twin forces of cultural/demographic creolization and civil rights struggles coalesced to promote cricket as a popular transracial cultural expression. The desire of coloured and black communities to play cricket their own way seemed to have grown in direct proportion to the white élite's determination to establish it as the exclusive sport of the propertied, the educated, and the 'well bred'. By mid century, versions of the game were being played and celebrated at all levels of society. It is debatable whether the blacks and coloureds 'loved' it simply because the white élite did, or whether in the absence of other mass activity it captured their creative imagination and proved useful in their cultural and political struggles. The important point is that all sections of society valued its physical form and moral messages. This is precisely why its growth was characterized by a dichotomous political history of intense ethnic contention and the nonviolent search for an idyllic area of social life.[3]

The body politic, of course, was no more than the ideological superstructure of the plantation based establishment that kept firmly in sight the concepts of white supremacy, the power and privilege of private property, and the attendant fear of, if not hatred for, racial/social egalitarianism. The absorption of cricket in the 'psychic world' of the colonial structure, therefore, meant that major redefinitions of the game's values had to take place. If cricket was the finest gift of nineteenth century English humanist culture, best played by persons of a particular moral attainment and social status, why then should it be influenced by the social consideration of keeping blacks in their 'place' within the plantation society? The answer, of course, is quite clear given our understanding of West Indian ideological history. In exactly the same way that whites defined a political system in which less than 10 percent of the population was enfranchised as democratic, a place was found for blacks within the cricket culture that enhanced the divisions of labour insisted upon by plantations. Against this background are to be seen the peculiar features of early West Indian cricket culture, particularly its élite origins, and subsequent social democratization.

Undoubtedly, this social and political history explores the institutional and ideological formation of plantation organization. In explaining this history,

4

the dependent mentality of the colonial élite is as important as their use of culture as a principal political strategy. Indeed, the two ideological practices when placed together constitute but one side of the dialectic; the other being the cultural resistance and affirmation of disenfranchised colonials who eventually claimed their right to cricket and re-promoted it as a symbol of liberating, politicized mass culture. Power, here, as Humpty Dumpty suggests, being shown to be no more than one's right to define and to have one's definition accepted.

It is not surprising that Barbadian creole planter society seemed most determined to import and entrench metropolitan cricket culture. They had already defined their island home as 'Little England' and 'Bimshire', and held steadfast to the view that they were Englishmen in a far-flung 'shire' separated by a large sea and a few centuries. As far as they could see these divisive elements were insufficient to erode their cultural rights, and they took great pride in defining themselves as the most loyal colonial subjects of the Crown; the worship of the cricket culture, then, was one way in which they expressed a boastful fidelity. But colonists in other territories had long captured a greater share of the London sugar market, and dominated the executive of the West India Committee, two developments that forced Barbadian whites to accept a more pragmatic view of their relations with the metropole.

In the early nineteenth century, the print media in the colonies were called upon to assist in the popularization of the cricket culture. Announcements of games were carried alongside references to the sale of slaves and the price fluctuations of sugar and other goods. Such announcements spoke aggressively of a new and exciting leisure system within colonial propertied society – all part of the overall cultural benefits of freedom and mastery. That these earliest references are specific to the endeavours of the garrisoned imperial military suggests that this group played the leading role in the pioneering of the game. In Barbados and the Leeward Islands, troops awaiting instructions to put down rebellious blacks or keep out the acquisitionist Napoleon, played cricket. It enabled them to handle the stress of frontier society, and more importantly to imagine through play the meaning of being at home.

Earliest Clubs and Contests

What seem to be the earliest references to an organized cricket match within the West Indies press appeared in the *Barbados Mercury* and *Bridgetown Gazette* on 10 May 1806 and 17 January 1807.[4] The latter entry was an announcement by the treasurer of the St Ann's Garrison Cricket Club inviting members to a special dinner after a game. Two years later the *Gazette* carried notice of a "grand cricket match to be played between the Officers of the Royal West Indies Rangers and Officers of the Third West Indian Regiment for 55 guineas a side on the Grand Parade on Tuesday, September 19". The match was arranged to start "immediately after 'gunfire' on the morning and continue until 8 o'clock a.m., then to resume at 4:30 p.m". The Royal Rangers were required to wear "flannel and blue facings" and the Third Regiment "flannel and yellow facings".

St Ann's Cricket Club, then, seemed to have been a pioneering West Indian social institution. Barbadian whites welcomed it, and appreciated the wider implications of its presence. The proprietor and editor of the *Barbadian*, Abel Clinckett, though admittedly consumed with reporting on the abolition of the apprenticeship system, and the onset of 'full' legal freedom for blacks, found time in May 1838 to editorialize on the importance of this cricket club to the imperial mission. He wrote:

We understand that to promote the gratification of the soldiers of St Ann's Garrison, as well as the sake of their health, the Commander of the Forces has sanctioned their engaging in the truly British, and manly sport of cricket. A great match, we are informed, will be played on Monday next at 6 o'clock [a.m.] – the 78th Regiment against the Garrison.[6]

This was a single-innings game, and the next week it was reported in the same paper that the 78th Regiment had won the game having scored 91 runs to the Garrison's 53. An important issue to be noticed here is that the Garrison team was made up of lower ranking soldiers. This attracted the attention of Mr Clinckett when he stated that such social mixing of men of different classes showed "the good feeling" entertained by officers for their soldiers.[7]

If the St Ann's Club can claim to be the incubator of Barbadian/West Indian cricket, it can also be justly proud of the rapidity with which the culture spread to neighbouring districts infecting élite communities with which it had close contact. Again, the *Barbadian* informs us in 1849 that 'gentlemen' in the parish of St Michael, in which the garrison was located, had constituted themselves into two 'well organized cricket companies' – the 'City' and 'St Michael' clubs. The editor described the first game between these clubs as an affair watched by "highly respectable ladies and gentlemen" that "evinced great spirit and extreme goodwill".[8] The game was played on a specially prepared field at Constant Plantation, owned by Mr Prettijohn, who also provided tents and refreshments for spectators.

It soon became the norm for cricket clubs to be patronized by imperial governors and other high ranking administrative officials. Located among the sugar fields, these cricket grounds represented more than just entertainment for whites but the agency of a cultural renaissance that swept throughout the colonies. In 1857 the *Barbadian* claimed to have made a public appeal for the financial and social support of cricket among all sections of society. The governor, meanwhile, had made it a matter of duty to attend the match between Codrington College and the gallant 49th Regiment, bringing with him to the proceedings the full authority of colonial and imperial respectability. In the same year the Jamaicans, who had also been playing on their plantations, began the formal institutionalization of cricket when they established the St Jago and the Vere and Clarendon Cricket Clubs. These organizations, like their Barbadian counterparts, were confined to the propertied élite classes, and both coloureds and blacks were excluded from membership.

In 1863, the Kingston Cricket Club was established in Jamaica – the first major urban-based organization – with the soon to be notorious Governor Eyre as patron. The significance of this development is twofold. First, that as was the case in Barbados, cricket could now claim to be an urban institution. Secondly, the 'heavy' official support the game received from the outset ensured its promotion as an activity that conferred or indicated social honour. The *Barbadian* was therefore not generating any scandal or controversy when it reported the following on the visit of Prince Alfred (second son of Queen Victoria) to Barbados in 1861:

Thursday, H.R.H. was supposed to rest from the fatigues of pleasure which had been inflicted on him; but instead of taking a siesta, he went to the Garrison to play cricket with the Officers, making his rest merely a change of amusement, and that by a recreation requiring so much energy and activity as cricket does.[9]

West Indies cricket, then, was a game played by royalty, and on such occasions colonials (black, coloured and white) came out and celebrated, if not the gentler social side of empire, the meteoric rise of a major cultural force within their midst.

The members of the black community had been encouraged from the slavery period to use their 'free time' in full indulgence in the sort of cultural activity that did not in any way appear to whites as informed by a spirit of resistance. Any cultural expression that whites feared or considered rebellious was outlawed. By the end of slavery, then, a complex entertainment system was to be found within the plantation villages – an established tradition that was also characterized by the adoption and adaptation of European forms to their own material and ontological condition.

The African-derived performance and celebratory social system absorbed the cricket missile – tamed and domesticated it as part of the culture complex. With their propensity to collectivize cultural ritual and to blend comic, heroic and tragic drama within the single form, blacks brought spectator theatre and participatory festiveness to bear upon the idealization of the physical and artistic elements of cricket. Cricket, then, found a soft and safe resting place within the residual African ontology. Blacks needed only a little encouragement, and they received just this. The early records attest to this fact in the clearest manner. Take, for instance, the view of the Revd Grenville John Chester whose literary sketches on the black poor of Barbados in the aftermath of slavery are frequently cited by social historians. He tells us in 1869:

The labouring classes in Barbados are badly off for amusement. Tops and marbles seem almost the only sports of the school children, but when encouraged they take kindly to cricket. But it is hard to find places to play in, and parochial cricket clubs are either above or below the notice of the local clergy. Thus dancing is almost the only amusement, and the people dance well and gracefully.[10]

TABLE 1 LEADING CRICKET CLUBS IN BARBADOS AND JAMAICA, 1850–1900

Name	When established	Colony
St Jago	1857	Jamaica
Vere and Clarendon	1857	Jamaica
Lodge School	1850s	Barbados
Codrington College	1850s	Barbados
The Garrison	1850s	Barbados
Kingston	1863	Jamaica
Harrison College	1877	Barbados
Wanderers	1877	Barbados
Kensington	1878	Jamaica
Pickwick	1882	Barbados
Leewards	1880s	Barbados
Windwards	1880s	Barbados
Bellville	1890s	Barbados
Melbourne	1892	Jamaica
Spartan	1893	Barbados
Garrison Club (Up Park Camp)	1898	Jamaica
Lucas	1898	Jamaica
St Georges	1890s	Jamaica

Black Exclusion

So here we have it. There was little assistance and no comfortable space within the early cricket culture for blacks, at a time when plantations were creating room for the proliferation of whites-only clubs, and the established schools had placed cricket at the centre of the academic agenda for white children. The racial division of space, however, did not prohibit black children from developing their skills and appetites for the game. The ways in which they adapted and developed technological instruments for the game to suit their environments point to the innovative consciousness that had long informed their survival strategies. If poverty is no enemy of ingenuity, then the cricket technology devised by blacks in the mid nineteenth century constitutes supportive evidence. Algernon Aspinall, historian of the nineteenth century British West Indies, describes the cricket gear of Jamaican blacks: "Black people are particularly enthusiastic about the game. It is quite common to see tiny black children innocent of clothing indulging in it with all the assurance of their elders, using, however, sugar canes for wickets, coconut palm leaf for a bat and whatever they can lay their hands on for a ball."[11]

What was true for mid nineteenth century Jamaica remained the case for most of the West Indies into the mid twentieth century. The instruments of the poor remained unaltered for over a century while their capability consistently improved. With respect to early community practices, Aspinall states that "black spectators of cricket matches are very demonstrative, and it is not at all unusual to see many of them rush out on the ground and leap and roll about from sheer excitement."[12] Aspinall also made reference to A.F. Somerset's observations of vociferous West Indies cricket crowds during the 1895 tour of an English team.[13] In the Barbados match, he stated, the England captain was forced to use a whistle to get the attention of his fieldsmen, so noisy and festive was the crowd.

The intensification of anti-black racial prejudice in the postslavery period, in part a response of whites to the expressed sociopolitical and economic expectations of blacks, meant that cricket in its infancy was socialized by values of race hatred and conflict. While the blacks worked for whites in the canefields, whites refused to play with blacks on the cricket fields. They watched each other, but kept their distance.

As the century progressed, however, and the civil rights movement won some constitutional and moral battles, the pressure mounted to lower the racial barriers to the cricket world. By the end of the century, some middle class coloured men played for white clubs or formed their own. (See Table 1.)

In turn, they would engage black teams in 'friendly' games – but these teams were not generally invited to the clubhouses for refreshments during or after the game. It was within this ideological environment that the institutional formation of the cricket culture matured.

Barbadian teams competed for a Challenge Cup from 1892 and Jamaican teams did so from 1893. At first, the Challenge Cups allowed for the display of cricket skills only from the white clubs, but gradually coloured and black players and clubs performed their way into the competition. The establishment of a network of cricket clubs had a great deal to do with the transformation taking place in West Indian social life at the end of the century. The convergence of a multi-ethnic urban professional middle class of whites, coloureds and blacks challenged the dominance of the planter–merchant élite within the cricket culture. In Jamaica, for example, St Jago, and Vere and Clarendon Clubs were represented exclusively by the planter élite, while the Kingston Club catered for their wealthy urban mercantile allies. The Kensington Club maintained a membership that was largely upper middle class, urban and white, but Melbourne Club was the facility of the coloured professional classes who, from the slavery period, considered attractive the skin-lightening miscegenation approach to social mobility into élite white society.[14]

Not surprisingly, then, Melbourne Club harboured as strong anti-black attitudes as the whites-only clubs – the colourism that separated the different shades of non-white society being as potent ideologically as the racism which divided blacks and whites. Not one black person, noted Soares, could be found among the 58 members of the club in 1894.[15] Whereas in Jamaica, Melbourne used the technicality of a complex fee structure to rationalize the absence of blacks from the club, in Barbados white officials categorized blacks as professionals not suited to participate in amateur competitions.

The plantation based society of Barbados could claim an older history than that of Jamaica, Trinidad, Demerara or the Windward Islands. As a result its ruling class insisted upon the social projection of race/colour/class stratifications with greater precision and illiberalism. The formation of Wanderers Cricket Club in 1877 represented the planter élite's social need for an institutional agency to distinguish their cricket from subordinate 'others'. The Pickwick Club that followed in 1882 was the response of a collective of small planters, middling merchants, and professional whites on whom Wanderers had closed the membership list.

The Spartan Cricket Club, like Melbourne in Jamaica, was the institution of the racially oppressed but socially respectable coloured families. With a few whites and blacks admitted to its membership, Spartan's mission was to democratize Barbados cricket and discredit the long-standing ideology of white superiority. Its first president was the distinguished Conrad Reeves, the mulatto chief justice, whose sense of racial pride was matched only by his loyalty to the political agenda of the white élite.

In both Jamaica and Barbados the black working class remained locked out from these institutionalized arrangements in spite of having established a reputation for producing very skilled professional players. The late nineteenth century "Barbadian professionals", noted Hughes, "were groundsmen, young men employed as grounds bowlers, and occasionally helpers and hangers on, in other words, labouring class black Barbadians".[16] These players, in spite of or probably because of, their ability were excluded from Challenge Cup competitions whether they played as 'guests' of established clubs or as a team. Whites would occasionally hire them as individuals or as teams to play in 'friendly' games as a means of providing excitement for spectators or to sharpen their own game. But there remained at the end of the century no respected institutional home for working class players.

Cricket's Impact in the Early Years

West Indies cricket, then, by the end of the nineteenth century, had been transformed from a minority élite 'English' sport into the region's first expression of popular mass culture. By mid century it had broken out of the mould represented by garrisoned English military men, and had spread into the plantations, villages and towns of the colonies. In so doing, cricket traversed a wide geographical space and slowly embraced all social classes and races in ways never before witnessed in the region. "Every self-respecting colony", noted Aspinall at the end of the nineteenth century, "has one or more cricket clubs, and the keenest interest is taken in the game especially during the winter months in alternate years, when an Inter-colonial Cricket Cup is competed for by representative teams from Barbados, British Guiana and Trinidad".[17] Initiating its social sojourn as an instrument of the imperial cultural mission, cricket soon became the leading leisure institution of a colonial élite in search of new methods of social differentiation. Seized by blacks and coloureds, it became the focus around which an intensive civil rights war was waged as they sought the democratization of social culture as well as organizational autonomy.

At the beginning of the nineteenth century, then, cricket was a distraction for a few resident Englishmen and at the end it was the region's premier cultural expression of the popular imagination. This process mirrored much of what was taking place within West Indian society as the socially liberating aspects of the emancipation event of 1838 began to impact upon social relations and structures. Bruce Hamilton, in a 1947 publication, *Cricket in Barbados*, captured with precision West Indian cricket culture at the turn of the century:

> If, as is often asserted, the game as played on the village green is the backbone of English cricket, at least equally valuable contribution to West Indies cricket has been made by the contests fought out on a few square yards of pasture, with a quite well-prepared pitch on the only piece of level ground, but only one half-split ball and two old bats to go round, square leg out of sight in a gully, silly point standing on an outcrop of rock and natural boundaries in the form of grazing goats and sheep. In Barbados at least the poorest black man has certainly no less love of the game than his white brother of rustic England, with a far deeper understanding of it and skill in playing it. Everyone who has practised cricket in the island is aware that any bare foot boy hanging about the ground is likely, if he is tossed a ball, to bowl at least reasonably well with it . . . It is not a question of intelligence; it simply is that a love of cricket (as distinct from interest in any sporting activity that is given publicity) is confined to a small section of Englishmen, whereas in the West Indies it is implanted in the hearts of the entire people.[18]

This achievement for blacks, so aptly described here for Barbados was one hundred years in the making and is guarded today by a popular will that is 'old testament' in its judgement. That Barbados won the Intercolonial Cricket Cup six times in the first eleven contests after 1893 (Trinidad four and Demerara one) is perhaps indicative of their early lead in the institutionalization of the game. But what is really important is that by 1900, a general distribution of cricket capability and enthusiasm was finally achieved also in those territories where club formation had been slowest in taking root.

NOTES

1. See Immanuel Wallerstein, *The Politics of the World Economy* (Cambridge: Cambridge University Press, 1984), 165–80. Also, "The national and the universal: can there be such a thing as world culture", in Anthony D. King, *Culture, Globalization and the World Economy* (London: Macmillan, 1991), 91–107; G. Beckford, "The dynamics of growth and the nature of metropolitan plantation enterprise", *Social and Economic Studies* (*SES*) 19, no. 4 (1970); L. Best, "Outlines of a model of pure plantation economy", *SES* 17, no. 3 (1968).

2. See Brian Stoddart, and Brian Stoddart and Keith Sandiford, in Section One of Hilary Beckles and Brian Stoddart (eds.) *Liberation Cricket: West Indies*

Cricket Culture (Kingston: Ian Randle Publishers; London: Manchester University Press, 1995); C.L.R. James, *Beyond a Boundary* (London: Hutchinson, 1963).

3. See Maurice St Pierre, "West Indies cricket: a cultural contradiction?" *Arena Review* 14, no. 1 (1990): 13–25.

4. *Barbados Mercury* and *Bridgetown Gazette*, 10 May 1806 and 17 January 1807; See also Warren Alleyne, "Cricket's beginnings in Barbados", *Sunday Sun*, Barbados, 17 March 1991.

5. Ibid.

6. Cited in Bruce Hamilton, *Cricket in Barbados* (Bridgetown: Advocate Press, 1947), 7.

7. Ibid.

8. Ibid.

9. Ibid., 8.

10. Revd Grenville John Chester, *Transatlantic Sketches, 1869* (Bridgetown: Barbados Heritage Series, National Cultural Foundation, 1990), 32.

11. Algernon E. Aspinall, *The British West Indies: Their History, Resources and Progress* (London: Pitman, 1912), 153.

12. Ibid., 153–54.

13. Ibid., 154.

14. See Dave Soares, "A history of the Melbourne Cricket Club, 1892–1962", MA thesis, Department of History, University of the West Indies, Mona, Jamaica, 1987; H.G. McDonald, *The History of Kingston Cricket Club, 1863–1938* (Kingston: Gleaner, 1938); F.L. Pearce and T.L. Roxburgh, *The Jamaica Cricket Annual* (Kingston: DeSouza, 1897); Anon, "The history of Melbourne Cricket Club", *The Sportsman* 2, no. 1 (1929).

15. Soares, "A history of the Melbourne Cricket Club", 17–18.

16. Ronnie Hughes, "A nineteenth century cricket development in 'Little England' ", in Barbados Cricket Association, *100 Years of Organised Cricket in Barbados, 1892–1992* (Bridgetown: Barbados Cricket Association, 1992), 2.

17. Aspinall, *The British West Indies*, 151.

18. Hamilton, *Cricket in Barbados*, 62.

2

An Anglo-American Apprenticeship

Origins of Intercolonial Contests

The Americans have come back into focus. It was just over 100 years ago that West Indians set out on a grand historic cricket tour of North America. It was the first time that the newly constructed institution, named The West Indies Cricket Team, had departed the region on what seemed more like a fact finding tour. It was an American apprenticeship served in preparation for a later epic mission – the quest for an English encounter. When in 1993, the West Indies Cricket Board (WICB) declared that North America would be the core target of its strategic development plan, the historical significance of the 1886 tour gained new meaning. The announcement jerked the historicized mind, and connected references that speak to the discontinuities that have shaped modern Caribbean development. Since the West Indian gaze has long been fixed on North America as a place of betterment and opportunity, the discontinuity in cricketing relations seems phenomenal and demands an explanation.

It is instructive to note, at the outset, that use of the term 'West Indies' in reference to a given territorial space is imperial in origins, and preceded the popular use of the term 'West Indian' (an indicator of consciousness and identity) by at least two centuries. Though records suggest that the imperial description of persons resident and born in these territories as West Indians was commonplace in the eighteenth century, it was only in the mid nineteenth century that their 'creole' voice was clearly heard and confidently used within metropolitan sociocultural, political and economic spheres.

Determining to a large measure the organizational history of West Indian cricket is the fact that the sugar plantation culture and its supportive imperial structures had integrated and considerably homogenized the social world and life experiences of West Indians during and after slavery. Sugar economy,

15

mercantilist trade theory, the ideology of white supremacy and black resistance determined the framework of everyday life in the Indies, and shaped the meaning of what social anthropologists first described as West Indianness.

By the 1840s planter-merchant communities across the region had moved away from the earlier practice of cutthroat competition among themselves for the largest share of the London sugar market, and had adopted a policy of cooperation which was coordinated by their London based lobby, the West India Committee. Though suggestions of political integration did not find favour with territorial legislatures, the social élite had recognized by then that economic cooperation could also be enhanced by social activities that necessitated intimacy and interpersonal familiarity.

The development of West Indies cricket organizations, then, was determined by the evolution of the sociopolitical consciousness and outlook within and across white colonial societies. By the late nineteenth century, the game had emerged as the principal social mechanism of interaction for the trans-colonial élites who now visited each other on a regular basis, not as farmers and merchants, but as cricketers. West Indianization as a socially exciting cultural process within ruling class society, therefore, first took form within the ambit of the cricketing world.

Before a 'West Indian' team could be assembled, however, it was necessary to intensify and widen the base of the cricket culture within individual territories. It was also essential that these territories play each other on a regular basis and in the process allow for the establishment of a regional knowledge base about particular players, and specific local conditions that would influence performances. Players and organizational supporters, also, needed to be assured that the economic basis of the cricket culture could support inter-colonial activity. Since, of course, the early years were exclusively those of the amateur, the financial matter was critical as players were required to pay for their own games and the travel involved in regional contests.

In all of this, the year 1865 is important. Though West Indian history students would know it as the year in which land hungry Jamaican blacks rose up at Morant Bay in search of secure access to land, and were massacred by local and imperial military forces, they may not know however that it marks the first occasion that representative teams from two West Indian colonies played each other in cricket. In this contest the teams were from Demerara and Barbados and the two innings game was played on 15 and 16 February at the Garrison's ground in Barbados. The home team won by 138 runs in spite of low scores made on both sides.[1]

It was, of course, a historic moment surrounded by celebratory extravaganza. Bridgetown employers released workers for the afternoon to encourage their attendance at the match and to participate in the festivities. In September the same year, a Barbados team visited Demerara for the return match; again the home team won in a closely fought contest. Six years later, in 1871, two teams from these colonies clashed once again in Barbados. Again, the home team won after being set a winning target of 59 runs which they scored for the loss of two wickets.[2]

The pioneering contest between teams from Barbados and Demerara opened the way for a range of other intercolonial contact across the West Indies. In 1879, for example, a team of masters and students from Harrison College in Barbados toured St Kitts and Antigua where they won all games against the Leeward Islanders whom they considered neophytes. In September 1883 Demerara sent another team to Barbados where they played a two-day game against a side made up largely of players from the Wanderers Cricket Club that was formed in 1877. The match was described as the "scene of bustle, confusion, and jollity, for there a thirsty aristocracy did congregate".[3]

During the early part of 1890 Trinidad was finally integrated into the touring cricket fold. After being unable to accept several earlier invitations from Demerara and Barbados, Trinidad agreed to participate in a triangular 'cricket festival' in Barbados with these other two colonies. On this occasion, commercial interests in Barbados showed their commitment to the game when no fewer than "eighty Bridgetown firms" agreed to close for the afternoon "on all four days when Barbados was playing the visiting colonies". With strong home support, and excellent bowling from the young (soon to be legendary) Clifford Goodman, the Barbadian team won the tournament.[4]

Jamaica followed suit and joined the West Indies touring network in 1891 when a team from the Garrison Club in Barbados visited Kingston. An all-Jamaican team, drawn largely from the Kingston Club, competed with the Barbados based soldiers. With Jamaica now in the ranks, inter-West Indies cricket contests included the major sugar producing territories. Two years later in 1893, an Antiguan team visited Barbados, and Trinidad played host to a visiting colonial side for the first time, the circumstance under which Queen's Park Cricket Club sprang into prominence. Teams from Barbados and St Vincent exchanged visits in 1896, and a Barbadian team visited St Lucia. Also in that year, Jamaica sent a team on a début West Indian tour. On this occasion the Jamaicans played against teams in Barbados and Demerara. During the Barbados match a toast was raised to the health of

C.W.K. Chandler of the Jamaica side, a Barbadian who, a decade earlier, had distinguished himself as a bowler for Harrison College.

Interregional cricket, then, as a social and organizational experience, was well entrenched by the end of the nineteenth century. This regional structure, however, was built upon the competitive cricket culture that had developed in particular territories. In 1892, the Barbadians had put in place a competition among clubs for a Challenge Cup, and Jamaica did likewise the following year. It was also in 1892 that a well organized tournament between Barbados, Trinidad, and Demerara for the Intercolonial Challenge Cup was launched. By the mid 1890s, therefore, white élite cricketers were competing for both colonial and intercolonial Challenge Cups.

It is important to note, also, that by this time the concept of a representative West Indies team was already well established in cricketing circles. It was commonplace to see references within the regional media to a West Indies team, though it was recognized by all concerned that the exclusion of black players from such selections would ultimately bring into question the relations between race, colour and class ideologies on the one hand, and the power of merit and social justice within the gradually democratizing political order on the other. The issue, of course, was one that centred around the manner in which planter-merchant hegemony determined the projection and political actualization of West Indianness. Though occasionally in the 1880s some colonial teams did include an exceptionally talented coloured or black player, the core concept of a West Indian team was formulated exclusively by the sugar interests.

First 'Overseas' Tour: North America

The year 1886 was the first occasion that a 'West Indian' team was selected to play in an extra-territorial match. An all-white team went on a tour of Canada and the United States where the cricket culture could claim a longer pedigree than in the West Indies. As early as 1844, Canada and the United States had clashed in their first 'international' – 24 years before the much acclaimed Australian Aboriginal tour to England in 1868.[5] English teams toured Canada and the United States in the summer of 1859 by which time the Canadians had declared cricket the national sport.[6] English teams also toured the United States in 1868 and in 1872; on the latter occasion none other than the legendary Dr W.G. Grace took part, scoring an expected and impressive 142 against a Toronto side. Australia toured Canada for the first time in 1878, so

TABLE 2 WEST INDIANS VS YOUNG AMERICA, PLAYED AT PHILADELPHIA ON 7 AND 8 SEPTEMBER 1886

WEST INDIANS

First Innings
E.M. Skeete c Schwartz b Brewster.............2
W.H. Farquharson c Downs
   b Brewster 6
R.H. Steward c Downs
   b C.A. Newhall 8
J. Lees b C.A.Newhall 33
P. Isaacs b Clark 13
G.Wyatt c R.S. Newhall b Brewster. 0
E. N. Marshall b Brewster 1
W. Collymore b Clark...................................1
J. J. Burke not out 10
T. Skeete c Dixon b Brewster 1
L. Fyfe c Clarke b C.A. Newhall 1
Extras 13
Total 89

Second Innings
E.M. Skeete c & b Brewster 11
W.H. Farquharson b Brester 4
R.H. Steward b C.A. Newhall 3
J. Lees c Patterson b Brewster..............37
P. Isaacs c Clark b Brewster 16
G. Wyatt b Brewster 64
E.N. Marshall b Brewster 14
J.M. Burke not out 6
L. Fyfe not out 6
Extras 14
Total 175

YOUNG AMERICA

First Innings
F.E. Brewster lbw b Marshall 70
N. Downs b Lees 12
R.S. Newhall c Farquharson, b Burke 83
C.A. Newhall run out 31
T.H. Dixon c Lees b Burke 8
E.W. Clarke Jr. b Farquharson 28
J.H. Patterson c Wyatt b Burke 5
H.L. Brown b Stewart 34
H.H. Firth st Wyatt b Stewart 0
E. H. Hance Jr not out 5
A.F. Schwartz st Wyatt b Stewart 0
Extras[7] 8
Total 284

that when the West Indies team arrived eight years later, the Canadian public was long accustomed to periodic 'international' cricket.

The 1886 West Indies tour of North America was the brainchild of George Wyatt of the Georgetown Cricket Club in Demerara. As expected, the team was drawn from the 'Big Four', though eventually Trinidad could not send its selected players. The touring party eventually consisted of seven Jamaicans, two Barbadians and four from Demerara. It was captained by Wyatt, and the appointed vice-captain was L.K. Fyfe of Jamaica. In all, 13 matches were played. The West Indies team won 6, lost 5, and 2 were drawn; on the whole it was a fairly mixed sort of tour from the point of view of results (see Table 3).[8]

The first match was scheduled for 16 August against the Montreal Cricket Club, whose secretary had been instrumental in securing the fixtures. By then, none of the Barbadian players had arrived, and only one from Demerara. The team had travelled separately, and substitutes were raised from spectators who had journeyed long distances to witness the West Indian North American début. The match against the Halifax Wanderers on 18 and 19 August met a similar fate. The missing players arrived late on the 19th, and the West Indies played as a complete team for the first time in the match against the Ottawa Cricket Club on the 20th.

Successes in Canada were followed by a string of defeats in the United States. The *Philadelphia Times* of 4 September, described the West Indies as offering "a somewhat indifferent showing", being defeated by "a rather weak eleven" by 10 wickets. In the match against the Belmont Cricket Club "they were compelled to hunt leather for many long hours", and the general local opinion seemed to be that no one should be surprised by their "poor work against the strong organizations" they met in Philadelphia.

The match against the Young America Cricket Club (Stenton, Philadelphia) played on 7 and 8 September almost ended in disaster for the West Indies, but they were able to hold on to a draw after trailing on first innings by 195 (see Table 2).[9] The draw was described as a "slight concession" to the West Indies which "filled them with pride". The game was played before a small crowd mainly of "carriage parties, who, after a brief stay, and upon hearing that the Young American men were doing quite well, drove to other and more interesting pursuits". The West Indies team departed Philadelphia in considerable doubts about its standard of play and whether they could ever match the cricketing abilities of the Americans.[10]

Sections of the press were not without sympathy for the West Indians and explained their poor performance in terms of generally unfavourable circumstances of the tour. One journalist noted:

The islanders are not accustomed to American wickets, their own being harder, rougher and faster. Again, they are under too great a strain. They play cricket day after day, and generally spend their evening in enjoying the hospitality of their hosts. These are the principal reasons why they have failed to do themselves justice.[11]

More concerned cricket journalists were hard pressed not to cast judgement on the overall West Indian standard of cricket. The *Philadelphia Times*, therefore, offering an analysis of the touring party, noted deficiencies.

TABLE 3 VISIT OF WEST INDIAN GENTLEMEN TO CANADA AND THE UNITED STATES, 1886
RESULTS OF MATCHES – PLAYED 13: WON 6, DRAWN 2, LOST 5

Opponents	Where played	When played	West Indians		Opponents		Remarks
			1st Ins	2nd Ins	1st Ins	2nd Ins	
Matches won (6)							
Halifax Wanderers	Montreal	18 & 19 Aug.	319	...	113	64	An innings & 142 runs
Ottawa CC	Ottawa	20 & 21 Aug.	67	80	67	54	26 runs
Toronto CC	Toronto	23 & 24 Aug.	167	...	71	57	An innings & 39 runs
Ontario Association XI	Toronto	25 & 26 Aug.	51	109	101	43	16 runs
Merion CC (return)	Ardmore, Pa.	1 Sept.	111*	...	107	...	4 wickets,* 6 w.d.
Longwood CC	Boston	10 & 11 Sept.	97	39	95	23	18 runs
Matches drawn (2)							*Remarks*
Montreal CC	Montreal	16 & 17 Aug.	60	101*	112	130	* 4 w.d.
Young America CC	Stenton, Pa.	7 & 8 Sept.	89	175*	284	...	* 0 w.d.
Matches lost (5)							*Lost by*
Hamilton CC	Hamilton	27 & 28 Aug.	114	63	116	63	7 wickets,* 3 w.d.
Merion CC	Ardmore, Pa.	31 Aug. & 1 Sept.	54	36	86	6*	10 wickets,* no w.d.
Belmont CC	Elmwood, Pa.	2 & 3 Sept.	74	116	222	...	An innings & 32 runs
Germantown CC	Nicetown, Pa	4 & 6 Sept.	74	148	310	...	An innings & 88 runs
Staten Island CC	Staten Island, NY	13 & 14 Sept.	74	132	165	42*	8 wickets, * 3 w.d.

Generally speaking, however, the team is deficient in bowling talent, and were it not for good, steady fielding, the scores against them would be larger than they are. To sum up, the visitors are playing under many disadvantages, but, making every allowance possible, it is clear that they are not up to the form of the leading local clubs.[12]

In short, the West Indies cricket team, on its first overseas tour, was well humiliated and made to feel quite inferior to various American cricket clubs. Performance in Canada was satisfactory, but the United States proved a formidable challenge.

A summary of the tour by Captain Wyatt, however, painted a less grim picture. Noting that for many the proposed tour was perceived at home "as rather a farce", he made reference to the pioneering nature of the project. Despite being "sneered and laughed at by many more than most people imagine", the team was able to experience the culture of an overseas tour, and build confidence among the cricket fraternity. It was not the strongest West Indies team, noted Captain Wyatt, though it might very well have been the wealthiest. Players were expected to personally fund their own trip, and this financial arrangement excluded a fair number of more talented players. The entire cost of the tour amounted to "near £1,000", an average of £71 or $340 per man for nine weeks. The cost for players from Demerara and Barbados amounted to more than those from Jamaica on account of the short journey of the latter.[13]

The West Indians had followed the English into North America, had not done as well, but were looking forward to an exciting future. Captain Wyatt, the middle order batsman from Demerara, who averaged 9.13 on tour, made comments that signalled the developmental vision held by this touring party for West Indies cricket:

The ball has been set-a-rolling now, and if the result of our recent tour gives us many visits in the West Indies from our Canadian and American friends, and wakes up our Island neighbours and our own Colony to move about amongst each other and further afield, in the interest of the noble game, something tangible and well worth having will have been gained, and the writer fully and well recompensed for what trouble he has taken in the matter.

But a hint to our island neighbours must be given. Some proper and really strong move must be made to secure permanent and good cricket grounds everywhere in the West Indies where the game is to take any standing, and let us hope that nowhere will this latter not be the case. In Barbados especially, the rendezvous and headquarters for all passenger steamers, there ought certainly to be the best ground in the West Indies, and we trust that the 'blot' (for such it is) of not having such a ground will not continue much longer.[14]

22

The following year the Americans returned the visit, but played against terri-torial sides rather than a West Indies team. It was a weak team and was defeated by Trinidad, Demerara, Jamaica and Barbados. The Barbados and Jamaica matches were billed as 'America vs Barbados' and 'Gentlemen of America vs All-Jamaica' respectively, but the evidence was now clear that the Civil War had ravaged American cricket culture leaving it a poor third to baseball and football.

Preparing for An England Tour

West Indians were now looking towards England as the direction to go in the consolidation and internationalization of their cricket. England, of course, was recognized as the premier cricketing nation on account of its claim as the 'inventor' of the organized game. It was also undeniably a case of white West Indian colonials seeking approval and recognition of their achievements from their 'motherland' in this cultural arena. By the early 1890s, they seemed frantic (similar to the Australians two decades earlier) in the quest for approval from the Marylebone Cricket Club (MCC). They desperately wanted a contest with England, but the English were slow in responding.

Both Wyatt of Demerara and Fyfe of Jamaica, captain and vice-captain respectively of the first 'West Indies' team, sought separately to arrange West Indies tours of England in 1888 and 1889. Their efforts were not successful, and it seemed then that the region's first encounter with England would take place under the circumstance of a touring English team playing against indi-vidual colonies. This occasion finally came when Slade Lucas assembled an English eleven which arrived in the region in January 1895.

Implicit within the thinking behind this first encounter was some measure of English contempt for West Indian cricketing abilities. The touring team was made up of low-level amateurs with one, maybe two, recognized players – hardly a first class eleven. Yet, thousands of West Indians came out to greet them with great fanfare wherever they went. English perception of West Indian standards was confirmed by the tour results. The English teams won 10 of the 16 matches and lost only 4. In front of a crowd in excess of 6,000 at Kensington Oval, Bridgetown, the Barbados team was beaten. St Vincent, not yet considered a cricketing colony, however, succeeded in defeating the Englishmen.

Reports in the West Indies indicate that colonials, in spite of receiving a sound thrashing by the English team, were overcome with excitement by the experience. References suggest that colonial sport writers expressed in no uncertain terms the sense of low self-esteem seemingly evident among West Indians with respect to the English. In their losing game, Barbados scored 517 in the second innings, a West Indies record at the time, and an achievement that presented an opportunity for the local press to unilaterally claim colonial 'arrival', and to indicate in a self-denying sort of way, reverence for standards supposedly established by their opponents. In Bridgetown the *Times* of 9 February 1895 reported:

Englishmen at home and abroad must have learnt with mixed feelings the news wired on Tuesday evening announcing to the world pre-eminent achievements that Barbados batted the whole day and had, at the call of time on Tuesday evening, still 3 wickets to fall with the score standing at the magnificent total of 359. Three centuries and a half would have been as fine a cricketing feat for a Colonial team that could possibly be accomplished in the presence of English batsmen and bowlers of renown, that would cause any Colonial combination to be inordinately proud of. But when it comes to be thought of that a team of cricketers in this little England beyond the seas could put in the field capable of greater things, though having for their opponents stalwarts hailing from the home of cricket, it seems to us to suggest a something not dreamt of in our cricketing philosophy. A West Indian batting record has been established in the cricket annals of these parts, and whatever the pride and elation we feel in knowing that it has been given to Barbadians to chronicle that fact in their history, cannot but be pardonable. That Barbados possessed the ability to compile 517 runs in a single innings was what the most judicious observers of our boys' play or even the most sanguine spirits among us would have described as belonging more to the region of exuberant imagination than to be within the bounds of possibilities.[15]

Immediately following the departure of the Lucas team, West Indians rejoiced on hearing the news that arrangements were being made in England for other touring teams to test the "colonial cricket steel". In 1896 two English teams, one led by A. Priestly (later Sir) and the other by Lord Hawke, arrived in the West Indies. Popular opinion was that both teams were stronger than the Lucas XI, though all were still considered amateurs.

The family linkages of empire being what they were, Priestly's team contained Dr Gilbert Elliot, a Barbadian, who refused to play in the Barbados match on the grounds that he could not compete against his own country. The Hawke team also included a West Indian: Pelham Warner, the distinguished Trinidadian. Both teams did well against colonial sides. Jamaica and Demerara received humiliating defeats, while Trinidad won two matches against each side. The Barbadian team won 2–1 in three games against the Priestly side, and lost one of the two games against the Hawke side.

The impressive record of the Trinidad team, which had hitherto been considered the weakest of the 'Big Four', drew particular attention for one special reason. Pelham Warner, star batsman of Hawke's side, who scored a hundred against the Barbados team, studied the matter closely and concluded that Trinidad's victories were due to the inclusion of two black professional bowlers, Wood and Cumberbatch.[16] This was a new and critical development in West Indies cricket, and signalled the beginning of the non-racial democratizing process in selection policy.

Multiracialism and the Colonial Dilemma

Black professionals had long been excluded in 'all-island' teams for 'friendly' games. Without black players, it was recognized, the Trinidadian team was no match for Barbados and Demerara. Warner considered this development of great importance to West Indies cricket. He concluded that only the integration of blacks into colonial and West Indies teams could raise the standard, increase competitiveness, and liberate the culture for the quantum leap into world recognition.

It was the 'illiberalism' of the racist mentality in Barbados and Demerara especially, Warner argued, that continued to insist upon the suffocating all-white race policy. Furthermore, he said, the talent of black players was necessary to "make the game more popular locally", and could assist in assuring "great and universal enthusiasm amongst all classes of the people". The first West Indian team selected for a proposed tour to England, he insisted, should include "four or five" black players, since this would be the only way to prevent embarrassments against county teams.[17]

The late 1890s, then, witnessed calls for the introduction of blacks into intercolonial cup competitions and West Indies touring teams. With a voice as influential as that of Pelham Warner, West Indian cricket élites felt compelled to listen and rethink selection policies. There had been no opposition in England to the presence of blacks in competitive cricket. By this time, such crude expressions of racial ideologies were confined to the colonials who found it particularly difficult to consider blacks as equals in any sphere of social activity. During the 1890s, Barbados had stated its refusal to play against Trinidad in the Challenge Cup if they included black players. In the 1897 competition the truth of Warner's argument was accepted when Trinidad arrived in Barbados without its black bowling stars and was massively beaten by an innings and 235 runs; centuries were scored for Barbados by H.B.G. Austin (129) and Gussy Cox (161).

If Trinidad had not learnt their lesson by this time, white Barbadians had received the message when in 1899 Spartan, the coloured middle class team, won the island's Challenge Cup, defeating traditional whites-only teams, and undermining their ideology of white supremacy in cricket culture. The rise to dominance of Spartan within Barbados cricket indicated to all that racism in West Indies cricket was a major inhibiting factor and an embarrassment to the ideals of cricket culture. The Trinidadians had initiated the policy of selection on merit, and now, at the end of the century, the word was out that ammunition for the future growth of West Indies cricket was to be found in large quantities within the black communities.

The recognition of this fact raised a number of questions concerning the social organization of West Indies cricket. Would whites accept blacks as equals within the boundary, and in the social activities beyond it? Were facilities available to blacks to acquire the 'personality' required of colonial representation? Would whites allow blacks access to leadership in this vital area of West Indian life? These questions generated controversy throughout the region, while the English cricket world listened with a mixture of amusement and horror.

Responding to the debate over the relative quality of black and white cricketers in Barbados, a leader writer for the *Reporter* argued that "there is absolutely no provision of playgrounds attached to primary and elementary schools" attended by black children, and yet their fidelity to the methods and values of the game was well inculcated. Blacks, it was understood, had established their own cricket culture about the 'gullies' of plantation villages and streets of urban ghettos.[18] Their game was learnt at the community level rather than formally within the school system. For them, cricket had become as instinctively cultural as religion and the performing arts.

Behind Spartan's success in 1899, could be found a spring of black talent waiting to be liberated. Professional black teams, such as the Fenwicks and Carrington cricket clubs, both working class organizations, represented this plank within Barbados cricket. It was known that these teams did defeat established Challenge Cup sides, but were excluded from formal competition on the basis that they were professionals, though it was also known that racial prejudice was the principal reason.

By the end of the century, then, blacks were poised to force their way *en masse* into first-class colonial cricket and therefore to secure selection eligibility for West Indies teams. Everything was in place to attain these ends. When, in 1899, it was announced that Lord Hawke had invited a West Indian team to tour England in the summer of 1900, the time for the grand 'English' début of multiracial West Indies cricket had arrived.

26

First Tour to England

P.F. Warner's brother, R.S. Warner, was appointed to captain the West Indies side. A selection committee, representing all the West Indian cricket territories, met in Trinidad in January 1900 with the mandate to choose a representative team. Shortly thereafter the news came: five blacks were selected to the touring party of 15. These players were Fitz Hinds (Barbados), W.J. Burton (Demerara), C.A. Ollivierre (St Vincent), and S. Wood and G.L. Constantine (Trinidad). Pelham Warner wrote:

It has been decided to include black men in the coming team, and there is little doubt that a fairly strong side can be got together. Without these black men it would have been quite absurd to attempt to play first-class counties, and no possible benefit would have been derived from playing those of the second class only. The fielding will certainly be of a high class. The black men will, I fear, suffer from the weather if the summer turns out cold and damp, as their strength lies in the fact that their muscles are extremely loose, owing to the warm weather to which they are accustomed. Woods takes only two steps and bowls as fast as Mold! Englishmen will be very much struck with the throwing powers of these black men, nearly all of them being able to throw well over a hundred yards. On the whole, I feel pretty confident that the team will attract favourable attention all round, and my view is, I know, shared by many sound judges of the game. The visit of any new team to England is always an experiment, attended with more or less possibilities of failure; but that they will be a failure I do not for a moment think, and in any case West Indian cricket will be greatly improved.[19]

The tour was not given first class status as there seemed to have been considerable belief among English officials that the West Indians were not ready for 'serious' competitive cricket. *Wisden* described the tour as an "experiment", but P.F. Warner had no doubt that by its end the West Indians would be ready for first class status.

The English press warmly welcomed the "second-class" West Indians but criticized heavily their apparent "slipshod and lazy" attitudes. The *Boy's Own Paper* (*BOP*), however, was particularly concerned to inform its readers about the "great novelty of the presence of coloured men playing on a cricket field in England", and indicated that before the tour began there had been much comment that the blacks would go on to the field "without boots and in a very sparse attire". W.L.A. Coleman, surveying the sociological contours of the tour, wrote in *The Cricketer*:

Apparently the coloured members of the team were much impressed with England and they indicated that in the West Indies the question was being asked as to whether white and coloured cricketers should play together in the same team. It had been the form to allow only white cricketers to play in cup and inter-colonial matches in the West Indies and the *BOP* editor ventured to suggest that "on the return home, many of the islands must have found themselves in a very awkward position over the matter. If, for instance, any of the coloured players are good enough to represent the team in an international match, it is difficult to see how they can be refused opportunities of playing at home". This throws interesting light on the prevailing attitudes in the West Indies and how, at the time, their cricket was dominated by the whites. The manager indicated that the coloured players had apparently "very quickly fallen into English ways" and that "they gave no trouble whatever during the tour. Indeed, they lived in the same hotels and were treated exactly like the white members". Woods is purported to have said "what a lot of white people they have got in this country", when playing at Crystal Palace.[20]

The performance of the team was not particularly impressive. It suffered consecutive defeats in its first four county matches, and was slaughtered in the sixth game against Gloucestershire, whose first innings total of 619 included three centuries and a partnership of 201 made in an hour. In one over, Jessop who scored 157, struck six fours, during which the blacks on the team, according to Warner, "sat down on the ground and shouted with laughter at the unfortunate bowler's discomforture".[21] In this game they were defeated by an innings and 216 runs. Its best performance was against Surrey whom they defeated by an innings and 34 runs with Wood returning figures of 7 for 48 and 5 for 68, and Cox and Ollivierre putting on an opening partnership score of 208 runs. The tour was, however, a major historic occasion for black

TABLE 4 COMPOSITION OF THE WEST INDIES TOURING TEAM TO ENGLAND, 1906

Name	Country	Race*
H.B.G. Austin (Captain)	Barbados	White
G.C. Learmond	Trinidad	White
W.J. Burton	Demerara	Black
L.S. Constantine	Trinidad	Black
J.J. Cameron	Jamaica	Black
R.C. Ollivierre	St Vincent	Black
O.H. Layne	Barbados	Black
J.E. Parker	Demerara	White
C.P. Cumberbatch	Trinidad	Black
C.K. Bancroft	Barbados	White
G. Challenor	Barbados	White
P.A. Goodman	Barbados	White
S.G. Smith	Trinidad	White
A.E. Harragin	Trinidad	White

* The term is used in the popular sense, i.e. the extent to which a person is understood to look more like one race than another.

players, and more importantly, the beginning of modern nonracial West Indies 'international' cricket. All that was left was to consolidate the achievements of this start.

In December–January 1904–5, an English team arranged by Lord Brackley, toured the West Indies capturing the spirit of a return bout. While in the region Lord Brackley was clearly impressed with the improvement in the West Indies game since 1900, and made arrangements for a second West Indies team to tour England during the following summer. He also insisted that the tour be designated first class – with a few second-class fixtures to satisfy reluctant commentators.

The 1906 intercolonial Challenge Cup competition was held in Trinidad, and immediately after its completion a selection committee comprising Messrs Gail and Belgrave (Demerara), P.A. Goodman and H.A. Cole (Barbados), and A.E. Harragin and G.C. Learmond (Trinidad) met at Queen's Park Cricket Club to select the West Indies team for the tour. The 14-member team chosen was considered an improvement upon the 1900 team, more balanced and stronger in each department. This time the blacks were not in the minority (see Table 4).

The English cricket press welcomed the team on arrival at Southampton on Monday 4 June, and remained divided throughout the tour on its designation as a first-class outfit. The members of the first West Indian first-class 'integration' team – still not Test standard (that came in 1928) – were described by the English press as follows:

1. H.B.G. Austin (Barbados), captain. A graceful bat with an especially good drive. He uses his weight to advantage, and although not too good a starter, he ought to make a lot of runs. 1904–5 batting average, 33.40.

2. C.K. Bancroft (Barbados). He is in residence at Cambridge as the team arrives in England. A wicket-keeper who is said to be very alert with the gloves. He kept well against Lord Brackley's XI and is also a steady bat. 1904–5 batting average, 9.00; 3 caught and 2 stumped.

3. G. Challenor (Barbados). A member of a famous cricketing family who should score a fine average. He is an attractive bat who combines brilliant batting with sound defence. He is young but most promising.

4. P.A. Goodman (Barbados). A 1900 tourist, who, with four centuries, was regarded by some as the best bat in the side. He has a good defence and can hit hard. He makes a pretty cut and uses his wrist well. He can bowl medium pace right hand with a break from leg. A capital slip. 1900 batting average, 28.15; 1904–5, 45.00. 1900 bowling, 5 wickets at 54.00; 1904–5, 7 wickets at 14.42.

5. O.H. Layne (Barbados). A professional and fast right hand bowler who can make the ball bump and is none too pleasant to play on a bad wicket. He is a fine long field with a dashing return and is a sound careful bat. 1904–5 batting average, 23.66, bowling 12 wickets at 28.50.

6. G.C. Learmond (Trinidad). A 1900 tourist, he has in turn been identified with Barbados, Demerara and Trinidad. A splendid bat, who having to keep wicket, failed to do himself justice on the previous tour. He has now cultivated cutting, is a useful slow change bowler and a capital field in the slips. 1900 batting average, 9.10; 1904–5, 18.00.

7. L.S. Constantine (Trinidad). A 1900 tourist, another of the old brigade who proved himself very strong on the left side and can bat with power. He fields in the slips and can bowl right hand medium pace if required. He was consistently good with the willow against Lord Brackley's XI, being second in the averages. 1900 batting average, 30.50; 1904–5, 36.80.

8. J.J. Cameron (Jamaica). A student at Edinburgh University and a fine field at cover point; a useful change bowler and sound bat.

9. A.E. Harragin (Trinidad). A player who can punish all types of bowling. He captained the Trinidad team this season and had fared particularly well in the intercolonial matches. A brilliant man in the country, fast and a sure thrower. 1904–5 batting average, 17.87.

10. S.G. Smith (Trinidad). He is regarded as the crack bowler of the side. A left hander with easy delivery who can make the ball break either way, and who sends down a deceptive fast ball. He can hit with vigour and precision and cuts well. He is a good field in the slips. 1904–5 batting average, 12.55, bowling 20 wickets at 13.95.

11. C.P. Cumberbatch (Trinidad). A professional who may be looked on as the mainstay of the attack. He bowls fast right arm, with an off break, the balls rising very sharply from the pitch. He has a good defence and is a safe field. 1904–5 batting average, 12.00, bowling, 24 wickets at 11.45.

12. J.E. Parker (Demerara). A slow bowler of the Armstrong type, with a field placed on the on-side; a fair defensive batsman and excellent slip.

13. W.J. Burton (Demerara). A professional who is a fine right hand medium pace power with plenty of break and a deceptive flight. He secured a fine record on the 1900 tour and hit well on several occasions. He is a sure field. 1900 batting average, 11.64; 1904–5, 9.60. 1900 bowling, 78 wickets at 21.55; 1904–5, 20 wickets at 16.90.

14. R.C. Ollivierre (St Vincent). He is one of the famous brotherhood and a hard hitter. He is quite the Jessop of the Indies, but combines the penchant of A.N. Hornby for short runs. Being the reserve wicket-keeper and a capital fast bowler, he is a good all round exponent. 1904–5 batting average, 26.50; bowling 21 wickets at 12.57.[22]

TABLE 5 WEST INDIES IN ENGLAND, 1906 – TOUR RESULTS [23]

Opposition	Dates	Venue	Results
W.G. Grace XI	June 11–12	Crystal Palace	Lost by 247 runs
Essex	June 14–16	Leyton	Lost by 111 runs
Lord Brackley's XI	June 18–20	Lord's	Lost by 2 wickets
Minor Countries	June 21–23	Ealing	Won by 215 runs
Surrey	June 25–26	The Oval	Lost by 10 wickets
Wiltshire	June 29–30	Swindon	Lost by 86 runs
Hampshire	July 2–4	Southampton	Lost by 6 wickets
South Wales	July 9–10	Cardiff	Won by 278 runs
Kent	July 12–1	Catford	Lost by an innings and 14 runs
MCC	July 16–17	Lord's	Lost by 6 wickets
Derbyshire	July 23–25	Derby	Lost by 6 wickets
Scotland	July 23–25	Edinburgh	Won by 4 wickets
An England XI	July 26–28	Blackpool	Drawn
Durham/ Northumberland	July 30–Aug 1	Sunderland	Won by 145 runs
Yorkshire	Aug 6–8	Harrogate	Won by 262 runs
Leicestershire	Aug 6–8	Leicester	Lost by 24 runs
Norfolk	Aug 10–11	Norwich	Won by an innings and 118 runs
Nottinghamshire	Aug 13–15	Nottingham	Drawn
Northamptonshire	Aug 16–18	Northampton	Won by 115 runs

Overall results: Lost, 10 games; Won, 7 games; Drawn, 2 games

The insightful assessment of the tour given by Gerry Wolstenholme leaves no doubt that for most English spectators and officials the tour revealed the two faces of empire and imperial ideology.[24] On the one hand it was necessary to encourage the colonials in a paternal sort of way even if to put them in their subordinate place by example of defeat. On the other hand, given the racial ideology endemic to empire, and the fact that the West Indies team had now for the first time acquired the image as a black force in spite of white leadership, elements of the press considered it necessary to cast the contest within a racial paradigm.

The team, on arrival, was invited to dinner by their sponsors, the West Indian Club, at the seemingly appropriate Imperial Restaurant. The official scaffold of imperial hospitality in place, Sir Cavendish Boyle, chairman of the evening's proceedings, toasted the team with language that removed any doubt about the perception that West Indies cricketers in England were part of a wider scheme of empire consolidation and promotion. The West Indian guests were admonished:

You are to show of what good stuff the children of Britain living in the beautiful climes known as the West Indies are possessed . . . I hope you pull together, train together, bowl together, bat together, field together for the honour of our sunny homes and add another link in the chain of oneness and wholeheartedness which binds the sons of Great Britain with the children of the greater Britain in that undefeated, age undaunted, whole – our British Empire.[25]

In reply to Sir Boyle, the West Indies captain indicated, particularly to the press, that his team was a revolutionary exercise in resource organization as it was drawn from five colonies "thousands of miles apart" and had never played before as one.[26]

The performance of the team, like its 1900 predecessor, started poorly but showed marked improvement as the tour progressed. The first game was against the W.G. Grace XI, on 11 June, at Crystal Palace – the same date and venue as the first match in 1900. The West Indies was trashed by 247 runs. In the second match against Essex they lost by 111 runs, and the third against Lord Brackley's XI, a second-class game, they lost by two wickets.

Following their first defeat, the press went to work promoting the argument that the West Indians were not a first-class lot, and that the decision to offer them this status was premature.

One reporter stated: "The West Indians gave a poor display of fielding. They dropped no less than seven catches (a rather kind estimate); they did not seem to be able to catch anything except the train to take them home". [27] After the game against Brackley's XI, one cricket reporter complained that "all their bowlers are as mild as the weather itself". A caricature showing the West Indian team as represented by a monkey-like black child being spanked by W.G. Grace, appeared in the press. On the whole, the literary image of an African world – black primitives and white masters – was unleashed, in spite of the claim by Jeremiah Coleman, chairman of Surrey, that the "visit tended to create Imperial good fellowship".[28]

The match against the MCC at Lord's on 16 July, the tenth of the tour, provided another opportunity for the press to harangue the West Indians. They were defeated by six wickets after giving the home team 87 runs to win. In an article by cricket journalist H.D. Sewell, under the caption "What is the matter with the West Indian Team?", readers were informed:

Once again the West Indies have failed to do themselves justice – as a side . . . It is a most extraordinary thing that the side, as a side, cannot get going in cricketer's phraseology. Is it just all the difference between first and second class, I wonder. I was chatting with one of the Kent XI and he wondered why they did not get more runs. He said their field was badly placed and only the coloured men are good catchers. They are certainly a mysterious side – and I cannot help thinking they may one day do something surprising.[29]

Following this tour, however, the concept of a first-class multiracial West Indies team was well established. Finally, they were elevated to Test status for the 1928 tour of England in which three official Test matches were played. By this time West Indies cricket had moved a long way from the planter–merchant culture in which it was incubated, though the management and other economic relations remained firmly in the hands of this group.

The working classes, however, had brought their cricket from the gullies of their villages to the international stage and had impressed wherever they went as excellent representatives of the modern game. In so doing they had broken the barriers of institutionalized racism and forged the way towards a new democratic ethos. As in all liberation struggles, determination and commitment to an ideal was necessary. Cricketers, then, led the way in many respects, and have demonstrated that in the West Indies cultural resources cannot be divided on ideological terms if maximum efficiency is to be attained with their use.

NOTES

1. Bruce Hamilton, *Cricket in Barbados* (Bridgetown: Advocate Press, 1947), 25.
2. Ibid., 30.
3. Ibid., 39.
4. Ibid., 39.
5. George Plumtree and E.W. Swanton (eds.), *Barclays World of Cricket: The Game from A–Z* (London: Willow Books, 1986 ed.), 78.
6. Ibid., 127–28.
7. G. Wyatt, *The Tour of the West Indian Cricketers, August and September 1886* (Demerara: Argosy Press, 1887), 7. Additional data cited below with respect to this tour are also from this book.
8. See also: Hamilton, *Cricket,* 32–4; Dave Soares, "A history of the Melbourne Cricket Club, 1892–1962", MA thesis, Department of History, University of the West Indies, Mona, Jamaica, 1987.
9. Wyatt, *The Tour,* 62, 63, 67.
10. Ibid., 68–69.
11. Ibid., 63–64.
12. Ibid., 64.
13. Ibid., 92.
14. Ibid.
15. *Times,* 9 February 1895, Barbados Archives.
16. Hamilton, *Cricket in Barbados,* 53.
17. Ibid., 56.
18. Ibid., 63.
19. Cited in Michael Davie and Simon Davie (eds.), *The Faber Book of Cricket* (London: Faber, 1987), 37.

20. W.L.A. Coleman, "The first West Indians", in *The Cricketer*, edited by Christopher Martin-Jenkins (June 1988).
21. Ibid.
22. Gerry Wolstenholme, *The West Indies Tour of England, 1906* (Blackpool: Nelson, 1992), 7–8.
23. Ibid.
24. Ibid., 24.
25. Ibid.
26. Ibid., 35–37.
27. Ibid., 13.
28. Ibid., 15.
29. Ibid., 20–21.

3

Pelham 'Plum' Warner's Project

The Making of a Colonial Cricketer

In many respects the legendary Sir Pelham Warner was at once a special creation and a senior statesman of West Indies colonial cricket in its formative democratizing stage at the beginning of the twentieth century. In him, we see the colourfully textured ways in which colonialism struggled to embrace and promote organized cricket as popular culture. As a fully enfranchised member of white élite West Indian society, Plum Warner, as he was generally known, represented cricket excellence on and off the field, and was respected as a leader of the game in its many aspects. Significantly, he led an ideological campaign, in the calm and subtle manner expected of the late Victorian scholar-cricketer, to throw open the gates of West Indian cricket to all men of talent and social quality irrespective of their race, colour or class. He was hailed in the West Indies as a supporter of cricket's democratic impulse, a promoter of popular participation at all its levels, and an advocate of its finest, humanist values.

Plum was born at Port of Spain on 2 October 1873, the son of Charles B. Warner, attorney general of Trinidad, who was born at sea between England and Barbados on 19 October 1805, two days before the battle of Trafalgar. His father had married twice, had 18 children, and was 68 years of age at Plum's birth. As an Eton student, Charles had played a little cricket, but Plum was to receive his formative cricket instruction from black servants about the house, and at school in Trinidad and Barbados. Reflecting on his childhood, he wrote: "I cannot remember when I was not keen on cricket, and I used to practise often before breakfast in my night-shirt on a marble gallery which made a perfect wicket, bowled to by a native boy who did all sorts of jobs about the house and garden, and who assured my father that I should be a good bat when I grew big." [1]

Like most children of the Trinidad élite, Plum received his primary education at home under the guidance of a governess; it was during this time that 'native' boys were his playmates. At the age of nine he attended the premier secondary school in the colony, Queen's Royal College (QRC) – at the time a multiracial institution for the propertied classes and a few scholarship winners from the less financially secure classes. Cricket culture was very much at the core of the academic programme at QRC, and other such Caribbean schools. Before Plum's time the school had already established a solid reputation as a cricketing centre in the pedagogical tradition of the English public schools. West Indian cricket, therefore, was developing along two distinct social tracks – both of which were part of Plum's social formation. The 'native boys', who bowled to their social superiors, encouraged him, and QRC provided the first context for his engagement in the organized game.

During his Trinidadian childhood Plum was aware of the race and class discord that characterized West Indian society and cricket, and throughout his life did many things to oppose its wastefulness and the injustice it bred. But his socialization as a youth was designed to produce a faithful servant of white supremacy and empire, and scholarship and cricket resided at the centre of the educational strategy. In early 1886, at the age of 13, his father, aware of the more distinguished reputation of Harrison College in Barbados as a boys school modelled on Eton, transferred him there under the headmastership of Horace Deighton, a Cambridge graduate. Sandiford, in assessing the impact of these Victorian styled Caribbean schools on social culture states that:

... the cream of the élite schools was Harrison College in Barbados, which emerged as one of the most famous secondary schools throughout the world during the administration (1872–1905) of Horace Deighton. Several Old Harrisonians distinguished themselves as classical scholars at Cambridge and Oxford. How successful Deighton was in propagating the doctrine of athleticism is manifest in the history of West Indian cricket. Not only did Harrison College produce many generations of brilliant scholar-cricketers but its alumni managed to convert the entire Barbadian society to the cricket cult before the century had ended. Several Old Harrisonians then became classics teachers and cricket masters in secondary schools through the English-speaking West Indies. They were the apostles who successfully disseminated the cricket gospel in such islands as Antigua, Dominica, Grenada, Jamaica, Tobago, Trinidad and St Vincent. During the late-Victorian age, cricket thus became a most significant feature of Caribbean life.[2]

At Harrison College "cricket was indeed the only game", Plum recalled. There was a little rugby and tennis, "but cricket was the game". At 13, he made the First XI, and played against the Lodge School – their chief opponents, as well as against the soldiers at the Garrison. Cricket and classics held the boys at

Harrison College and the Lodge in competitive, ritual engagements, and Plum set about the task of being a master of both.

Harrison was almost entirely a day school, but there were a dozen or so boarders from other West Indian islands. If QRC was distinctly a multi-racial school, Harrison was not. There he met and became friends with the cricketing sons of the Barbados planter-merchant élite – "the Challenors, the Piles, the Howells, the Skeetes, the Spencers, the Sealys, the Evelyns, and the Hicksons". "I owe much to Harrison College," Plum admitted, "for it was there that the foundations of any skill I may have acquired at cricket were built . . ."[3]

At age 15 years, Plum was at Eton, and playing cricket for the Second XI. The adjustment was an easy one. The journey from QRC to Harrison to Eton was movement between institutions that stood for the same principles of educational and social development. The cultural space between colony and metropole was conflated as young colonials like Plum interfaced the sugar fields at home with the playing field of the mother country. It was in this integrated cultural world that he received the guiding concept of his life: "keep a straight bat and a modest mind, and you will go far".

Race and the Imperial Order

A month after graduating from Oxford with a degree in law, Plum sailed back to the West Indies. It was 1897, and he was a member of a touring team assembled and led by Lord Hawke – described as the Odysseus of cricket on account of having taken touring teams to Australia, South Africa, India, the USA and Canada. Little did Plum know that six years later he would be appointed captain of the first team the MCC ever sent abroad. As treasurer and president of the MCC, Lord Hawke was well placed to bring together West Indies and English cricket – and to use the services of a West Indian born batsman as the bridge between the two cultural spaces. Plum made an important 119 in the opening match of the tour in Trinidad, his home community, gaining the approval of the locals who claimed him as their "little boy" who returned with "de Lord". He was embraced in front of his team by his childhood nanny, Kitsey, who seemed oversatisfied that "her little boy became a big cricketer".[4]

During the Hawke tour, 14 matches were played. The visitors won nine, lost two (both to Trinidad captained by Plum's brother, Aucher), and drew three. Plum's observation on the contests, however, was instructive: "It was clear that the West Indies would one day be formidable opponents for they were natural cricketers", and were "inspired by intense enthusiasm and love of the game".[5] During the tour Plum established his reputation of an outstanding batsman, a matured player and keen competitor. On returning to England in May 1898, he scored his first hundred at Lord's – 108 not out for the MCC vs. Yorkshire – the first century made on that ground by a West Indian born cricketer. The innings was described by *Wisden* as "splendid batting".

In September the same year he led a side to the USA, playing games in Philadelphia, Staten Island, New York and Baltimore. The following year he joined another Lord Hawke side on tour to South Africa. There he scored a match winning 132 against the colony at Johannesburg, and established on both sides of the Atlantic world a reputation as a distinguished West Indian born English cricketer. As a white West Indian committed to the British Empire playing and administering cricket within its boundaries was as natural as criss-crossing the globe in promotion of imperial cultural hegemony. He also had the pleasure of playing a game in England for a West Indies team against Leicestershire, at Leicester, in which he scored 113. But his cricket tours to South Africa, India and Australia, before the West Indies were granted Test status in 1928, fitted perfectly into his version of the imperial order of things.

Plum's cricket tours outside of the empire, however, did pose other sets of political and cultural challenges, though the ultimate objective was very much the same. A tour to South America in 1926–27 took in Rio de Janeiro, Santos and Montevideo. On all occasions, the steamer on which the team travelled flew the MCC flag, a "unique honour . . . on any ship in any sea", Plum noted.[6] The team played seven matches in the Argentine, one at Montevideo, and then, crossing the Andes, played at Valparaiso and Lima. Not a single game of the tour was played within British territory, "another proof", noted Plum, that "cricket has set a girdle round the earth, and that it has become the interest not only of the British race, but of half the world".[7] The British consul in addressing the tour party at Buenos Aires described the players as "ambassadors, not only of cricket, but of empire". President Dr Alvear of Argentina, and President Lequia of Peru, received the players, and made reference to the importance placed upon cricket within British culture. Both presidents, however, detached the warm welcome afforded the cricketers from any association with notions of British imperial expansion.

Suitably, Plum and his colleagues ended the tour within the Caribbean at Panama. On entering the black communities along the Canal Plum was informed that there were several cricket clubs – nine in Colón and the others spread over the country. These were established and maintained by West Indians contracted to work on the construction of the Canal since the 1870s. The West Indians, on recognizing Plum as a fellow countryman honoured him with a 'creole dinner' after which he presented them with a bat and "congratulated them on the splendid way in which they were keeping the flag of cricket flying".[8] In the Argentine the toughest team Plum met was captained by one C.H. Gibson of Eton and Cambridge but the West Indian players he saw in Panama were cut socially from the same cloth as those he had advocated for the West Indies team during the tours to England in 1900 and 1906. These working men, Plum knew, would carry into the future the torch of cricket culture in a way never before experienced.

Plum's social understanding was that white and black cricketers in the West Indies, and those in England, for whom he was a conduit, were held together by ideological bonds symbolized in the social and cultural practice of cricket. According to Sandiford, Plum sought to identify a high moral ground for empire, but was sensitive to the contradictions evident within the concept as it related to the politics of race hatred and colonial exploitation:

Pelham Warner, a native of Trinidad, disagreed in the 1890s with the racist policy of Barbados and Demerara. He sincerely believed that the black professionals added a vital dimension, as the bowling of Cumberbatch and Woods for Trinidad had just shown. He thought that the West Indies should send a composite team to England soon, but bluntly added that if the black men were excluded "it would be absurd to attempt to play the first class counties". Warner was sure that a combination of nine white players and five blacks could give the majority of English counties very stiff competition indeed. This advice was only partially followed in 1900, when a few token blacks were selected among the first West Indian cricketers to tour England. This gave the editor of the *Athletic News* a chance to observe that the "men of colour" were hopelessly out of their element in a coldish summer, "although it must be said that neither in the West Indies nor in England could this type of player ever hope to bring the same amount of intelligence to his game". This was the orthodoxy of that age which served to keep the West Indies out of Test cricket until 1928.[9]

Cricket, Warner believed, should symbolize social progress and justice, and not the endemic racial oppression and class alienation that was challenged by radical socialist and anti-imperial insurgents. He spoke of the fairness of the game's value system and believed that it was an important vehicle on which West Indians of all ethnicity could travel into a more democratic future.

If, in 1906, the black cricketers sent on tour to England had weakened the force of colonial opposition to their participation, the English in beating the team were keen to demonstrate their interest in keeping all colonials – black and white – in a subordinate position. A.E. Morton, popular English cartoonist, did not miss the opportunity to capture the politics of ethnic relations that surrounded the tour. Though blacks were never a majority in any side, Morton, and most journalists, managed somehow to construct a black image of the team for popular social consumption. Morton's cartoon which depicted W.G. Grace in white flannels whipping a terrified black monkey-like figure placed over his lap, represented the general racist attitudes that lurked beneath the surface of the English welcome.

The West Indians got their first 'whacking' yesterday.

This A.E. Morton cartoon comments on the West Indian defeat at Crystal Palace in the first game of the 1906 tour

Furthermore, the representation of W.G. Grace as an imperial officer disciplining an insolent, childlike native located cricket in England at the centre of colonial discourse, particularly the legitimacy of colonial rule and white superiority ideology. A cricket postcard which showed a barefoot black girl dressed like a rag doll bowling to a black boy attired as an agricultural labourer entitled "Happy Little Coons" became very popular during and after the tour.[10] The iconography was distinctly racist and reflective of late Victorian attitudes to blacks who through cricket were seeking to develop a closer association with imperial culture.

The game played at Lord's against an MCC Club and Ground XI, however, indicated more significantly the bonds already forged in the emergence of an Anglo-West Indian cricket sensibility. The MCC team included two West Indians – Plum Warner (the captain) and E.L. Challenor, brother of the 18-year-old George Challenor of the West Indies team. In the game George top scored for the tourists in the first innings with a patient innings of 59 (Cumberbatch also made 59) from a total of 240, and Plum did the honours for the MCC with a polished performance of 87 from a 269 total. Sydney Smith dominated the West Indies bowling with a haul of five wickets for 78 runs. The West Indies were bundled out for a meagre 115 runs in the second innings leaving the MCC a mere 87 runs for victory. These runs were made for the loss of three wickets.

Smith had impressed throughout the tour and was invited by Northamptonshire to join their club. He did so and became the first player for the county to score 1,000 runs in a season and also the first to do the double. He captained the team in 1913–14 and after a total of 117 games with the club emigrated to New Zealand where he played with Auckland. Charles Ollivierre, Vincentian star of the 1900 tour, had also opted to play county cricket, and with Smith constructed the foundation on which West Indian cricketers would build monuments within the park of English county cricket.[11]

Plum in 1900 had foreseen these developments in West Indies cricket, and his disappointment that the West Indies were not granted Test status until 1928 spoke to the potency of the wider imperial agenda to which he was a critical subscriber. His vision, however, was not born purely of intellectual insight. Rather, it had to do with his earlier exposure to West Indies players as a member of Lord Hawke's team during the tour of 1896–97, particularly to his fellow Trinidadians. Though Plum was the outstanding batsman of Hawke's team, falling short of 1,000 runs by 16, he had considerable difficulty with the black Trinidadian pacemen, J. Woods and C.P. Cumberbatch. He also had problems with Clifford Goodman, the white Barbadian pacer. In these three men, the West Indies had as good a pace attack as any, and Plum recognized their importance to the West Indian cause.

White Batsmen, Black Bowlers

The success of Woods and Cumberbatch was the barometer by which West Indians came to measure their suitability for first class cricket. Both men, James noted, with no opportunities had made themselves bowlers whom most English counties would have been glad to have. Recognizing that Plum was an active campaigner for West Indian multiracial cricket, and a leading MCC batsman, James paid particular attention to how he performed with the bat against the black professionals:

P.F. Warner did not fare very well against them. He got 74 before falling to Cumberbatch in his first innings against the pair, and in his next three innings Cumberbatch had him twice for small scores. The pity was that only Woods came to England, for Cumberbatch would surely have succeeded. During his tour Lord Hawke had said that a team of West Indian cricketers was good enough to go to England, and play against the counties, and on this hint a tour was arranged.[12]

Unlike Plum, however, W.G. Grace was more impressed with the West Indian batsmen during the 1906 tour, and had singled out George Challenor and Captain Harold B. Austin – the two white Barbadian aristocrats – as men of the future.

If in Challenor Grace saw a future batting star, it was recognized all over the West Indian cricketing world that Austin was the master organizer and natural leader of the pioneering West Indian efforts. His appointment to lead the team in 1906 seemed inevitable given his prominence as a 'big' player with a shrewd eye for development details. Austin was one of five brothers, three of whom played cricket for Barbados and the other two for British Guiana. Born into an upper class merchant family, the Austin boys played their game wherever their economic interest took them.

Harold, like Plum, was a Harrison product of the time when Principal Horace Deighton was enthusiastically promoting the game. In 1899, after he had established his reputation as a leading batsman for Wanderers Club and Barbados, he went off to help the English fight the Boers in South Africa. On his return in 1902 he consolidated his reputation as a batsman and cricket administrator. His investment in cricket was total; he loved the game and dedicated his personal financial resources to its advancement.[13] Unlike most players in 1906, he was able to pay his own way comfortably, and this fact was of critical significance in consolidating his leadership. Money in those days bought selection advantages, and West Indian cricket was dominated by the rich and influential.

The development of West Indies cricket in the years after the 1906 tour confirmed the accuracy of Grace's perception. English teams visited the region between 1907 and 1911 and presented opportunities for West Indians to fine tune and display their cricketing skills. On the 1909 tour white Barbadian batsmen, Percy Goodman, P.H. Tarilton and George Challenor, plundered the English bowling, and Andre Cipriani of Trinidad emerged as the hero of a new breed of coloured fast bowlers who paved the way for the legendary George John and Learie Constantine. The 1911 touring team was also roughly treated by Barbados and Trinidad, with Austin, Challenor, Constantine, Cipriani and Tarilton blazing trails through its bowling attack.

If the consensus on both sides of the Atlantic was that the 1911 side was weak, and expected the treatment it received, this could not be said of the 1913 touring team which included many established county players:

It was a very good team, but West Indies cricket was now of a high standard. Barbados, by itself as powerful in batting as most English counties, made scores of 520 for 6 and 447, winning by an innings each time. Tarilton and Gibbs each scored a century, and George Challenor two. Challenor's 109 was a grand innings, the first half played on a tricky wicket, the batsmen opening out as the wicket improved. But R. Challenor, C.A. Browne, and H.W. Ince (like the Austins, the Challenors were all fine cricketers) all scored heavily, and the English bowling could do little with them.[14]

By this time, West Indies first-class cricket was well on the way, and deserving, as Plum had expected, to be awarded Test status. But it was not to be. This was to come much later, and after two additional postwar tours to England.

The Fight for Test Status

Plum was swimming against the tide in his effort to promote the West Indies to Test status. The 1900 tour was not granted first class status, and though the 1906 tour was elevated, there remained racial attitudes within the English cricket establishment that viewed West Indian players as inferior and inadequate. The racism at the heart of the British Empire had been demonstrated on the cricketing field much earlier. The first Australian tour to England was in 1868, but this was a team of Aboriginals, put together by an Englishman, Charles Lawrence, their coach and manager. They were not defined as *the* Australian team, as blacks were not allowed by white colonials to represent the colony. The team did reasonably well, winning 14 of the 47 matches: 19 were drawn and 14 lost.

Ten years later, when *the* Australian side visited England, it was an all white outfit. The colony had been granted Test status the previous year in 1877, and the first official Test was played between the two teams at Melbourne. Likewise, the white South Africans were granted Test status in 1889 when England opposed them at Port Elizabeth. But in their 1894 Test tour of England, the white South Africans excluded the black cricketing genius Krom Hendriks because they did not wish to play with or against blacks. The English understood and accepted their policy as consistent with their own thinking and sense of imperial order.[15]

White Barbadians and black Trinidadians constituted the nuclei of post-war efforts at raising cricket standards in order to secure Test status for the West Indies. Arrangements were made in 1919 for a competition between the two colonies to commence the following year. This contest provided the opportunity for both new and experienced players to perform before local fans, and to build social relations for the future. Performances were predictable. Barbados scored 623 for 5 in one match, Percy Tarilton making an extraordinary 304 not out in less than two days. W. St Hill from Trinidad emerged as a star batsman, but it was J.A. Small who stood out as their most improved player, shifting his focus from medium-fast bowling to middle order batting.

Tarilton had established himself with Challenor as the leading opening batsmen in the West Indies. Unlike Challenor, he was a patient and cautious strokemaker whose first instinct was the defensive play. But like Challenor, he was a child prodigy. A middle class white boy from rural Barbados, he attended the Lodge School and played in the first division in the Challenge Cup for his school at age 11. By the time he was 16 he was already one of the best opening batsmen in Barbados. The 304 not out against Trinidad set a Barbadian first-class record which was broken in 1944 by Frank Worrell. Throughout the 1920s he and Challenor plundered West Indian bowlers. The Trinidadians, especially, bore the brunt of their force on several occasions, particularly in the 1927 season when the pair put on a 292 partnership. In 1923, on the tour to England he was already 38 and past his best, but his 109 not out against Nottinghamshire represented evidence of his considerable skill. [16]

THE TOUR TO ENGLAND, 1923

To some extent the immediate postwar matches were trials for the upcoming 1923 tour to England. While for blacks the selection process was far from satisfactory, it was understood generally that performances in these games would constitute the basis of consideration for inclusion in the touring party. Expectation of the granting of Test status was the subject of popular discussions, and players had reason to believe that tour results would be the determining factor. When the side was declared in early 1923, there were few surprises. H.B.G. Austin, as expected, was to carry the side, and comments that he was over 40 and too old were set aside by the widespread recognition that he was still one of the most reliable batsmen in the region. The other

Barbadians were G. Challenor, H.W. Ince, P.H. Tarilton and G. Francis. From Guiana, came C.R. Browne, and Trinidad provided G. John, V. Pascall, G.A. Dewhurst, L. Constantine and J. Small, while Jamaica sent out J.K. Holt, R.K. Nunes and R. Phillips. The little known George Francis of Barbados was chosen over the feared Herman Griffith to bowl the new ball with John on the recommendation of the captain, a decision that surprised spectators. Learie Constantine, whose father had been a pioneer in the 1900 and 1906 tours, was regarded as a genuine all-rounder and brilliant fielder. Altogether, the team was expected to perform at the highest level – certainly beating most county sides and establishing the argument for West Indies Test status.

The team, however, performed moderately at best. The batting failed miserably, though glimpses of brilliance were seen from time to time. The bowling was impressive, occasionally superb, and brought respectability to the overall performance. Sympathizers blamed the weather by drawing attention to the often wet and cold conditions. But this was hardly a satisfactory explanation. Challenor did well because he was a player of considerable class. The 1,556 runs scored at an average of 51 surprised no one, but merely confirmed what W.G. Grace had said in 1906. Small occasionally showed form, but the failure of Ince and Tarilton, and the below average performance of Austin (av. 25) exposed the team to frequent ridicule. West Indians at home read the scores in shame and dismay. They had seen these batsmen dominating good bowling in recent years at the regional level, and noticed that they did not spare the bowlers of touring English teams. Suddenly, they appeared ordinary and unreliable against bowling that was not understood as demonic.

The tour, however, was a turning point for the culture of West Indian fast bowling. The speedsters impressed wherever they went with tenacity and accuracy. Francis and John established a reputation as a powerful and respected pair, each taking over 100 wickets. C.L.R. James noted:

P.F. Warner and a few others said quite openly that an English side of that year would have been glad to have Francis and John. Francis was the deadlier, and from his first match had a series of astonishing analyses, clean bowling an unusual number of batsmen for under double figures. John at the start was not so deadly, but John was approaching forty and past his best. In 1917, 1918, 1919, there could have been few finer fast bowlers. C.R. Browne, medium right hand, took 75 wickets in first-class matches and maintained a high level of excellence all through, while Pascall the left-hander, if not always deadly, took 51, and bowled very well . . . The finest performance was in the last match at Scarborough against an England XI which included Hobbs, Rhodes, G.T.S. Stevens, Ernest Tyldesley, J.W.H.T. Douglas, P.G.H. Fender, in fact a team not far removed from an English Test side. Having 31 to win, Francis and John bowled against the English XI in so determined a fashion that six wickets were lost before the runs were made, and that only with the help of all the luck that was going.[17]

The tour, furthermore, served to consolidate an ethnic division of labour which was rooted in plantation culture, and had shaped cricket's social relations in the West Indies since the mid nineteenth century; it determined that white men should bat and black men bowl. The ideological assumption behind this technological specialization was the climatic theory of plantation development which held that white men could not labour at high productivity levels under a tropical sun, and that black men could – hence the slave trade and African populations in the colonial worlds of the Americas. Fast bowling, was, in the scheme of things, considered a process of brutish hard labour while batsmanship was an art – or science – that emerged from the workings of the intellect.

George Challenor

Putting this reality aside, Challenor was rated a batsman of great class. Perhaps, more than any other player, he established West Indian batsmanship at the world level. He was already 35 during the 1923 tour. Described as having a classical style, and aggressive, Challenor also possessed a sound defence. It was for him a splendid tour. He scored eight impressive hundreds, including an aggressive 155 not out against Surrey. Following the tour he continued his domination of bowling attacks at home. In the 1927 domestic season he hit a magnificent 220 off Trinidad and 105 against Guiana. By this time he was considered the greatest batsman the West Indies had produced. In England, the comment was often heard that the century he struck off Nottinghamshire in his 1906 début tour, at the age of 18, was among the finest played there by a débutant.

Challenor, it has been said, was "born rich and batted like a millionaire". Like his captain in 1923, H.B. Austin, he was born in Barbados into an upper class white merchant family. He was the youngest of four brothers, all of whom played first division cricket for Wanderers Club. He attended Harrison College, and showed his batting ability before entering his teens. All who saw the young George knew that he was destined for greatness, but there was insufficient exposure to international cricket to develop his outstanding skills. He, nonetheless, flew the West Indian flag, and answered with his bat the questions asked about the ability of the island cricketers to hold their own internationally.

The 1926 tour of an MCC team to the West Indies also served to display the general rule of white batsmanship and black bowling that guided the development of the first class game. Austin, Nunes, Tarilton, Challenor, St Hill and Wiles performed well with the bat, and C.R. Browne scored an aggressive, high speed century against the tourists at Guiana. Constantine symbolized the spirit of West Indian fast bowling and fielding athleticism. He was expected to bowl all day while taking up the fielding position at cover-point, and yet be ready to produce a swashbuckling innings. By 1928, he had emerged the global icon of black cricket, the first truly great West Indian superstar. Nonetheless, he took instructions on the field from white men of considerably lesser talent whose selection often, even as players, could not be argued on the basis of cricketing performance.

Winning Test Status

The decision to grant the West Indies Test status came in 1928, and in the spring of that year trial matches were organized in Barbados to pick the team that would play three Tests against the MCC in England during the summer. This was the grand moment for West Indies cricketers, long overdue, Plum Warner and others argued, but momentous nonetheless. Some 50 years of touring North America and England, gathering experience and consolidating a first- class team culture, had come to maturity. The MCC finally agreed that the Test encounter was the appropriate context within which to meet the West Indies.

The leadership of the first Test side was given to R.K. Nunes of Jamaica. He had been vice-captain to Austin for the 1923 tour, and had scored a brilliant 140 not out for Jamaica against the 1926 MCC touring team of Lord Tennyson. At age 34, he was one of six players who had toured in 1923; also, he had been a founder member in 1926 of the Jamaica Cricket Board of Control. The batting was led by Challenor, F.R. Martin, M. P. Fernandes, W.H. St Hill, C.A. Roach, and Constantine; Captain Nunes held the gloves and batted at number 4. He had a horrid tour as a wicketkeeper, captain and batsman. In the first three Tests he scored just 87 runs from six innings, put down a number of chances, and lost each of the three matches by an innings. The 3–0 'whitewash' meant that the West Indies could only but improve, but Nunes's role in the entire unfortunate affair did not escape the critics who considered him aloof, out of touch with his players, and not compelling Test material.

The first Test was played at Lord's on 23–26 June. Batting first, England made a formidable 401, with E. Tyldesley, who had toured the West Indies more than once and knew the bowling attack, scoring a patient 122.

Constantine picked up 4 for 82 and Francis, losing much of his pace, 2 for 72, with Herman Griffith, J.A. Small and C.R. Browne also chipping in with 2 each. The West Indies batting did not stand up to the English attack led by Larwood, Tate, Freeman and Jupp, and was all out for 177 in the first innings. When asked to bat again they managed to score an embarrassing 166.

The defeat by an innings in the first Test was repeated in the second Test played at Old Trafford, 21–24 July. Batting first, the West Indies reached 206 thanks to a fifty partnership between C.R Browne (23) and O.C. Scott (32) batting at 8 and 9 respectively.England piled up an oppressive 351, and the West Indies facing a deficit of 145 could only muster 115 in the second innings, with St Hill top scoring with 38 and four batsmen, including the opening pair of Challenor and C.A. Roach each failing to score. In the West Indies first innings A.P. Freeman picked up five for 54 and five for 39 in the second.

The third Test at the Kennington Oval, 11–14 August, was more of the same for the West Indies. They batted first and compiled a modest 238 despite the fact that Captain Nunes did not trouble the scorers. England responded with a massive 438, led by a crushing 159 by opener J.B. Hobbs who had missed the first Test but had signalled his intention with 53 in the second. Griffith 6 for 103 from 25.5 overs, and Francis 4 for 112 from 27 overs, were impressive but Constantine's 0 for 91 from 20 overs, Scott's 0 for 75 from 14 and Small's 0 for 39 from 15, indicated the extent to which England showed their dominance over the West Indies as a batting force. Led by an even 200, West Indies were scattered for 129 in the second innings. England won the series 3–0, defeating the West Indies by an innings and 58 runs, an innings and 30 runs, and an innings and 71 runs in the first, second and third Tests respectively.

George Headley

There was, however, an enormously bright light shining through the West Indies cane fields in the name of George Alphonso Headley. Plum Warner might not have known in 1927 when he toured Panama and met with migrant West Indian workers on the Canal that the community had produced young Headley. Had Plum seen him in action in Jamaica in 1927, however, he would have recommended his selection for the West Indies Test team in 1928. Headley was born in Panama in 1909 of a Barbadian father and Jamaican mother. He did not go to Jamaica until the age of ten, following a stay of four years in Cuba where his parents had also migrated in search of work. As a teenager, his cricket ability was the subject of village talk and he was invited to join the St Catherine Cricket Club where his first-class game developed.

When Lord Tennyson's XI arrived in Jamaica in 1927, young Headley, just 18, was selected to play against it for Jamaica. In one game he scored 211 out of 348, and reports circulated through the West Indian cricketing world that a batting genius had been found. The forces of white supremacy that claimed batsmanship as its privilege and special preserve in West Indian cricket showed no anxiety about selecting the young Headley for the inaugural Test tour. He continued, however, to impress against touring English sides while dominating local bowlers in colonial contests. The thrashing received by the Test team in England in 1928 opened the opportunity for new players to be admitted, and Headley was selected to make his Test début against England in the 1929–30 West Indian tour.

Headley's arrival was in some respects quite revolutionary. The first specialist batsman hailing from the black working classes in West Indies Test cricket, he was sent in to bat at number 3; no black player could reasonably expect to bat this high in the Test batting order. These were esteemed positions reserved for the plantocracy and its mercantile allies. The lower social orders were presumed to occupy corresponding positions in the batting line up, and the public understood this as the natural order of things beyond the boundary. Headley's arrival, then, was welcomed by the working classes as a kind of saturnalia, the sign of things to come – the beginning of the democratic process that would turn the colonial world upside down. As for his team mates, he was charged with holding up the batting department against the English bowling attack and with removing the possibility of another humiliating white wash.

The Barbadian-Jamaican-Panamanian did not disappoint. In the first Test at Bridgetown, 11–16 January 1930, he scored 21 and 176 in the drawn game. The second innings score of 176 runs was made from a total of 384, and the débutant was immediately proclaimed by the locals as the best batsman in the West Indies. His scores of 8 and 39 in the second Test at the Queen's Park Oval were insufficient to prevent the West Indies from sliding to defeat, rekindling memories of the 1928 tour. By the third Test at Bourda, however, Headley retaliated, and secured for the West Indies its first Test victory. With scores of 114 and 112 in the Test, Headley had so far made three hundreds in three Tests on his début tour. While C.A. Roach's 209 runs in the first innings total of 471 had set the stage, Headley's second innings total of 112 from a total of 290, landed the West Indies a victory by 289 runs.

Travelling home to Jamaica for the fourth Test, Headley was to save the West Indies from its greatest embarrassment to date. Batting first, England whipped up a hurricane and piled an enormous 849 runs on the West Indies.

This was the game in which A. Sandham broke the record for the highest individual score in Tests with his 325 runs. West Indies in response were all out for a miserable 286, but England with a lead of 563 opted to bat again and made 272 for 9 declared, setting the West Indies 836 runs to win. Headley refused to be intimidated. He stood his ground, scoring an aggressive 223 in six and a half hours out of a total of 408 for 5. Batting with Captain Nunes they added 228, and when rain ended play on the last day, spectators were left debating who would have won the game (and the series) had it gone to time. Despite Sandham's record breaking innings, Headley was undoubtedly the man of the drawn series. West Indies cricket had finally produced a batting star who was arguably the 'greatest'.

The following year, West Indies made their début tour to Australia for a five-Test series. Headley maintained his number 3 spot in the batting order. The great Don Bradman was his opposite number in the Australian side. The Headley-Bradman comparison did not escape the attention of the media who went to considerable length to generate a literature on their relative batting strengths and weaknesses. It was no small matter that the little man from the West Indies was considered in such high esteem. Could it be that the West Indies, granted Test status just two years earlier, could make claims to possessing the greatest batsman in the world? In any event, what would such a claim say about the nature of West Indies cricket?

Both men got off to a poor start in the Test series to the utter disappointment of spectators. West Indies batted first in the first Test and Headley was caught off Grimmett for a duck and stumped off the same bowler for 11 in the second innings. Bradman batted only once in the match and was caught by Captain Grant off Herman Griffith for 4. Australia won the Test by 10 wickets erasing the 172 required to win without losing a wicket. Grimmett took 7 wickets in the West Indies first innings and 4 in the second. The second Test was more of the same. Bradman batted once and was removed by Francis for 25; Headley did no better, scoring 14 in the first innings and 2 in the second. The Aussies won the Test by an innings and 172 runs.

As if by design, the third Test saw both men rising from the shadow of failure and disappointment. Bradman had scored 223 before he was removed by Constantine; the Australian first innings total was 558. Headley in turn ran out of partners when the West Indies collapsed in the first innings for 193; he was left stranded in the middle on 102 not out. The next highest score for the West Indies was 21, made by Martin batting at number 2. Headley also top scored in the second innings with 28 from a total of 148, which guaranteed the West Indies defeat by an innings and 217 runs. Australia went on to win the fourth Test, this time by an innings and 122 runs, due in large measure to a first innings score of 152 by Bradman that overshadowed Headley's 33 and 11 in the first and second innings respectively.

With the score in the series standing at 4–0 in favour of Australia, the West Indians entered the fifth Test at Sydney facing a total disgrace, compounded by the fact that they had travelled an enormous distance to receive it. Headley's 105 in the first innings, and Bradman's duck in the second (bowled Griffith) saved what was left of West Indies pride. The Australians received their first defeat at the hands of the West Indies. Headley's 105 was so brilliant an innings, said the commentators, that the great Don rose in applause. While appreciative of the considerable praise, however, Headley lamented the fact that he had no choice but to treat C.V. Grimmett with the respect he had earned.

The West Indies, then, went off to a less than praiseworthy start in Test cricket. But there was much to be proud about in various aspects of their game. In Headley, they had as reliable a class player as any in the world. Constantine was undoubtedly the world's greatest all round cricketer, and in Francis, Constantine and Griffith they had a feared pace attack. Yet the components of the team were not welded together to frame a sturdy structure. English commentators spoke about the "usual batting collapses", and sports reporters referred, as if to a rule, to the batsmen's fickle and inconsistent performances.

While many new players were awaiting their chance to make a contribution, social forces beyond the boundary inhibited the free flow of talent into the side. The team remained riddled with racism and class arrogance, and players from different social backgrounds did not feel each other's needs because no natural channels of communication existed between them. In general, whites did not socialize with non-whites off the field, and blacks were divided among themselves by attitudes derived from their reading of how privilege operated within colonial society.

James and Constantine Confront White Supremacy

Both Plum Warner and C.L.R. James saw these issues clearly in 1933 as the team made preparations for the summer tour to England. Their performances in the series, James suggests, would be dependent upon how these social and ideological issues were handled. The team was led by G.C. Grant, an old Cambridge Blue, and this according to Plum enhanced their social stature among the English.[18] James did not think that there was any shortage of skill or ability in the team. But the social world that surrounded and informed the game needed to be ruled out of play. He wrote shortly after the team arrived in England:

Let every good West Indian know that, after watching cricket here and carefully weighing my words, I have no hesitation in saying that in cricket, as in many other things, West Indians are among the most highly gifted people one can find anywhere. The English have money, thirty times our population, vast organization, every conceivable advantage. Yet with all that, we could hold our own. Our trouble is that we have not yet learned to subordinate everything to winning. Under modern conditions to win you have got to make up your mind to win. The day West Indian whites, Browns and Blacks learn to be West Indian, to see nothing in front to right or left but West Indian success and the means to it, that day they begin to be grown up.[19]

This statement represents a confirmation of what Constantine had written the same year; that the West Indies cricket team was a home for race and class antipathies, and that this was the principal reason for its poor performance.

Both Constantine and James had good reason to question the political, and therefore tactical, thinking of Captain Jack Grant. While they accepted, like many other critics, that Grant was a leader of some cricketing ability, it did not follow that he would do the right thing by West Indies cricket against England within the context of the controversies that surrounded the 1933 tour. Popular opinion in England was that its players were hard done by in the 1932 body-line series against Australia; and that body-line bowling was not in the best interest of cricket. The English feared that the West Indies would engage them in a body-line war. Plum recalled the events of 1933 as follows:

The West Indies were here in 1933 . . . It was not, however, a happy season, for the body-line controversy was still simmering, and cables continued to pass between the MCC and the Australian Board of Control. A special committee was appointed, with Lord Hailsham, the President of the MCC, as Chairman, before which I gave evidence. Some people thought that I got the wrong perspective, but that I was correct in opposing this type of bowling was proved by subsequent happenings. The cricket world for the moment was upside down, and nerves were frayed. Even in the University Match body-line was used by Farnes, and one Oxford batsman was bowled off his jaw, while another hit the wicket after being struck on the neck . . . Wisden had strong comment on all this, and people began to realize that even if body-line was within the law it was not in the best interests of cricket.[20]

James, an admirer of Plum, had no time for this line of argument which he considered unreasonable in so far as England were the chief culprits in the body-line war, and had gone all out to intimidate the Australian side. As far as he was concerned the facts of the case spoke for themselves, "The English had no mercy on the Australians", he said, and when the tour was all but over, and the Ashes won, nearly every English writer and cricketer "with the most bare-faced effrontery" condemned body-line bowling. When the Australians had been complaining from the outset, these same persons "shrieked to high heaven that there was nothing in it and the Australians were merely squealing". The West Indians, James thought, had the fast bowling and "English batsmen were "childishly helpless" against it.[21] He was worried, however, about the responses of the West Indian captain and management. Constantine had already expressed his concern that white West Indian cricketers did not challenge their English 'cousins' in the same aggressive way that black players did on account of the politics of race and empire that bound them together

James was emphatic on the matter. The important question was, he said, whether "Grant will allow himself to be frightened by these English critics". "If he breaks the morale of his fast bowlers by expressing doubt as to whether the tactics of Constantine and Martindale are fair, the West Indians should flay him alive", he argued. Furthermore, James said, "This is our chance and if weakness and lack of sense of realism in the high command makes us lose it, then our blood be upon our own head".[22] We do not hear from James whether the West Indian pacers bowled body-line and met with his approval during the Test series, but Plum tells us that "Constantine and Martindale . . . employed it in the Test match at Old Trafford, and Hammond had his chin laid open". In the same match, he said, "Jardine played a magnificent innings of 127, but one ball from Constantine missed his jaw by a fraction of an inch".[23]

The West Indies, nonetheless, suffered another humiliation in the three-Test series. The first Test at Lord's was a disaster for their batsmen who in two innings were unable to reach England's first innings total of 296. Defeated by an innings and 27 runs in the low scoring match they were able to secure a draw in the second Test at Old Trafford largely on account of a dogged 169 not out by Headley, who with Barrow (105), helped the team to a face-saving total of 375. Headley's failure in the third Test (9 in the first innings and 12 in the second) exposed the batting, once again, to the ravishes of England's attack. The team went down by an innings and 17 runs, managing to score only 100 and 195 in the first and second innings respectively in response to England's total of 312.

The absence of Constantine from the first and third Tests was a significant feature in West Indies poor showing. On contract to a Lancashire League team, he was unable to participate fully in the tour, but his presence in the drawn second Test made a considerable difference. In the first innings he scored an important 31 runs batting at number 6, followed by a top score of 64 runs in the second innings. Though he took only one wicket (Hammond) in England's innings, his 25 overs for 55 runs, and two catches (off Martindale's bowling) added to the all round performance needed to shore up the team.

The return tour by the English team to the West Indies in 1934–35 saw an important change of fortune, and a seminal development in West Indies cricket. The West Indies were able to win their first Test series, defeating England 2–1 in the four matches. England won the first Test at Kensington Oval by four wickets in one of the lowest scoring matches in Test history. Batting first, the West Indies made 102 to which England responded with 81 for 7 declared. West Indies in reply made 51 for 6 declared and England inched home at 75 for 6. West Indies won the second Test by 217 runs at Queen's Park, and drew the third at Bourda. The fourth and final Test saw the West Indies rising to an unprecedented height thrashing England by an innings and 161 runs at Sabina Park. Headley's 270 not out pushed the West Indies to a massive total of 535 to which England responded with 271 and 103. It was a moment of triumph for the West Indies that seemed to finally justify their status as a Test team. Martindale and Constantine gave yeoman service as Francis, John and Griffith had done before, but Headley's performance with the bat, building upon the lead provided by Challenor, made all the difference to a side that seemed unable to make big scores consistently.

The question of leadership, however, continued to haunt the social world of West Indies cricket. There is no doubt that the white communities across the region considered cricket 'their' game to which the involvement of blacks and Asians was requested on terms set by them. The argument was made, furthermore, that had the West Indies team been all white during the tours to England of 1900 and 1906, Test status would have been granted earlier. The record of English racism against blacks was well established. The MCC was not keen, for example, to engage South African black cricketers. In the West Indies supporters and admirers of the MCC excluded blacks from most established clubs, and many fine cricketers were denied the opportunity of playing for their colony and by extension the West Indies. When H.B. Austin took Francis, a groundsman in Barbados, to England in 1923 as a pace bowler there was considerable resentment among whites. Francis was still excluded by his race from first division cricket in Barbados. There were many others who had 'dried and died on the vine' of racism in the West Indies.

An important implication of this social circumstance was that when Test status was granted, the best possible team was not selected for the inaugural tour. West Indians to a man knew that for the next ten years or so the best team was not selected to play Test cricket. The early thrashings received must therefore be explained, in part, in terms of a selection process that paid insufficient respect to the principle of merit. This was certainly the case with regard to black players, and might very well have been the case with less financially secure white players.

But in terms of the captaincy, the social circumstances of cricket culture were even more stark. The Grant brothers who led the team in the 1930s could not have made the side on merit alone; no one could legitimately claim an advantage over Constantine or Headley with respect to the right to lead. G.C. Grant, on his first tour as captain in the Australia series of 1930–31, scored in Tests 53 not out, 71, 6, 15, 8, 10, 0, 3, 62 and 27 not out; on tour to England in 1933, he scored in Tests 26, 28, 16, 14, 4 and 14; against England at home in 1934–35, he scored in Tests, 4, 0 not out, 8, 23, 16, 5 not out, and 77. His career ended with a Test average of 25.81, and his brother R.S. who replaced him against England in the 1939 tour ended with a Test average of 22. Before them, captains such as Nelson Betancourt, Maurice Fernandes, Mervyn Grell and E.L.G. Hoad were not cricketers of Test quality.

That R.S. Grant was called upon in 1939 to lead world stars such as Constantine, Headley and Martindale was a straight case of white supremacy ideology in action in West Indies cricket. Headley was the popular choice in the region, and Constantine was the father figure who had earned the right to lead by virtue of his monumental contribution to the regional and international game. The sense of enormous injustice that surrounded the 1939 tour never left the consciousness of any of these players. Constantine spoke publicly about it, and Headley reflected upon it privately with trusted friends. Martindale and Francis never got the respect due them as two of the greatest fast bowlers of all times.

Plum's commentary on the 1939 tour effectively set Headley and Constantine above and beyond their team mates as outstanding superstars of world cricket. In his own subtle style, Plum indicated the magnificence of them both, and provided a context within which to view their marginalization within the leadership of West Indies cricket. He stated:

The West Indies were a good side, under the captaincy of R.S. Grant, with J.M. Kidney as Manager, and their tour went well, with large crowds to watch these able and attractive cricketers; but because of the situation their last six matches were cancelled, their final appearance being against England at the Oval on August 19, 21 and 22. England won at Lord's by eight wickets, the games at Old Trafford and the Oval being drawn. Headley had his crowning triumph at Lord's with two centuries (106 and 107), and this great batsman scored 1 745 runs, with an average of 72.70, for the whole season. He carried the side on his shoulders, so far as batting went, and C.B. Fry suggested that he should have been christened Atlas, and not George. He had good support from K.H. Weekes, left-hand, J.B. Stollmeyer, and L. Constantine. The last also bowled well, changing his pace from a cleverly flighted slow to an occasional fast ball, and his fielding still remained that of the best fielder in the world.[24]

Test cricket was interrupted by the World War II, and did not resume for the West Indies until 1948 with the MCC tour of the region. The immediate postwar years witnessed several important ideological and social changes, particularly within the British Empire, and these in turn found their way into the world of imperial cricket.

The seminal development was the sight of George Headley leading out the West Indies team in the first Test match at Barbados on 21 January 1948. He was not appointed captain with tenure for the series because in the second Test at Queen's Park the team was led by G.E. Gomez, and by J.D.C. Goddard of Barbados in the third at Bourda, Georgetown. But it was the first time in Tests that a black man had led the West Indies and throughout the region it was hailed as a moment of considerable political significance. Headley did not perform with the bat, scoring 29 in the first innings and batting at number 11 in the second innings, 7 not out. He did not lose the Test, however, which ended in an unobtrusive draw.

Constantine also had his moment of glorious recognition in the immediate postwar years. One of the features of wartime cricket in England was the success of the one-day match which attracted large crowds on Saturdays. But the games which did most to raise emotions and capture public imagination were those played at Lord's between England and the Dominions. These games conferred considerable prestige upon players, as it was considered an enormous honour to play in the presence of royalty.

The 1945 game was played on 25–28 August, and Plum Warner was a principal organizer. Once again, Plum confronted the forces of history; he invited Constantine to lead the Dominions side, and granted him an enormous honour long denied him in the West Indies. Plum sets out the circumstances as follows:

Before this match started a difficulty arose when Hassett, who was to have captained the Dominions side, was taken ill and unable to play. His place as captain was filled by Constantine, the great West Indian player, who was the senior international cricketer on the side. In this country, certainly on the cricket field, colour does not excite the feeling and prejudice that exists in some other parts of the empire. It was, however, necessary to secure both the consent and cooperation of the rest of the Dominions side, and I went to their dressing room. I chose my words with care, referring to his seniority and position in the cricket world. I think I sensed that for a moment there was some slight hesitation, but after a very prominent member of the side had agreed that it was a proper choice one and all fell into line. On leading his side into the field Constantine had a great reception.[25]

Plum's project, then, was now complete. He had spoken in 1900 and 1906 about the need for a democratic approach to cricket in the West Indies, and finally, in 1945 he acted to bring some justice and dignity to one of the great men of the game who had benefited so much from his liberal politics.

The struggle for ethnic equality in West Indies cricket, therefore, had much to do with the application of the concept of merit to the selection process. It is a narrative that runs through the story of Pelham Warner's sojourn from his West Indian roots through the lofty corridors of imperial authority and high office at the MCC. He was a defender of empire and an ambassador for cricket, but he was a West Indian who did the best he could, under difficult circumstances, to see that his fellow countrymen got the recognition they deserved.

NOTES

1.   Pelham Warner, *Long Innings: The Autobiography* (London: Harrap, 1951), 14.
      Warner died on 30 January 1963. In 1950, he was president of the MCC, 47
      years after captaining their first touring team in Australia. The members' stand
      at Lord's is named in his honour. He also captained Middlesex, and was an
      MCC Test selector. Warner was also a prolific cricket writer, broadcaster and
      publisher. Among his many books are: *Cricket in Many Climes; Cricket Across
      the Sea; How We Recovered the Ashes; The MCC in South Africa; The Book of
      Cricket; England v. Australia; Imperial Cricket* (editor); *My Cricketing Life;
      The Fight for the Ashes in 1926; The Fight for the Ashes in 1930; Cricket
      between the Wars; Lord's, 1787–1945;* and *Gentlemen v. Players, 1806–1949.*
2.   Keith Sandiford, *Cricket and the Victorians* (London: Scolar Press, 1994), 150;
      "The Victorians at play: problems in historiographical methodology", *Journal of
      Social History* 15 (Winter 1981): 271–88; "Sport and Victorian England: a
      review article", *Canadian Journal of History* 18 (April 1983): 111–17; "The pro-
      fessionalization of modern cricket", *British Journal of Sports History* 2
      (December 1985): 270–89; "Cricket and the Barbadian society", *Canadian
      Journal of History* 21 (December 1986): 353–70; B. Stoddart, "The élite schools
      and cricket in Barbados: a study in colonial continuity", *International Journal
      of the History of Sports* 4 (December 1987): 333–50; Vamplew, W. "The

peculiar economics of English cricket before 1914", *British Journal of Sports History* 3 (December 1986): 311–26.

3. Warner, *Long Innings*, 15.
4. Ibid., 43.
5. Ibid., 44.
6. Ibid., 123.
7. Ibid., 123.
8. Ibid., 124.
9. Sandiford, *Cricket and the Victorians*, 155.
10. See Gerry Wolstenholme, *The West Indian Tour of England in 1906* (Blackpool: Nelson, 1992), 13, 22, 34.
11. Ibid., 33.
12. C.L.R. James, *Cricket* (London: Allison and Busby, 1986), 17.
13. See "Profile of George Challenor", in Barbados Cricket Association (ed.), *100 Years of Organised Cricket in Barbados, 1892–1992* (Bridgetown: BCA, 1992), 64.
14. James, *Cricket*, 25.
15. Sandiford, *Cricket and the Victorians*, 153–54.
16. "Profile of Percy Tarilton", in Barbados Cricket Association (ed.), *100 Years of Organised Cricket*, 116–117.
17. James, *Cricket*, 28.
18. Warner, *Long Innings*, 143.
19. James, *Cricket*, 35.
20. Warner, *Long Innings*, 143–44.
21. James, *Cricket*, 34.
22. Ibid., 34.
23. Warner, *Long Innings*, 143–44.
24. Ibid., 156.
25. Ibid., 156.

The landing of the first English cricket team at the harbour at Bridgetown, Barbados, 28 January 1895

Cricket being played by children in South Africa in the nineteenth century

Children playing cricket at the end of the nineteenth century in Antigua.
Behind them are typical wattle and daub houses, built of sticks and plastered mud

H.C. Griffith,
Barbados, born 1
December 1893.
Fast bowler who
toured England in
1928 and took 103
wickets at 23.68
each.; had an
excellent 1930–31
Australian tour.
Photo taken
during the 1933
tour to England

G.N. Francis, Barbados, born 7 December 1897. Fast bowler, one of the best produced in the West Indies. Toured England in 1928 and Australia in 1930–31; shared the new ball

Below, left: L.N. Constantine, Trinidad, born 21 September 1902. First West Indies superstar cricketer; great fast bowler, hard-hitting batsman and excellent fielder

Below, right: Learie Constantine in action on the 1939 tour of England at age 36

C.A. Roach, Trinidad,
born 13 March 1904.
Very popular opening
batsman who also toured
England in 1928 and
Australia in 1930–31;
also a medium pacer and
excellent cover fielder.
Photo taken on tour to
England in 1933

George Headley, Jamaica,
born in Panama, 30 May
1909. Photo taken on 1933
tour to England

George Headley in action on the 1939 tour to England

The Grant brothers from Trinidad.

Right, G.C. Grant, born 9 May 1907. Captained the West Indies on the tour to Australia, 1930–31. Photo taken on tour to England in 1933 which he also led

Below, R.S. Grant, born 15 December 1909. Captained tour to England in 1939; an allround cricketer, he was the younger brother to G.C.Grant

E.A. Martindale,
Barbados, born
25 November
1909. Toured
England in 1933
at 23 years old.
Very fast bowler
who helped to
establish the
tradition of West
Indies fast
bowling; also an
aggressive
batsman

I. Barrow, Jamaica, born
6 January 1911. A wicket-
keeper/batsman, he
toured Australia in
1930–31. Photo taken on
the 1933 tour to England

C.B. Clarke, Barbados, born 7 April, 1919. Excellent spinner and googlie bowler; also a fair batsman. Photo taken on the 1939 tour to England

John Goddard, Barbados, born 21 April 1919. Captain on the tour to England in 1957

G.E. Gomez, Trinidad, born 10 September 1919. Steady, reliable batsman and accurate medium pacer. Photo taken on the 1939 tour of England.

J.B. Stollmeyer, Trinidad, born 11 March 1921. Stylish opener who used his wrist a great deal, and a useful slow bowler. Developed into a stalwart of West Indies cricket.

Photo taken on 1939 tour to England on which he was the youngest member of the team.

4

Political Ideology and Anticolonialism

Constantine's Vision

Contests of cultural legitimacy within contexts of racial domination are located at the centre of all readings of colonialism. The colonizer recognizes the importance of cultural actions and identity in the making and unmaking of colonial authority, and seeks to maintain delicate balances over time despite resistance and general turbulence in social relations. Colonial cultural policies are always tentative, in part the effect of uncertainty about the significance of cultural democracy upon the dispensation. Official society is never sure if the integration of the colonized into its organized cultural institutions will facilitate or undermine the effectiveness of its rule. Incremental, but closely restricted access is generally the result; in turn this process generates further expectations and turmoil. Chris Searle, in a splendid essay which examines the relations between the spread of cricket throughout the British Empire during the nineteenth century, and the consolidation of white supremacy ideologies within these subjugated territories, defines West Indian cricket, in contrast to that found in other areas, as a "game of resistance".[1] Its inner logic, symbols, moments of transformation and connections to popular struggles, he tells us, punctuate and flavour the radical political history of modern Caribbean peoples.

Searle insists, furthermore, that cricket, at an early stage, became an area of revolt; the heroic figures that occupy the crease being made from the same politicized materials as revolutionary writers such as C.L.R. James, George Lamming and Edward Brathwaite. For him, cricketers and artists alike contributed to the "same anti-imperialist cultural momentum" that resides at the centre of the West Indian radical tradition. For this reason, therefore, he concludes that "cricket could never be a mere past time or weekend affectation

69

for the black player of the Caribbean. It was a means of struggle and achievement and it is a powerful expression of Caribbean progress and nationhood."[2]

Undoubtedly, Searle's approach to the study of West Indies cricket culture is informed by a number of critical assumptions about the nature of the region's political history and how such a history has facilitated the structuring of social experience and ideological consciousness. Furthermore, it is informed by the methodological employment of post-Hegelian dialectical analysis, particularly the Marxian concept of hegemony and counter-hegemonic struggle within the superstructure. These analytical tools and concepts allow Searle to hold steady 150 years of West Indian cricket history for an internal pathological analysis which, in turn, is placed within the specific context of conflict and co-option within the British Empire and the wider modern world system.

The late C.L.R. James, to whom Searle's essay is dedicated, pointed us in this general direction with his early political and philosophical writings. His ideas concerning the ideological character of West Indian civilization, clearly articulated in his 1938 analysis of Toussaint L'Ouverture and the Haitian Revolution, are also to be found within the political and intellectual infrastructure of his pioneer 1963 text (*Beyond a Boundary*) on West Indies cricket culture.[3] With James, as with so many other writers who prioritize the role of cultural struggle within social change, one feels the intensity of his analytical search for a dialectical solution to the mechanistic formula which showed that in the West Indies, history made cricket, and cricket made history. Points of origin and beginnings had to be identified in order to grasp the ideological meaning over time of this basic truth. In other words, the formula, simply stated, said little, but internally examined, it says everything.

A concept of West Indian history, then, seems the appropriate place to begin a search for the internal motion and ideological meaning of the cricket culture. Here we assert, with reference to a notion of what is the 'essence', that no matter how many times and how many ways we toss the coin of West Indian history, more often than not it comes down on the side of resistance rather than accommodation. The implication of this view is clear, certainly with respect to the issue of popular consciousness and political action. It says, principally, that though the experiences of West Indian people have been shaped by the need to come to terms with powerful hegemonic, colonial and imperialist structures and ideas, their essential response has been one of the antisystemic resistances.

Whether it was during the period of the Amerindian-European encounter, or the subsequent slavery epoch, the majority of West Indian inhabitants have sought to define their own existence in terms of an appropriation of space that could be autonomously manipulated in the building of discrete realities of freedom. Cricket, then, became enmeshed in all these considerations, and represented an ideological and cultural terrain on which this very intensive battle was fought. This is precisely why James was able to argue that the cricket history of the region is but a mirror within which its modern social undertakings can be examined and assessed. It is also expressive of the manner in which colonized West Indians took the plough share of empire and turned it into a sword which they later placed at the throats of the imperial order.

As far as the mid nineteenth century English sponsor of cricket in the empire was concerned, "cricket was an essential and symbolic part of the imperial order and manners".[4] Could they have envisioned that West Indian recipients a century later would promote cricket as an agent in the dismantlement of the imperial order and a symbol of liberation? Perhaps not, but it is necessary to be clear on what is made of the present state of affairs, as 'confessed' by Searle, an English middle class radical intellectual:

There is no doubt that for some English and Australian cricket 'experts', sunk into the conservative traditions of the sport, the prospect of an exceptionally fast Caribbean man with a cricket ball carries the same threat as a rebellious, anti-imperial black man with a gun. They want him suppressed, disarmed – he fits nowhere into their rules and ways of the game and only challenges them.[5]

For anyone who seeks nothing but 'a simple game of cricket', none of this can be understood. Indeed, it is outright disturbing of the senses. But if Englishmen and West Indians find themselves thinking that what lies 'beyond the boundary' is important to the contest , if not to determining the nature of it, then the question of what we do about concepts of guns and warfare must be answered, and there is no better way to do this than with a presentation of the relevant historical facts of the case.

The politics of West Indies cricket, and the history of West Indies politics in the century after emancipation in 1838, were driven by the same basic consideration. This, according to Learie Constantine was: "how to keep the black man in his place" and maintain white institutional hegemony.[6] There is nothing particularly contentious about this assertion. The apartheid policy that survived the slavery period remained in place, with minor constitutional adjustments that had varying sociopolitical impact across the region, well into the twentieth century. Cricket entered the Caribbean vein in much the way that the concept of representative government did. Both were considered

71

by the importing white élites as their private cultural property, with the ideological effect of disqualifying black participation in cricket in colonial competitions.

The politics of the ancient plantation system, then, had determined the ideological foundations on which West Indies cricket rests. The struggle for the political franchise by blacks would follow the same course as the efforts to break down the boundary that separated the cricket cultures of whites, browns and blacks. Cricket was, therefore, a highly politicized business, riddled with the expressed ideological concerns of the time. The desire of blacks to penetrate the formal structures, and then to dominate them by sheer weight of numbers and quality of performance, determined the evolution of both cultures – politics and cricket. It is in this sense, then, that the most sensitive observers of West Indies cricket during the nineteenth and twentieth centuries have commented on the importance and potency of political activity beyond the boundary.

During the nineteenth century, when West Indians had developed their game to the regional level, the imperial cricket culture was understood to be another area of life in which whites engaged in gentlemanly competition devoid of overt political rancour. White élites in the West Indians, Australians, Canadians, Americans and Southern Africans played each other as often as they could, and clamoured for exchange arrangements with England, the perceived centre of cricketing philosophy and methodologies. The political exclusion of non-whites, and the reasons offered to rationalize the consequences, meant that the disenfranchised peoples confronted cricket at the outset as an activity associated with racial élitism, respectability and ideological authority. Their response to it was one of ambivalence, an indication of the pressure of historical circumstances that evokes from the colonized both admiration and hostility for the culture of the oppressor.

It is interesting to note that creole white West Indians, unlike their counterparts in Canada, the United States and South Africa, did not develop the ideological position that a cricket defeat by England, in particular, constituted a severe blow to their rising national consciousness and sensibility. Cricket had survived the revolutionary independence process in the USA, but not the Civil War a century later. By then, American political leadership was bent on subduing English cultural influences, and sought to 'create' their own nation-games, language, political institutions and social values. Cricket disappeared along with several things English, and was replaced by football and baseball, symbols of a new, independent nation.

The Canadians were tugged along by American influences, while Aussie nationalism embraced cricket as a politicized weapon in their anticolonial and independence struggles, which explained in part the bloody trench war fought between the two teams in the 'body-line series' in 1932–33. Never before had international cricket contests assumed such militancy, and by the time it was over all involved were clear that its motivating forces came, not only from within the internal process of the game, but as a result of ideological infiltrations from beyond the boundary. West Indian whites, who by this time were still the dominant representatives of West Indies cricket, shuddered at the idea of West Indian independence, and their continued subservience in political life shaped the ideological profile and posture of West Indies cricket.

While Australian nationalists were flexing their muscles in the 1932–33 'body-line series', and sending serious political messages to Westminster, black West Indians were taking note. The Garvey movement, insisting on black political and economic enfranchisement, had integrated the masses in ways hitherto done only by the sugar plantations on which they 'slaved'. Black nationalism became the cutting edge ideological force throughout the West Indies, and by 1938 the masses had confronted local whites and the imperial state in a series of rebellions during which they demanded the political franchise, social reform, and access to economic resources. It was a revolutionary decade for the West Indies, and cricket, the people's primary cultural form, became infused by this ideological temperature.

As is always the case radical struggles are fought on the ideological as well as the organizational level. The simultaneous nature of these actions ensures that political directions are guided by the contents of consciousness. The question of black racial oppression in West Indies cricket, especially after 1928 when Test status was achieved, was placed on the front burners of West Indies politics. This issue occupied the popular imagination in much the way that the struggle for legal trade unionism did. Only concerted political organization was required. The ideological point was won. The West Indies team, captained and managed by "whitemen of dubious cricketing ability", had become politically problematic. Blacks were being told in no uncertain terms that they were invitees of the establishment which was "composed of plantocrats, professionals, and merchants, to a man white or a generous part of white", who were "a class fearful of successful black endeavour".[7]

During the 1930s, according to Cummings, the presence of George Headley and Learie Constantine, superlative black West Indies players from Jamaica and Trinidad respectively, laid the foundation for the political struggle. Michael Manley saw very clearly the relationship between the 1937–38 workers' rebellion and the black struggle within West Indies cricket.[8] Searle noted that the display of genius by Headley within the context of the workers' uprising "meant that cricket became a black man's game and the challenge was against white interests who controlled it".[9]

The challenge came at two levels, references to both of which are to be found in the writing of Learie Constantine. First, the ideological position of white cricketers and administrators, that contest with England was essentially a nonpolitical event in which cousins exchanged mutual admiration, had to be defeated and rejected. Black West Indians did not share the outlook of their white team mates, and this divided and weakened West Indies cricket. The division was political, and had to be removed by political means. Constantine wrote:

Of all Test playing combinations the West Indies team alone is composed of men of different race. And there lies a difficulty which I believe few of the West Indian selectors themselves realize. As I shall have occasion to point out more emphatically in a moment, Test Match cricket to day is no sort of game. It is a battle. And to win you need not only the strenuous effort of individual players: the work of each player must be backed by a sense of solidarity, of all the others supporting him, not only actually but, so to speak, in the spirit. The lack of this is the chief weakness of the West Indies team in big cricket. We have not been able to get together in the sort of spirit which says "Look here, we are going out today against those fellows and it is war to the knife!" It is difficult for us, but not by any means impossible. I have played on West Indian sides which had that spirit and I have played on sides which had not. Until all members of a West Indies side realize that every consideration must give way before the necessity of uniting in spirit and in truth to win through a series of Test Matches the West Indians will not play the cricket that I know they can play. Much depends on the players, much more depends on the leadership, which must itself be above pettiness, sympathetic, and yet be strong and command respect from all in the team.[10]

Constantine had doubts as to whether white West Indian cricketers could feel the same intensity of purpose as blacks, especially with regard to contests against England. He did not doubt their ability as players. In fact, he had the highest regard for the genius of H.B.G. Austin and George Challenor, in particular. For this reason, he moved to the second position, which was that high quality black leadership of the West Indies team was necessary in order to infuse it with those aggressive ideological and psychological considerations and feelings found beyond the boundary. If cricket resides at the heart of the West Indian social view, he said, then their exploits on the field should reflect all those emotional concerns than inform their vision.

The linkage of these two issues within Constantine's analysis suggests that West Indies cricket was hamstrung by very serious political concerns. Cricket, he said, is the "most obvious, and some would say the most glaring, example of the black man being kept 'in his place', and this is the first thing that is going to be changed".[11] The 1933 West Indies team which contained black stars such as E. Martindale, B. Sealy and George Headley was captained by G.C. Grant, the Trinidadian Cambridge Blue, who supported the view that England was the motherland that deserved loyalty and respect from its colonists in all areas of life. The leadership of the West Indies team by persons of this political ilk, Constantine intimated, had "rotted the heart out of our cricket. I only hope before I die," he wrote, "to see a West Indies team, chosen on its merits alone, captained by a black player, win a ribbon against England."[12]

The attainment of black leadership dreamt of by Constantine would not be easy. As far as the establishment was concerned too much was at stake; the political implications would be severe and long lasting. It would be a battle fought on many fronts, and determined by that party beyond the boundary – the West Indies public, for whom it had become a religious sort of activity. They, of course, knew the historical background. Communities throughout the region could speak with passion and conviction about this or that player whose ambitions died on the vine on account of white domination of the game. They knew also that whites had taken the view that cricket was 'their' game and that blacks should accept subordinate roles.

There was, of course, only one West Indies team. But cricket culture indicated that there were many social demarcations. For whites, the issue was a simple political one. They controlled political and economic power throughout the region, and it was only logical for them to believe that in representation at the 'international' level they should retain their portfolio. Black radicals, then, who understood these ideological dimensions, realized that only the highest political campaign, rooted within the wider anticolonial, black nationalist movement, could secure their objective.

C.L.R. James, by the 1940s a seasoned anticolonial activist in the West Indies, and veteran Pan-Africanist revolutionary, came forth and made this struggle a top regional priority. He possessed all the relevant skills to lead this campaign. He knew the issues, saw their relevance to West Indies liberation, and was an activist by political instinct. In his typical literary style, he described the 1958 political movement for black leadership under Frank Worrell as follows:

Once in a blue moon, i.e. once in a lifetime, a writer is handed on a plate a gift from heaven. I was handed mine in 1958. I had just completed a draft of this book up to the end of the previous chapter when I returned to the West Indies in April 1958, after twenty-six years of absence. I intended to stay three months, I stayed four years. I became the editor of a political paper, the *Nation*, the official organ of the People's National Movement of Trinidad, and the secretary of the West Indian Federal Labour Party. Both these parties governed, the one Trinidad, the other the Federation of the West Indies. These were temporary assignments, as I made clear from the start. Immediately I was immersed up to the eyes in 'The Case for West Indian Self-Government'; and a little later, in the most furious cricket campaign I have every known, to break the discrimination of sixty years and have a black man, in this case Frank Worrell, appointed captain of a West Indies team. I saw the beginning, the middle, but I am not sure at all that I have seen the end of violent intervention of a West Indian crowd into the actual play of a Test match. The intimate connection between cricket and West Indian social and political life was established so that all except the wilfully perverse could see. It seemed as if I were just taking up again what I had occupied myself within the months before I left in 1932, except that what was then idea and aspiration was now in the open and public property.[13]

The Trinidad *Nation* became a Caribbean forum in which intellectuals and workers, politicians and lawyers, teachers and students participated in or followed the heated debate in which three issues were linked: (a) the politics of black nationalist decolonization; (b) movement towards nation state (singular or federated independence); (c) black leadership of West Indies Test cricket. This was undoubtedly the most historically significant movement of the century, and the politics of cricket was at the heart of the matter. Black leadership of West Indies cricket, political independence, and nationhood were all symbols of one historic process – the liberation of blacks from colonial bondage – and the cricket struggle was in the vanguard.[14]

It was, of course, much more than just the replacement of white leadership by black leadership. It was about the question of merit, democracy, and social justice. It was clear to all informed cricket observers in 1958–59 that Worrell was the obvious man for the job on the basis of merit. He did not qualify under existing social criteria. He was neither planter nor merchant, and had no intimate social relations with these communities. In fact, he had been a thorn in their flesh for some time for insisting that proper wages be paid to professional (non-élite) cricketers. But his cricket genius was obvious and the future of democracy in the West Indies required the populace to stand up on principle and reject blatant racial injustice.[15]

Public indignation, noted Michael Manley, "swept the cricketing world", as West Indians stood up and demanded that merit should not give way to mediocrity. C.L.R. James led them into an ideological crusade that signalled the end of the ancien régime. Cricket was now in the hands of the masses who had given breath to it at critical moments. Worrell was appointed captain in 1960 for the upcoming tour of Australia. He was the first black man to be appointed captain with tenure of the West Indies cricket team. Headley had captained the Barbados Test match in the 1948 home series, but this appointment was the grand historic moment, and it took a regional high profile political movement to accomplish it.[16]

White West Indians, Barbadians in particular, took the decision of the West Indies Cricket Board of Control (WICBC) very badly. They knew it was the end of the line for white domination. Adult suffrage in Barbados in 1950 led to a wholesale removal of white politicians from the Assembly in 1951. They knew Worrell as a man who did not buckle under the pressure of racism on the island. He spoke his mind, told them what he knew they did not want to hear, and adopted Jamaica as his home. As far as they were concerned, they had run Worrell out of Barbados. He could not get work in the economy which they controlled, and they called him a racist for criticizing their racial bigotry. Worrell was a political rebel with a cause, and white West Indian society moved against him.

It was not Worrell that white West Indians feared. It was the entire political process that had thrust him into the leadership position by discrediting mediocrity from their ranks. In most territories, whites rallied against labour unions, the formation of the University of the West Indies (UWI), adult suffrage and, most importantly, political independence. These institutions, they believed, were adding fuel to the flame raging in black hearts, while independence would leave them stranded in black majority states without the protective armour of the 'motherland'. Whites in general, then, took a grand political stand against the tide of democracy and freedom, which in turn meant that they could no longer support the West Indies cricket team against a white team. Race first was their dominant ideology, and in 1960 and 1963 many withdrew full support from the West Indies in their series against Australia and England respectively. In Barbados this was particularly obvious and stunning to visitors, though it was also evident in other places.

There is evidence to show, however, that the process of white withdrawal of support for the West Indies team had started from the time that blacks had attained numerical superiority with the team. Len Hutton, for example, the England captain of the West Indies tour in 1953–54, stated that while in Jamaica native whites persistently impressed upon him at social functions how important it was to them that the blacks did not win the series. Also, Keith Miller, the Australian allrounder who scored 137 in the 1955 Barbados Test, found that black and white team mates did not socialize on account of the intensity of anti-black racial prejudice on the island. He noted that during the Test white players did not invite the three Ws (Walcott, Weekes, and Worrell) to their homes when cocktails were prepared for the Australians, which was a source of embarrassment for the visitors.

The issue of anti-black racism in West Indies cricket was not only an affront to the Australians, but also to members of the English touring team in the 1959–60 Test series. E. W. Swanton, the distinguished English cricket writer, who accompanied the English touring party, had much to say about his own personal experiences in his 'memoirs' of the series. White members of the West Indies team, in addition to white natives who attended Tests, clearly offended Swanton in their expression of negrophobic attitudes. In summarizing the report on the tour he wrote:

This is a cricket book, not a treatise on West Indian problems, but there was one aspect of current life in the islands which one noticed more this time, in relation to the cricket, than on previous visits, and I must therefore mention it though, I hope, with due diffidence. I mean the matter of colour prejudice – in both directions – and what had been dubbed 'shade distinction'. Cricket in the West Indies was planted like the sugar, the citrus and the cocoanuts, by white colonists. They gave the lead, and when the coloured West Indians followed it with such gusto and skill it became a bond between them, as games should always be a bond between creeds and classes. The first West Indian teams to England before the first war contained some four or five coloured men, the rest white. By 1939, when R.S. Grant's team had to hustle back home ahead of the German submarines, the balance had been almost exactly reversed. Now it happens that the Test team is likely most times to be almost wholly coloured, though it by no means follows that men who have done so much for West Indian cricket, such as John Goddard, Jeffrey Stollmeyer and Gerry Gomez, may not have their successors among the teams of the sixties. All this is an inevitable evolution, the racial proportions being what they are. But the situation makes it the more surprising that one finds people apparently insisting on a certain line of policy, or the selection of a certain man, on grounds of colour, disguised or thinly veiled though their arguments may be.[17]

Swanton's call was for the removal of race politics from the game, and he celebrated the selection of Worrell as captain since it was not possible to find within the team a 'better example' of leadership. West Indian whites, he intimated, should let go of old, bankrupt ideologies and support 'their' team irrespective of the opposition.

In much the same way that West Indian people rose up against apartheid in West Indies cricket and assured Frank Worrell the captaincy, they swiftly moved against Captain Sobers in 1970 when he visited apartheid Rhodesia for two days and participated in a double wicket tournament with South African Ali Bacher. It had taken black West Indians a century of intense struggle against racism to place their cricket leadership in the hands of a working class player. They did not take too kindly to Sobers' trip which was conceived as offering support and legitimacy to a racist regime – especially since he met with Ian Smith and was reported to have said that the leader of the racist regime was "not so bad after all".[18] Throughout the West Indies public opinion called for Sobers' neck. How could the leader of the only popular West Indian institution – the cricket team – not recognize that since the 1920s the region's cricket culture had been highly politicized and ideologically charged to resist racial injustice?[19]

Sobers, unlike Worrell, his predecessor, was not attuned to the historical and ideological nature of his location within West Indies cricket. No one doubted his genius as a player, but the question was asked: how could he have inherited the finest gifts of a grand cricketing tradition without acquiring at the same time an understanding of its sociological and political characteristics? All along, Sobers' view was that he was a cricketer and not a politician, and that he hoped his action would assist in the promotion of multiracial sport. Two contradictions are evident here. First, as a result of high level political action the role of captaincy was placed within his grasp and therefore his situation was intrinsically politicized. Secondly, his desire to assist the promotion of nonracial democracy in a country where bloody armed struggle was taking place in order to remove apartheid meant that the cricket game in which he participated was obviously a major political intervention. Trevor Bailey, former English Test captain, and a Sobers biographer, completely misunderstood the nature of West Indies cricket when he stated that Sobers was "appointed to captain a cricket team . . . and not to lead an ideological crusade".[20] The weight of the evidence suggests, however, that Sobers was an integral part of an ideological crusade which had begun some 150 years earlier and had only began to bear fruit in his own lifetime.

If these matters were not clear to Sobers in 1970 they certainly were to Viv Richards a generation later. Like Sobers, Richards was the world's greatest batsman in his time, and on assuming the West Indies captaincy, found himself compelled to represent the ideological tradition established by Constantine, Headley and Worrell. He was clear on where he stood ideologically, and on the nature of his time. "The whole issue [of race/apartheid] is quite central to me," he wrote, "coming as I do from the West Indies at the very end of colonialism. I believe very strongly in the black man asserting himself in this world and over the years I have leaned towards many movements that followed this basic cause. It was perfectly natural for me to identify, for example, with the Black Power movement in America and, to a certain extent, with Rastafarians."[21]

Richards, therefore, took into cricket much of what cricket had given to him. His cricket and his politics fused into an ideological force that shaped his genius and determined the principled positions adopted with respect to apartheid and the South African cricket culture. While Sobers adopted and maintained the rather simple position that politics should not be involved in sports, Richards emphasized that "you cannot evade the point that playing cricket is in itself a political action".[22] From this position, he could not follow Sobers into Southern Africa. He says:

Once I was offered one million Eastern Caribbean dollars [US$1 = EC$2.60], and there have been all kinds of similar proposals [to play cricket in South Africa]. They all carried a political burden and in each case it was a very simple decision for me. I just could not go. As long as the black majority in South Africa remains suppressed by the apartheid system, I could never come to terms with playing cricket there. I would be letting down my own people back in Antigua and it would destroy my self-esteem.[23]

Many other players, of course, succumbed to the financial temptations and found themselves categorized as 'honorary whites' in order to play cricket in South Africa. Political consciousness, like cricketing ability, varies from player to player, but for Richards cricket allowed for his self-expression "in a way that is totally pure".[24]

The Sobers–Richards experience, then, is illustrative of the dialectical process of accommodation and resistance that resides at the core of Caribbean history. Within this dialectic the forces of resistance are invariably the greater, which is why 12,000 Barbadians had great problems with the 1992 'Test' between South Africa and the West Indies at Bridgetown.[25] A massive boycott of the historic single Test was planned before the South Africans arrived in Barbados. Eventually no more than 3,000 people attended the opening days when Test matches usually attract upwards of 12,000 per day.

Before the Test started on Saturday 18 April, the Pan-African movement of Barbados was referring to the WICBC as 'traitors' who, in league with West Indian governments, had "reneged on the duty which they owe to the exploited, suffering and struggling black people of South Africa".[26] The movement called for the boycott of the Test in a press release which said:

Virtually the only practical and effective way in which the Caribbean nations can contribute to the international isolation of South Africa and to the cause of the black South

Africans is in the field of sport in general and cricket in particular. It is therefore utterly shameful that the governments and cricket administrators of the region could so casually throw away the 'cricket weapon' and join the members of a privileged racial élite to frolic and make sport in the Caribbean sun . . . It is now left to the Barbados people to demonstrate that at least one island population is serious about their responsibility to the black struggle by boycotting the Test match and sending a stern message to the international community and the racist Government of South Africa.[27]

Richards, recently retired from Test cricket, took the view that no Test should be played against white South Africa until democratic systems were put in place, in spite of the fact that Nelson Mandela had urged West Indian governments and the WICBC to support the Test. Sobers, on the other hand, was a prime mover in the arrangement and was photographed at the Barbados airport hugging and kissing South African officials, led by the same Ali Bacher who had participated in luring him into Rhodesia in 1970. While large sections of public opinion felt that the very successful boycott was due to the exclusion of Barbadian pacer, Andy Cummins, from the West Indies team, it remains inescapable that the mood of the country was that West Indies cricket should not freely interface with 'white' South African cricket within the context of their domestic apartheid policy. Once again, West Indies cricket found itself in the vanguard of the political movement, dividing those who saw it as an activity to combat racism and those who considered that it could serve to a greater degree the interests of racists.

Given this ideological character and political history, it should not be surprising that cricket has been called upon to perform the task of healing the wounds and building the bridges of a fragmented nationalism that has been established in the wake of the passing colonial order. Bound historically by the sugar plantations' regime and now by the cricket culture, West Indians are aware, according to David Lowenthal, that "outside the world of cricket the West Indies is not a nation and does not act as one".[28] The political weight being carried, and the mission expected of West Indies cricket, then, are really quite extraordinary.

These matters were not lost on the West Indian Commission who in 1989 were mandated by Caricom governments to prepare a report in order to guide West Indian nations into the next century with a revitalized commitment to a sense of collective independence, sovereignty and nationhood. In the 1992 official report, a blueprint for change for the next generation, commissioners, led by Sir Shridath Ramphal and Sir Alister McIntyre, chancellor and vice chancellor respectively of the UWI, were very explicit in their reflection on information received from citizens about the political role and function of cricket. It stated:

When we lost a particularly vital World Cup match, a commentator tried to get a dismal, undedicated performance by the West Indies cricket team into what he thought might be the right perspective by saying: "after all, it is just another game". He made a fundamental mistake. To us it was not, it is not, 'just a game'.

No West Indian believer can afford to underestimate or neglect this game. It is an element in our heritage which binds us close and is seen as such both by ourselves and the outside world. When first Frank Worrell in that famous tour of Australia in 1960 and then later Clive Lloyd, followed by Viv Richards in the 1970s and 1980s, led the West Indies to a dominant position in world cricket, it built our stature as a people both in our own eyes and in the eyes of others. When we stood as one in the cricket boycott of South African apartheid it really mattered. And when we failed as a team in crucial games in the World Cup throughout the region we felt ourselves indefinably but definitely diminished as a nation in those performances.

The performance of the West Indian team in their miracle win in the historic Test match against South Africa revalidated the supremacy of cricket in the West Indian psyche as an enduring source of inspiration and as a demonstration of the fact that we do it better when we do it together.

It may be instructive that it was in a presentation made to the Commission on the sources of West Indian success in building a great cricket team in the late 1970s and 1980s that we heard what we thought was perhaps the most succinct recipe for success in all the endeavours we pursue as a community of nations acting together.[29]

As a result, the commission in making recommendations to governments with respect to the promotion of a federated nationhood, made 12 distinct proposals for the furtherance of cricket's contribution to the deepening of the regional integration movement.

But democratic, multiracial cricket and the political movement for integration and nationhood in the West Indies grew up together, often under the same parentage. They are therefore 'family', bonded and torn by emotional concerns that are found only in domestic conditions. V.S. Naipaul gives us an insight into this world when he eavesdropped on a discussion among West Indians at the Oval Test between England and the West Indies in 1963:

"What, they have politics in Grenada?" Laughter.
"Boy, I had to leave Grenada because politics were making it too hot for me."
"What, they have politics in Grenada?" Laughter.
"You are lucky to see me here today, let me tell you. The only thing in which I remain West Indian is cricket. Only thing . . ."
"I hear the economic situation not too good in Trinidad these days. All these damn strikes. You know our West Indian labour . . ."

"But the cricket ever returns . . ."

"My dear girl, I didn't know you followed cricket."

"Man, how you could help it at home? In Barbados. And with all my brothers."[30]

It is for reasons so described that Richards, the seminal ideological figure since Frank Worrell, was to discover within the context of the international game that cricket is "not some irrelevant, eccentric sport played by a handful of countries, but a game that gets right to the root of the societies involved".[31]

Richards' Mission

Postcolonial West Indies cricket, then, is a mass supportive festival culture in which nationalistic, liberationist ideologies are expressed. From inception it has been an effective instrument that indicated ideological forces within society, and at the same time functioned as a field on which the process of conflict and co-option was played out. Like every social fact, West Indies cricket is a perpetual creation of the men who practise and organize it, and who are, in turn, transformed by their very creation. Its political ideology is embedded not only in its moral codes, but within the historical struggle against colonial oppression and its social legacies. Furthermore, its ideological effects are witnessed daily within West Indian life, with the result that for most persons cricket is about life as 'lived' rather than endured. In all of this Viv Richards emerges the pivotal icon of the radical movement that swept through West Indian society during the 1970s.

C.L.R. James knew, in a way that few people did, how to cut away the tissue and expose the raw nerve. For some, his analytical, and often acerbic forthrightness, paid no attention to individual sensitivities, and sent shivers down many spines. He published no extensive essays, nor offered any detailed commentary on Viv Richards in the way he examined Learie Constantine, George Headley, Frank Worrell, Gary Sobers and Rohan Kanhai. This is not phenomenal. By the early 1980s, when Viv was at the height of his productivity, James was well advanced in age. His cricket writings had virtually ceased. The few comments he offered with respect to Viv, however, said a great deal, and were conceptually consistent with the methodology he used in earlier analytical assessments of the game's greats.

The specific context within which James made a final categorization of Viv was one he knew only too well; a West Indies tour of England in which a clash of old and new Atlantic cricket cultures and sensibilities would rendezvous in aesthetic celebration of performance excellence. It was the long summer of 1984. Five Tests were played, starting at Edgbaston in mid June, climaxing in a fifth Test at Kennington Oval in mid August. The West Indies, under Clive Lloyd's leadership, won at Edgbaston by an innings and 180 runs with Richards scoring 117. The second Test at Lord's was won by the West Indies by nine wickets with Richards top scoring in the first innings with 72; the third Test at Headingley they won by eight wickets. The fourth Test at Old Trafford the West Indies won by an innings and 64 runs, and the fifth Test they won by 172. H.A. Gomes had a marvelous tour, scoring 143 in the first Test, 92 not out in the second, and 104 in the third. Gordon Greenidge was similarly productive with innings of 214 in the second Test and 223 in the fourth.

At the end of the 5 –0 'blackwash' (another clean 'washing' was inflicted on England by the West Indies under Richards' leadership in the 1985–86 tour to the Caribbean). James examined the West Indies team that had swept England, and all other oppositions, as no team had done in the history of the game. He did it in his usual detached and clinical style, locating Richards within the specific performance circumstances of the series and the wider traditions of methodological excellence. First, his views on the team:

It is necessary to get down to principles. A winning team must be well established in certain departments. The team should have a good pair of openers. It should have three good batsmen, and it would do no harm if one of these is a great super batsman. By super batsman I mean one who is not disturbed by any bowling or any crisis. Super batsmen are rare, and a team can be a good team without having a man of that style.[32]

With respect to the composition of the batting department, James continues:

I look at their batting, and I think that there is one super batsman – that is Richards. Richards is undoubtedly a batsman who can be ranked with great batsmen of any time . . . Apart from Richards, frankly I do not see any outstandingly great batsmen on that West Indian side.[33]

Lloyd, Gomes and Greenidge he described as good players, competent and distinguished, but not 'great' in the sense of belonging to a category of rare players over which Sobers presides.

Few who have studied the game would disagree with this judgement. A player's capacity for scoring hundreds, James argued, is an insufficient feature in such a determination. Great players, on balance, should dominate all kinds of attacks under diverse circumstances. There is no structural weakness, no fatal flaw. Perfect adaptability is expected. The ability to answer all challenges and to place one's team in a position of authority are the hallmarks of the great player. Oppositions have always felt the psychological power of such players, a kind of charisma at the crease that enhances a spirit of defeatism in their ranks. James saw all these distinctive features in Richards, and was brief in summation.

Viv, in addition, was not just great, he was the world's greatest batsman of his generation. He also held a reputation within Caribbean society that extended beyond the boundary and connected to political and philosophical discourses that continue to engage students and academics seeking an understanding of the project of West Indian nation building and the postcolonial dispensation. As is often the case, subjective judgements underpinned much of what academics say about the relationships of individuals to society. It is always difficult to escape the line of reasoning that seeks to ascertain whether individuals did the best they could for their time. Each generation, says Frantz Fanon, has its mission which it can either fulfil or betray.[34] Viv knew and fulfilled what was expected of him by West Indian society. It is a story of a turbulent but rewarding journey to excellence that has its place within the classrooms of academies. It contains important principles of political and moral philosophy and speaks metaphorically to the tensions, paradoxes and contradictions of postcolonial social consciousness.

When I encountered Richards for the first time in 1976, a number of circumstances had positioned themselves at the centre of my being. The dejected West Indies cricket team had not long departed from Australia where they received the kind of whipping (5–1) that only old headmasters know how to administer. They arrived in England, still bruised and sore, to face those whose colonizing yoke our foreparents had recently thrown off in a firm but silent revolutionary fashion. I had just completed an undergraduate programme in historical studies at Hull University in Yorkshire where those like myself whom God had blessed with an adequate quantum of melanin were disenfranchised with respect to the local cricket culture.

As a student of history I knew only too well that it was not very long ago that a similar brand of ethnic prejudice and discrimination had applied to people of my ilk in the West Indies. When Lloyd's men arrived in England, then, the moment for me was charged with concern about past injustices, current anxieties, and future expectations. It was a time when my mind was still trying to evaluate references to the loss of Martin Luther King and Malcolm X on the one hand, and observations of the carnage that was taking place in

Vietnam, Angola, Mozambique, Northern Ireland and Zimbabwe – not to mention the brutality of the English police with respect to West Indian people in the inner cities.

It was a familiar West Indian type summer in England in 1976. There was a drought and water rations in some places. Richards was thirsty for runs and before he was fully unpacked started scoring hundreds. I watched him closely. I remembered my grandfather who was forced to make a living cutting the white man's cane on the white man's plantations in the white man's island of Barbados (home!). There was something in Richards' manner that reminded me of my grandfather; perhaps it was my grandfather's slow, graceful walk to the canefield, the rolling of the sleeves, and the precise but unpredictable swinging of the cutlass. But there was nothing agricultural about Richards, except that he was reaping that which those who went before him had sown. That is how the struggle for justice evolves everywhere. I understood the meaning of many things that summer.

From the beginning, Richards was businesslike in his demolition of English bowling. His powers of concentration and, above all, his haste made me wonder if he possessed a hidden agenda. It did not matter in the least; his was a level of mastery I had never seen before, and wished to see in all of our people's endeavours. I believed that he understood the seriousness of our condition and was prepared to act with all means necessary. We, the wretched of England's inner cities, had never seen the likes of it. Frank Worrell had signalled that an emissary would come from the Leewards; we waited as only believers know how. I examined him with all the skills available to me at that time. There have been many false prophets in the past, and many pretenders. Time was running out on us; we were about to be packaged as volatile, calypso sunshine boys who entertained on a good day but packed up and went home disgraced when the clouds came over. I therefore examined his method, his concepts, and his sense of purpose. I concluded that the survival struggle for West Indians with respect to postcolonial Englishness was placed at a higher level.

Sir Gary Sobers, it seemed to me, had gloriously entertained the in-crowd at Lord's with his genius; Richards, however, intimidated, mocked and perhaps humiliated such gatherings. It was political; he said so, and I knew it. The score had to be settled. He wore the colours of the Rastas, who said he was sent by the Conquering Lion of the tribe of Judah, Ras Tafari Makennon (Haile Selassie), the Redeemer from Ethiopia. With us, there is always religion and mythology within the politics. I felt that we were seeing what some said was the beginning of the glory. Bob Willis, Chris Old, Mike Hendricks,

Tony Greig, Derek Underwood and others who bowled for England, knew not what had befallen them. Richards broke all the rules, and tore up the Lord's treaty which said that 'hitting across the line' was an offence punishable by the withdrawal of approving adjectives. By the end of the summer, John Arlott of the British Broadcasting Corporation (BBC) was describing him as the "Lord of Lord's". For us, he was the 'king' of the Oval, Lord's, and all venues where cricket was played that summer. How can anyone forget Arlott's coining of the term, "intimidatory batting"? You had to see it to believe it; fast bowlers afraid to follow through in fear of losing their ears; infielders preferring outfielding; umpires standing well back; and the steady clicking of electronic scoreboards.

It is rare indeed that great men locate their genius within the social circumstances of their humble origins. It is also rare for great men to humble themselves before movements that surround them and which they could ignore to much profit. We felt then, that Richards was doing something for us. Each century, each double century, peeled away the optic scales accumulated over 400 years of inhuman subjection. The English were thrown into panic, not because of the aggregates – they had seen them before – but because they sensed that with Richards it was more than sport; it was the business of history and politics – the struggle against injustice and inequality. We assisted them to understand these things by our unfettered spectator responses. This worsened their condition, and I understood then the potence and social importance of strategic solidarity at the frontier.

In the course of that summer, we thanked our Antiguan brothers and sisters for sending Richards and we begged their forgiveness for not having been allowed to send more of his kind in the past. For me, it was a moment of new beginning. Many young West Indians felt compelled to do for their generation in diverse endeavors what Richards was doing on the cricket field. The articulation was clear, and the need was pressing. We were taken through a steep learning curve, and I decided to return to university for graduate research. I could not separate these things in my mind. Richards, you see, was an icon for those in my condition, and we were inspired by his self-confidence, ideological firmness, and determination. He delivered the goods, and this made us recognize the meaning of productivity in new and different ways.

Undoubtedly, Viv was a rare but not phenomenal type of West Indian cricketer. C.L.R. James would have said that his coming was anticipated, and would have been surprised had he not arrived. It has to do with a certain kind of reading of Caribbean history, its logic, internal dialectics, and ideological trajectory. It is not a question of mechanical determinism in an understanding of history. Rather, it has to do with how possible futures are perceived as a result of a careful scrutiny of historical evidence. It is not the art of the speculator. There is nothing random about it. It is the science of those who can feel and sense the evidence of things not seen.

Viv did not walk on to the cricket field in search of himself. Neither did he discover his consciousness within the contexts of sporting contests. He was sent in to do battle by villagers, not only those in Antigua, but all those from little places in this diaspora; people who have been hurling missiles at the Columbus project since it crashed into their history 500 years and ten million lives ago. His strut was not designed as part of a sterile social discourse that speaks of conceit and arrogance, but was an expression of a mind made up, hardened by a discarded plantation landscape that carries the marks of injustice and denial. He was determined to tilt the scales, even if marginally and temporarily, in favour of those whose view of the world is from the bottom up.

Preparation for such a task is never consciously done. There is no formal organization of ideas, and no exposure to texts that detail the visions of those who went before. Neither is there an awareness of the forces that conspire to fashion the consciousness from day to day. Ideas are encountered along the way, in a normal way in regular places, among people who see themselves as going nowhere, but who at the same time are always looking about themselves for emissaries. Villagers, from both town and country, have the vision of dentists; they smile in recognition of the perfect form, but possess keen eyes that easily spot the rot that indicates a painful flaw. It is a process of deep-seated collective responsibility, shaped by a culture of relentless criticism that is designed to assure high standards.

The geometry of these relations is now well known. The domestic and neighbourhood worlds that produced Viv's mentality, and the wider history of black people's survival, represent the base for his departure into the orbit of an empowering pan-Africanist vista. The behaviour of 'natural rebels', we have been told, is not learnt by trial and error; it is a kind of carriage, bred by generations of social expectation and uncritical acceptance of social responsibility. For sure, 300 years of colonial demand on the Antiguan land planted the ideology within Richards' being that 'arrival' and 'conquest' at Lord's – the centre of a civilization held in high esteem by those responsible for him – had everything to do with the collective West Indian midsummer dream. There is no contradiction in any of this. The lines were drawn before his time. His mission was to produce and secure a legitimate nationalist cartography that gave his people new undisputed boundaries and a land of their own.

Viv's autobiography, *Hitting Across the Line*, is precisely this – a mission statement, as well as an ideological account, the beginning and the end of a journey. It is a text that shows where the new boundaries are drawn, and where the land beyond the imperial line can be identified. At the same time it is more, much more. It belongs to an old tradition, but breaks new ground and can therefore stand on its own. Few autobiographies from the Caribbean have had the intellectual content to rise above the specific circumstances of their appearance to generate a life of their own. This statement by Richards, therefore, needs careful scrutiny. But we must begin with the idea.

It is a fact that in the West Indies the cricketer's autobiography represents the principal literary form of working class male expression. Men from the labouring classes have had little reason to prepare texts detailing the evolution of their lives. The cricketer's memoirs, then, are a unique literary form in which the voice of the villager is heard on its own terms, and more importantly, in its own tone. In recent years there have been many such publications, but none of them details a narrative that flows through the hardened veins of West Indian history. There are reasons for this, and here there are no surprises. It is a text that reflects the rugged journey from the game's colonial periphery to its imperial centre and demonstrates how and why polarities had to be exchanged. It documents a mentality committed to subversion and revolution; it speaks of self-assertion and liberation. It is the treatise of the villager who rejects other peoples' notion of his space, and who always knew that he was global and in possession of the information to prove it as well as the technology to demonstrate it.

Viv's journey in search of ideological ancestry would rendezvous somewhere in 1933 with the publication of Learie Constantine's autobiographic *Cricket and I*.[35] The lineage is clear, the resemblances are obvious, and we have no reason to doubt ideological paternity. Constantine's struggle was to free West Indies cricket from its colonial scaffold, establish the foundations of a 'nationalist' culture against the grain of divisive social racism. His political mission was to promote the concept of merit as the organizing principle of the selection process. He had no time for the 'cousin cricket' played between white West Indians and English teams. For him it smacked of colonial subservience and promoted a self denial of West Indian legitimacy. *Cricket and I* served as the voice from within the boundary of the progressive movement, and represented the clearest condemnation of the social forces that had denied George Headley his rightful place as captain of the West Indies Test team during the 1930s.

89

Since then the cricket autobiography has proliferated, but within a different genre. Most are generally accounts of selected encounters, important moments and performances within the general evolution of a career. At best they offer insights into publicly reported issues, but rarely touch the nerve as they are often written by ghost writers contracted from the British media. While their principal contribution lies in offering entry to individual mentalities, they are limited in contextual sensitivity and sociological meaning. *Hitting Across the Line* breaks radically with this literary form and connects to Constantine's *Cricket and I*, bridging a timespan of some three generations.

The title itself is a declaration of a new sense of sovereignty and independence, a rupture with an imperial tradition and a legitimization of an indigenous methodological approach. The tradition of batsmanship established by English technical experts disapproves violently of an approach that includes hitting across the line of the ball. Batting is understood as a side-on technology that loses its aesthetics and soundness when the ball is struck to the on-side if the line and trajectory is to the off side, and vice versa. Such transgressions are tabooed, and offending batsmen are described as lacking technique and correctness. It is this nineteenth century English tradition within which twentieth century West Indian batsmanship grew up and matured.

Viv's legitimization of 'hitting across the line' was in fact revolutionary, a unilateral declaration of cultural freedom. There are two issues here that require scrutiny. First, English opponents, more so than others, sought to contain Richards by setting defensive off side fields to which they would bowl. Indeed, setting an off side field is standard strategy in English first-class cricket, and bowling an off-line the norm for most types of bowlers. Two forms of counterattack are possible under such circumstances. The batsman could either try to penetrate a densely populated off side, or strike the ball across the line to the on-side wilderness. The latter is considered a high risk and low interest response, the former is approved, particularly as it requires precision of placement and the patience of Job.

Viv's cricket nature was to counter and discredit the integrity of such strategies. He would hit the ball across the line at will, invariably using a straight bat on contact, leaving opposing captains to deny the efficacy of their field placing. The destruction of bowlers' self-confidence, and the extraordinary rate at which he accumulated runs, speak to his innovative brilliance and conceptual genius. It was, of course, his remarkable hand-eye coordination that allowed for the effectiveness of this methodological departure. Tradition, he seems to be saying, is a safe haven for those of average ability; the way of the genius is to redraw the boundaries and discover new space.

This spirit of independence and departure was part of the West Indian social environment that shaped Viv's consciousness as a youth. The ideological discourse of black liberation as a pan-African imperative emerged from the region during the 1960s and early 1970s. In some places debates evolved into intense political mobilization and revolutionary politics. But everywhere, the youth began to speak a different language, ritualized their conduct in new directions, and searched for solutions to the culture of marginalization and exclusion that typified their condition. Theirs was a spirit of protest that filled the streets; communities, in town and country, began to march to the sound of ancestral drums.

It is evident, then, that Viv was as much part of this discovery as Walter Rodney who provided its leadership with historical context and clear ideological articulation. This is why *Hitting Across the Line* has to be 'read' as a manifesto of the progressive movement in much the same way that Rodney's *Groundings with my Brothers* is understood. They both evolved from the same set of anxieties and expectations that excited the faces of Caribbean youth in the morning of their new day. Both men infused their immediate worlds with visions and philosophies and transformed much of what they touched. Africans everywhere embraced them and sought to sustain the moral integrity and historical coherence of their interventions. The shape of Rodney's words and the echoes from Richards' bat connected to the rhythms and vibes of Bob Marley's music. For a moment – a lifting and painful decade – West Indians sniffed the future with all its epic possibilities. Rastafari came to the centre and provided the leadership. Viv was sympathetic to this arrival. He displayed the colours of the 'brethren' in new places and gave them enlarged dimensions and significance.

At the centre of this celebration of self-discovery was a constellation of ideas, some fully matured, others in the making. The uprooting of racism from the soils of an island civilization built upon it would not be easy, but it was necessary on principle to take a stand. "The racists", Viv says, "are people with a perverse kind of pride, who think we have no right to be competing on the same stage as them. My pride, for the record," he concludes, "is as big as that of any other man!" The pride of which he speaks has to do with the right to be different, to be respected, and not to be denied without just cause. Constantine used the same language in 1933, and was determined, as the owners of the Imperial Hotel in London discovered in 1944 when he took them to court for refusing him normal service on the basis of his race. But true pride for Viv had more to do with achieving results from the correct use of the collective intelligence of players in the pursuit of clearly understood and important objectives. "Success", he says, "does not have a lot to do with how much talent you have; what matters is how you manage to collect and nurture that talent."[37] The binding of a West Indian character that speaks with a single voice and rallies behind a single flag has proven illusive in most areas of interaction, and is still troublesome in cricket. "When we are separate, we are nothing", says Viv, a fact that seems to stand without contest, yet the nature of daily discourse within the region remains divisive and at times acrimonious.[38]

For sure, Viv's location of his world views within the pan-Africanist movement, at home and abroad, meant that his social experiences would be characterized by considerable political turbulence and extreme social reactions. Caribbean societies remain deeply divided, torn and tortured in fact, by positive representations of the African ontology. The economic domination of these societies by élites of European ancestry, whose historic imposition of their value system remains hegemonic, cannot readily accommodate ideological and political challenges that speak on behalf of black redemption. The considerable corporate power of these groups continues to define and guide public discourse with respect to the authority and capacity of the state to devise and apply national policy in favour of the psychologically fractured people of African descent. Ironically, non-West Indian white élites have had less difficulty in accepting the validity and necessity of a pan-Africanist epistemology. One result has been that Viv was able to establish positive and lasting relations with business élites around the world, while considerable tension and unease continue to surround his interactions with élite Caribbean society.

An important aspect of this ambivalence is found in the attitudes of Afro-West Indians themselves. Despite the formal projection of a political dialogue that rests upon the aspirations of black society with respect to social and economic inclusion, many blacks have had considerable difficulty with the articulation of an agenda that directs attention to their structural disenfranchisement. The majority of society seemed divided on what was described during the 1970s as the 'Black Power Movement'. The established media had no difficulty in convincing many blacks that the movement was constituted and led by 'racists', 'ethnic cleansers' and anarchists. To speak on behalf of democratic political programmes of black empowerment in these societies, where colonial legacies continue to be supportive of white supremacy ideologies and values, is to encounter the wrath of élite society, particularly the cruder version expressed by its non-white elements.

Richards, then, was undoubtedly a highly developed product of the second paradigm in West Indies cricket. The first paradigm was that of the nineteenth century in which cricket was the instrument of colonial exclusion, used by white élite society to distance itself from the black majority. By the 1930s, this model was under attack, and the rise of the 3 Ws (Weekes, Worrell and Walcott) against the background of Learie Constantine and George Headley signalled the rise of the second paradigm. During the 1950s and 1960s cricket became hinged to the process of anticolonial reforms and the movement to independence and nation building. The political projects – rise of nation states and cricket as a symbol of West Indian liberation – grew hand in hand and together account for the ideological positions taken by Viv on a number of issues. There is nothing surprising, then, about this summary of his philosophy:

The whole issue is quite central for me, coming as I do from the West Indies at the very end of colonialism. I believe very strongly in the black man asserting himself in this world and over the years I have leaned towards many movements that follow this basic cause. It was perfectly natural for me to identify, for example, with the Black Power movement in America and, to a certain extent, with the Rastafarians.

I cannot say that I have ever reconciled myself totally to Rastafarianism. However I have many Rastafarian friends and I have always despised the way they have been discriminated against. Even in Antigua I have been put down in the past for simply having Rastafarian friends. It was hinted once that my career might not progress as far as it might simply because I was friendly with Rastafarians. Now that is certainly a case of prejudice and it goes back a long way in the Caribbean, back to when the Rastaman was initially regarded as nothing more than a subversive influence. Many people in the Caribbean have treated them in a bad way.[39]

The question for Viv, then, is one of supporting just causes within the political morality of the immediate postcolonial culture that correctly insists ideologically upon social inclusion and collective empowerment.

The social manifestations of ideological disapproval with Viv, however, are propagated everywhere; they have never been subtle or discreet. It has to do with power and its reproduction – the very essence of decolonization in the ideological sphere – and is therefore for many a matter of life and death. Decolonization, says Fanon, "is always a violent phenomenon", even if only in the language of ideological discourse. It is violent because it is quite simply the replacing of a certain 'species' of men by another 'species' of men.[40] Richards narrowly escaped being nailed to the cross on this matter of replacing one type of man with another. Lloyd was established and had to be replaced; the WICBC waxed and waned on the question of Richards' succession.

Trevor McDonald, in assessing Richards' career, makes references to the persistent tensions between Richards and the WICBC, and makes comparisons with an earlier stage when difficulties existed between the establishment and Sir Frank Worrell. He suggests that Richards paid, and continues to pay, a price for his defiant position in promoting the radical tradition within West Indies cricket culture. Two generations earlier the young and ideologically aggressive Frank Worrell was severely criticized in Barbados and by WICBC officials, who felt that he was an arrogant, radical 'upstart'. Worrell eventually chose to depart from Barbados, and took up residence in Jamaica and Trinidad where the social culture seemed more liberal and accommodating of progressive mentalities.[41]

The ideological tension, then, between these two traditions within West Indian cricket, the conservative and radical traditions, would surface from time to time and find expression in the political postures of individuals. These forces are very well understood by the English, largely because as an imperial nation they are experienced in the matter of seeking out dissidents and putting down insurgents. As colonizers, they understand all too well the responses of the colonized, and have developed a powerful ideological machinery to discredit, defeat, and eliminate challengers. Robin Marlar, writing for the *Sunday Times*, 4 July 1993, against the background of the changeover from the Richards to the Richardson captaincy, says:

It is clear that the West Indies Board thought that when Vivian Richards retired it was time that the leadership of West Indies cricket shifted its centre of gravity away from black activism and back towards the mainstream of the international game. Haynes was too close to his predecessor to achieve this objective and the mantle passed to the younger less confrontational Richie Richardson.

This shifting of the centre of gravity in West Indies cricket, therefore, is as much part of the making of the modern nation as the ideological metamorphosis of political parties and trade unions. The 1990s witness a similar preference for conservative leadership in public invitations throughout the Caribbean, and constituted, for example, the cemetery within which the Grenada Revolution now rests.

Lloyd stayed as captain longer than he intended. His extended term came as the result of a request of the WICBC. He had named Richards, his vice-captain of five years, as his successor and received a reprimand from the Board for doing so. Richards was hurt, wounded to the core, by the politics of succession. He felt rejected by the hands he had supported and fought for. He belonged to one species of men, while his employers belonged to another. There was nothing extraordinary about this relationship. It constituted a metaphor for the discourse of political decolonization. In the West Indies, many champions of popular movements lie broken, dejected, and hidden from history, defeated at the greased hands of emergent middlemen who stepped forward to broker 'a peace' and took the largest 'piece' for themselves. Viv wrote:

I believed that at one time there was a conspiracy, of sorts, to prevent me from taking over the leadership of the squad. After we had lost the World Cup to India, Clive announced that he would be giving up the captaincy and that I would be his immediate successor. I had been his vice-captain for five years and I felt, at that particular time, that I had paid my dues. I had actually captained the West Indies, in Clive's absence, as far back as 1980 in England. Nobody knew the West Indies game more than me. I thought I had done my job as deputy very well throughout that period and, I am not trying to be big-headed, but the captaincy rightfully belonged to me. Clive knew this, which is why he stated it, on a couple of occasions. But Clyde Walcott, the touring manager of the side, told Lloyd that he should not have made those statements, that the West Indies Cricket Board had not, at that point, decided that I was to be captain. But I knew that was wrong. Clive had decided to quit and there was no way they should have persuaded him otherwise.

But they did and, although I know that Clive tried to ring me to tell me of his decision to carry on, he could not reach me. I heard the news on the radio when I was in Somerset. Of course, it was immensely frustrating for me, not because of Clive's decision to carry on, but because I knew why he had been persuaded to do so. I knew that there were people who did not want me to take over.[42]

When the ballot for the captaincy was finally held by the West Indies Board, Viv had won by a margin of one vote. Malcolm Marshall, young in years and tenure on the side, but aged as a professional, almost upstaged his mentor.

Despite Richards being an outstanding motivator of players, and having successfully rebuilt the team after the departure of Lloyd, Croft, Garner, Holding, Gomes and other stalwarts, and never losing a Test series in the process, cricket officialdom withheld its praise for his leadership. With a statistical record superior to that of Lloyd, the establishment continued to identify Viv as the sort of 'rebel' not be encouraged. This further denial of just reward, intensified the pressure on Richards, forcing him at times to appear injudicious in his off-field assessments and action. In Rob Steen's autobiography of Desmond Haynes, *Lion of Barbados*, he expresses sympathy and a rare understanding of the pressure applied by the English press in particular to Viv. Circumstances, he said, were sometimes planned to upset Viv. People wanted to get him, Haynes indicated, because he was the symbol of West Indian dominance.[43] He was a man under siege by an array of ideological forces that were never comfortable with persons of his ilk. He had friends, and sympathizers, but they were insufficient to keep off the pressure and allow him to go into retirement as a contented and graceful old warrior.

Michael Holding, in his autobiography, *Whispering Death*, offers insights into what he considered the predicament of Viv, and the paradox his leadership posed for players and administrators. It had nothing to do with his supreme ability as a player or his right to be captain. Holding stated:

Viv certainly had no challengers as Lloyd's successor. No one in the team stood out as potentially a better skipper. He was a strong character who set high standards of performance for his players, precisely because he was so fiercely conscious of what success meant for the West Indies and West Indian people. The upshot was that he came down hard on those who fell short of his expectations. His players didn't seem to warm to him and I detected in his latter years that individuals were playing more for themselves than for the captain. Man-management calls for tact, patience and understanding but these did not come easily for such a passionate man as Viv Richards.[44]

The view has subsequently been expressed that this divide (between Richards' lack of social tact and his abundance of cricket tactics) caused the premature retirement of Michael Holding and Joel Garner, and signalled the final restructuring of Lloyd's regime. On assuming the captaincy, Richards made clear to all his determination to continue with the "winning ways" achieved by Lloyd, but by doing things his way. He was a captain of strong views and an iron will, not always the best combination in circumstances, says Holding, that required a light hand and gentle touch.

The turbulence and ambivalence that surrounded his entry to the captaincy intensified during the period of his retirement. Richards had outlined to the WICBC and the public his wish for a phased departure from first-class cricket. First, he wanted to give up the captaincy of the Test side, and openly proclaimed Desmond Haynes, his vice-captain, as his successor. Secondly, he declared his desire to play in the Australia–New Zealand World Cup which was just weeks away. Neither desire was honoured by the WICBC. Richie Richardson was appointed captain and supported the selectors' decision to exclude Richards from the World Cup squad. Richards was bitterly hurt. Richardson had been the beneficiary of his training, advice and special favours. His compliance with the decision of the selectors was received by Richards as an act of cowardice, betrayal and capitulation. In Antigua, the home of both men, the word on the streets is that Richardson bit the hand that fed him, and cannot be forgiven.

Thrown into unexpected retirement from West Indies cricket, officialdom moved to make light weather of the fact that Richards had not only been the world's greatest batsman, and statistically the most successful of West Indies captains. He considers himself banished by the establishment, with no one speaking publicly on his behalf as a candidate for a post as manager or coach. He returned to the English county and league circuit where he had first come to global prominence. His class and form were shown everywhere he played, and these opportunities and experiences provided the kind of soft landing that West Indies cricket had unreasonably denied him. He is currently employed by the Sultan of Brunei as a coach and cricket consultant. It is a long way from home, but for Viv it is another stop in his sojourn in exile.

All of this constitutes another paradox in the journey of the 'Enterprise of the Indies'. Toussaint L'Ouverture died in Napoleon's jail in France, and Marcus Garvey, another truly great revolutionary hero, was driven out of the islands to die in the hands of the colonial oppressor that had opposed his every initiative. The return of Richards to the West Indies, however, will be more than a physical one – but a further step in the process of self-discovery and recognition of identity by people who at this time remain fractured in terms of historical consciousness. There is no doubt that the exile of Richards has had a dampening effect on the 'soul' of West Indies cricket. The masses of cricket spectators know it. This is why West Indians turned out to fill Sabina Park on 23 March 1996, to pay a final and respectful farewell to the 'Conquering Lion' during the UWI Vice Chancellor's XI game against the touring New Zealand side. As always, the masses of people have ways of knowing and feeling the unjust use of power by the élite, and more often than not do what they can to mitigate the effects of the injustice.

Richards, then, walks in a tradition we know well from the records of Caribbean oral historiography. His trajectory is that of the uncompromising spirit that gives no space to the reactionary forces that encircle efforts to mend broken minds. Elevated by the positive dreams of a people, he now exists in the margins of their nightmare, a place where heroes are buried in fast succession. Viv, however, has always been quick on his feet, and possessed of an extraordinary eye for 'reading' the moving ball and responding with precision timing. For these reasons, if no others, history is on his side, if not behind him, and he may strike back sooner rather than later.

NOTES

1. Chris Searle, "Race before cricket: cricket, empire and the white rose", *Race and Class* 31, no. 3 (January/March 1990): 343–45; See also Christine Cummings, "The ideology of West Indies cricket", *Arena Review* 14, no. 1 (May

1990), 25–33; Hilary Beckles, "Barbados cricket and the crisis of social culture", in Barbados Cricket Association, *100 Years of Organised Cricket in Barbados* (Bridgetown: BCA, 1992), 50–51.

2. Searle, "Race before cricket", 37.

3. C.L.R. James, *The Black Jacobins: Toussaint L'Ouverture and the San Domingo Revolution* (1938; reprint New York: Vintage Books, 1963); *Beyond a Boundary* (London: Hutchinson, 1963); "The *Black Scholar* interviews C.L.R. James", *Black Scholar* 2, no. 1 (September 1970), 35–43.

4. Searle, "Race before cricket", 31.

5. Ibid., 38.

6. Ibid., 35.

7. Ibid., 34.

8. Cummings, "The ideology of West Indies cricket".

9. Searle, "Race before cricket", 35.

10. Learie Constantine, *Cricket and I* (London: Allan, 1933), 172.

11. Searle, "Race before cricket", 217.

12. Learie Constantine, *Cricket in the Sun* (London: Allan, 1947); Searle, "Race before cricket", 34.

13. James, *Beyond a Boundary*, 217.

14. C.L.R. James, *The Case for West Indian Self-Government* (London: Hogarth, 1933); "The Caribbean confrontation begins", *Race Today* 2 (1970): 311–14.

15. Michael Manley, *A History of West Indies Cricket* (London: André Deutsch, 1988), 146.

16. Ibid., 39–40

17. E.W. Swanton, *West Indies Revisited: the MCC Tour of 1959–60* (London: Heinemann, 1960), 279–80.

18. Trevor Bailey, *Sir Gary* (Glasgow: Fontana/Collins, 1976), 137.

19. Ibid., 39–40.

20. Ibid., 140.

21. Viv Richards, *Hitting Across the Line* (London: Headline Books, 1991), 188.

22. Ibid., 186.

23. Ibid., 187.

24. Ibid., 186.

25. *Sunday Advocate* (Barbados), 19 April 1992.

26. *Weekend Nation* (Barbados), 17 April 1992.

27. *Ibid.*

28. David Lowenthal, *West Indian Societies* (Oxford: Oxford University Press, 1972), 229.

29. *Time for Action: Report of the West India Commission* (Black Rock: Barbados, 1992), 328.

30. V.S. Naipaul, "England v. West Indies, 1963", in *Cricket,* edited by M. Davie and S. Davie (London: Faber, 1987), 184.

31. Richards, *Hitting Across the Line*, 76.

32. C.L.R. James, *Cricket* (London: Allison and Busby, 1989), 298–99.

33. Ibid., 299.

34. See Frantz Fanon, *The Wretched of the Earth* (London: Penguin, 1967).

35. Constantine, *Cricket and I*, 21–42.
36. Walter Rodney, *Groundings with my Brothers* (London: Bogle-L'Ouverture Publishers, 1970).
37. Richards, *Hitting Across the Line*, 75, 87.
38. Ibid., 88.
39. Ibid., 188.
40. Fanon, *The Wretched of the Earth*, 27.
41. See Trevor McDonald, *Viv Richards* (London: Sphere Books, 1984), 15–23, 122–23; Ivo Tennant, *Frank Worrell: A Biography* (Cambridge: Lutterworth Press, 1987), 3–17.
42. Richards, *Hitting Across the Line*, 146.
43. Rob Steen, *Desmond Haynes: Lion of Barbados* (London: H.F. and G. Witherby, 1993), 13, 17, 19, 26, 102–103, 198–202.
44. Michael Holding, *Whispering Death: The Life and Times of Michael Holding* (Kingston: West Indies Publishers, 1993), 189–90.

5

Popular Art and Cultural Freedom

Ritualizing Resistance

Magnificently expressive of the anxieties of nationalist consciousness in the twentieth century are the drama, music and literature, both oral and scribal, of the West Indian masses. Nationalist identity and sentiments found eruptive articulation in spectator 'politics' that reveal both the depth and fragility of the new sovereign order. For many colonials this process was entirely surprising. It was not altogether clear at the end of the nineteenth century that within two decades the majority of West Indians would have embraced cricket and promoted it as their principal, popular, nationalist cultural activity.

Much clearer, however, was that traditional promoters of the game wished for no such objective. The intensity of the determination to maintain the heart and soul of the game by white élite participants stimulated the imagination of the excluded majority who understood the principles and ideas at the centre of the contest. By the interwar years cricket had ceased to be a minority game. The masses now saw their own players holding forth and challenging the best. Home-grown heroes were emerging everywhere, and stars were shining in rural villages and urban ghettos in ways hitherto unimaginable. They could now travel overseas as reputable players and engage 'gentlemen' at the highest levels; the status of 'professional' was one they could appropriate and use as a measure, and mirror, of their success.

Like Protestant Christianity, cricket was introduced into West Indian society and defined as part of the ideological armour of an aggressive English cultural imperialism. Neither was intended for the social consumption of the politically disenfranchised and materially impoverished black communities. Both were instruments of empire, imported and imposed upon colonial society by English officials and resident white élite who valued above all the political importance of formally organized social institutions.

The end of the nineteenth century, however, was a significant social moment for advocates of both cricket and Christianity. While nonconformist missionaries in particular traversed the region feverishly seeking a mass (black) membership for their churches, the colonial élite was doing all in its power to insulate cricket culture from the social effects of ideological egalitarianism. Élite whites wished to be satisfied, at least moderately so, that there was still one social institution whose doors remained closed to the lower orders, and in which 'gentlemen' could enjoy exclusively the social pleasures and privileges associated with their oligarchical ownership of private property.

The ideological positions adopted by the Anglo-colonial élite with respect to the politics of Christianity and cricket constitute a discursive context. A sophisticated appreciation of the value system of cricket, élite whites argued, was beyond the intellectual reach of Africans and Asians, whose participation was seen as detrimental to its development. In the ideological sphere, 'high' moral and aesthetical expression was appropriated and monopolized by the élite, while concepts that denoted crudity and primitivism were levelled against the labouring classes. Eurocentrism and racism, then, functioned as a formidable boundary that separated colonial social groups within the established church as well as on the cricket field.

In the twentieth century, however, West Indians of African and Asian descent confronted the 'imported/imposed' Englishness of the plantation-based cricket world with precise anticolonial, nationalist demands that had the effect of changing forever the social trajectory and meaning of the game.[1] Within this process of cultural domestication and working class aggression, the disenfranchised sculptured unique and distinct methodological and aesthetical forms of the game that reflected and promoted their social identity and concerns. In their varied roles as players, spectators and commentators, the working classes succeeded in determining and defining the popular images, politics and social considerations of cricket in ways that soon gained hegemonic cultural dimensions.[2]

While Englishmen, and their creole progeny, sought to imitate and fossilize cricketing images and behavioural patterns that originated with the Victorian gentry, the West Indian masses surrounded and infused the game with an aura and ethos derived from their popular struggles and residual cultural norms. Even before 1928, when the West Indies cricket team gained Test status, observers were keen to point out that Africans and Asians brought to the game a unique, dynamic, celebratory, theatrical presence.

With reference to an earlier period, for example, Algernon Aspinall, historian of the English in the nineteenth century West Indies, had commented on the "sheer excitement" and "demonstrative" expressions of "the black spectator". "It is not unusual", he tells us, "to see many of them rush out on the ground and leap and roll about from sheer excitement when a wicket falls on the side which they do not favour, or when a brilliant catch is made." A.F. Somerset, who toured the West Indies in 1895 with the Slade Lucas team, while comparing the participatory 'playing' of the West Indian crowd with its less verbose, more quietly consumerist English counterpart, stated:

A good ball dealt with brings a shout of 'played!' all around the ground, and to stop a 'yorker' evokes a yell that would not be given for a hit out of the ground in England. When that comes off a large part of the crowd spring on to the ground, throw their hands and umbrellas in the air, perform fantastic dances, and some of them are occasionally arrested by the police.[3]

In the Barbados vs England match of that tour, Somerset stated, the England captain was forced to use a whistle to get the attention of his fieldsmen, so noisy and festive was the crowd.

Performing the Language

This expressive physical and oral appreciation of performance had hardly changed in the years after World War II when West Indians prepared to take the cricket world by storm. In fact, it has been consolidated into that realm of popular recognition generally referred to as custom. Barbadian poet, Edward Brathwaite, captured the nationalist language and sound of the Barbados cricket crowd during a postwar Test against England:

Clyde [Walcott] back pun de backfoot an' prax!
Is through extra cover an' four red runs all de way.
"You see dat shot?" the people was shoutin';
"Jesus Chrise, man, wanna see dat shot?"
All over de groun' fellers shakin' hands wid each other
An' in front o' where I was sittin',
One ball-headed sceptic snatch hat off he head
as if he did crazy
an' pointin' he finger at Wardle [the bowler]
he jump up an' down
Like a sun-shatter daisy an' bawl
out; "B..L..O..O..D, B..I..G.. B..O..Y.
Bring me he B..L..O..O..D".[4]

This tradition of language, performance and sound 'speaks' directly to the variety of issues central to an ontological understanding of what is West Indianness. That the West Indian voice is clearly heard in the sound of the cricket crowd should indicate the basic truth of C.L.R. James' assertion that spectators take with them through the gates of cricket arenas the full weight of their history and visions of the future. This 'sound' of gathered West Indians, like the talking drums of their ancestors, is a secret code which is very easily misconceived and misunderstood by those not perfectly tuned to its transmission. It is a sound that fills the air and unites those whose mission it is to put together fragments of an old world in new, more resistant forms.

The indigenous literature, music, and dance of the West Indian cricket crowd, then, are cultural missiles that emanate from a complex, nationalist command centre within race/class consciousness. The inherent beliefs of the common people with respect to past and current achievements and injustices, as well as everyday fears and expectations, are often displayed at moments of 'play', and in ways which support Brathwaite's and Vidia Naipaul's view that cricket for many constitutes a level of consciousness and existence located somewhere above mundane matters of economics and politics. It is this historically informed matrix of consciousness, actions and ideology that continues to engage the creative art forms of West Indians. Cricket as the popular cultural occupation of the region, therefore, converts spectators into artists in a dialectical and symbiotic way, allowing for some of the finest expressions of music, theatrical performance and oral literature.

The nation language employed by the West Indian voice within the cricket arena, furthermore, is not only authentic, but perhaps more importantly, it is pure in that it remains spontaneous in its creative form and insists upon being uncensored. Its linguistic code is no different in meaning from the drumbeat call to arms by the enslaved on the plantation in an earlier era. At the same time it is also the infrastructure for a sophisticated literary play on the pressing sociopolitical issues 'beyond the boundary'. All together, as a discursive practice, they constitute a compelling element of an indigenous literary canon that rejects notions of the region as 'other' by the imperial centre and insists upon the existence of plurality in style and genre. The voice of the cricket crowd as heard, and interpreted, to which generations of established artists have responded, is therefore rooted in popular ideology and echoes levels of consciousness within the fragmented West Indian nation.

The oral and scribal text of the West Indian cricket culture, then, constitutes a storehouse of information on the native tongue, sound and senses. In terms of content this text has been fiercely anticolonial, even before the time when such an ideological position had not taken shape in the form of organized political activity. The earliest cricket crowd said as much about English colonialism as more recent political leaders on their soapboxes; working class calypsonians sent as many potent messages to Whitehall in their cricket songs as scholars did in their written texts. The metaphoric cricket poems, songs and prose of the region constitute an innovative literary and artistic style of communication that reinforces the significance of the game within mass society. It is this sporting activity that has given West Indian people as a whole their first mass heroes. While political or intellectual leaders may attain popularity within single territories, only the following of cricket heroes transcends national, ideological and generational boundaries. This reality provides a unique terrain for artists and intellectuals to speak to the region as one about itself as a unified cultural space.

Such an opportunity was not to be missed by an artist as penetrating and perceptive as Trinidad's Errol John. In his play, *Moon on a Rainbow Shawl*, the quintessential classic of contemporary Caribbean theatre, John speaks of the racial injustices within early twentieth century colonial society that found fertile soil in its cricket fields. In the script, Charlie Adams, who, just by an analysis of his name, is a 'regular' common kind of being – if not the first man in terms of biblical text – has a decidedly promising career ahead of him as a cricketer, possessing in his physical and mental faculties an abundance of skills and power of application. While representing his country on a tour of Jamaica, however, Adams expressed some measure of disgust at the discriminatory treatment meted out to black members of his team by their white hosts. For this social 'indiscretion' his cricketing career came to a cataclysmic end, with the consequence of his being unemployable, abjectly depressed and finally, a convicted, alcoholic criminal. Broken dreams and a shattered life led to Adams' 'social death' in a colonial community that was prepared to offer him 'recognition' on condition of self-negation and denial. What is important about this scenario from our viewpoint is not the written text, but the fact that John's father was himself recognized as a 'potential' who, during the 1930s, had experienced considerable frustration and humiliation at the hands of the 'white' cricketing authorities.[5]

Adams' dream was no different from that of most working class African and Asian West Indian boys from the 1930s to the present; to escape the poverty and racial oppression of their little world aboard the cricket vehicle – the one that took the most passengers from the ghettoes to the suburbs and beyond. Adams tells his story of hope, struggle and despair, and finally defeat by the 'savannah' colonial upper class of the Queen's Park Cricket Club:

Charlie: In my day, EPF – I use to get my bats second-hand. An' sometimes they had to last me from season to season, but my big talent was with the ball.
I used to trundle down to that wicket – an' send them down red hot! They don't make them that fast these days. The boys don't keep in condition. Today they send down a couple of overs – then they are on their knees. But in my time, John, Old Constantine, Francis, them fellas was fast! Fast! Up in England them so help put the Indies on the map.

EPF: I only saw you once on the green, Charlie. Yer was kind of past yer prime. But the ole brain was there! And batsman was seein' trouble! Trouble, man! And I say this to you now, papa – You was class!

Charlie: In them days, boy – The Savannah Club crowd was running most everything. People like me either had to lump it or leave it.

EPF: It ent much different now, Charlie.

Charlie: Is different – a whole lot different. In them times so when we went Barbados or Jamaica to play cricket they used to treat us like hogs, boy. When we went on tours they put we in any ole kind of boarding-house. The best hotels was fer them and the half-scald members of the team – So in twenty-seven when we was on tour in Jamaica I cause a stink, boy. I had had enough of them dirty little boarding-house rooms. I said either they treat me decent or they send me back. The stink I made got into the newspapers. They didn't send me back. But that was the last intercolony series I ever play. They broke me, boy.

EPF: [quietly] Fer that?

Charlie: I should of known mey place. If I had known mey place, EPF, I'd made the team to England the following year. And in them days, boy – the English County clubs was outbidding each other fer bowlers like me. But the Big Ones here strangled my future, boy.[6]

The collective memory of the cricket 'crowd' has in store cases by the dozen of 'potentials' who dried and died on the cricket vine on account of protesting such social injustices.

Bruce St John, 'nation poet' of Barbados, understood the tragic drama that lurks in the dark corners of the cricket culture. He urges the player, however, to be optimistic and to persevere against all adversity since, in the final instance, the crowd, like Christ of the New Testament, is understanding and sympathetic. Cricket, St John tells us, has assumed quasi-religious proportions for the Barbadian masses:

Le' muh tell yuh somet'ing Boysie boy,
De Lord got somet'ing to do wid cricket.
De wicket does remin' me o' de Trinity
God in de centre of de three,
Holy Ghost pun de lef' and Jesus
Pun de right an' de bails like a crown
Joinin' dem an' mekkin' dem Three in One.
De pitch lika an altar north and south

Wid de sun transfigurin' de scene
And de umpires like two high priests
Wid de groundsmen as de sextons, Yes, Yes . . .
Cricket is de game o' de Lord
Cricket is de game o' de Master
Play de game right, Boysie boy
An' you stan' a good chance hereafter.[7]

St John's utopian 'hereafter' refers less to the social honour and economic betterment dreamt of by Charlie Adams, and more to a perception that the moral values of the game if properly applied to social life tend towards the making of a Christian character that is readily embraced by the society.

St John's optimism and generosity, however, did not find its way into Edward Brathwaite's use of the cricket metaphor in his clinical (for some cynical) assessment of the West Indian personality. Brathwaite seems to share Wilson Harris's criticism of the West Indian mind as disunited, consumed in apathy and unwilling to be disciplined into taking responsibility for its destiny. In "Rites", the famous poem in which these themes are explored, Brathwaite confronts the question of indiscipline and irresponsibility:

I tole him over an' over
agen: *watch de ball, man,* watch
De ball like it hook to your eye

When you first goes in an' you doan know de pitch.
Uh doan mean to poke
but you jes got to watch what you doin';
this isn't no time for playin'
the fool nor making no sport; this is cricket!
But Gullstone too deaf:
mudder doan clean out de wax in 'e ear!
Firs' ball from Cass an' he fishin':
second ball an' he missin', swishin'
he bat like wishin'
to catch butterfly; though all Gullstone ever could catch
pun this beach was a cole!
But is always the trouble wid we;
Too afraid an' too frighten.
Is all very well when it rosy an' sweet,
but leh murder start an' bruggalungdung!
You cahn fine a man to hole up de side.[8]

On this matter, if not on any other, Brathwaite and Naipaul agree.

For Naipaul, West Indian cricketers, like politicians, lack the kind of mental preparation necessary for the attainment of creative accomplishments. For him, colonials are generally imitators and flippant in manner – nation builders are not. With reference to the 1963 West Indies tour of England, Naipaul places these words in the mouth of his fictional character:

> You know what's wrong with our West Indians? No damn discipline. Look at this business this morning. That Hall and Trueman nonsense, Kya-Kya, very funny. But that is not the way the Aussies won Tests. I tell you, what we need is *conscription*. Put every one of the idlers in the army. Give them discipline.[9]

Music, Melody and Messengers

If Brathwaite saw in cricket characteristic features of an unfit West Indian personality – one not yet ready for serious nationalist concerns – and was therefore unwilling to celebrate and savour the 'highs' of the game on account of the 'lows' that were sure to follow, calypsonians from the earliest days had no such reservations. They composed and performed melodies that captured the essence of historic moments in a way that newspaper reporters could not. In the first West Indies Test match at Lord's, against England, which was played in 1928, Learie Constantine, at age 26, took four wickets and three catches, and was involved in the dismissal of the first four English batsmen. To mark the occasion, Trinidadian calypsonian, Lord Beginner (Egbert Moore) composed the song:

> Joe Small and Griffith was
> excellent
> was magnificent
> And our cricketer, great Wilton St Hill
> Did not do well because he was ill
> He made a name for the West Indies
> Who he was? Learie Constantine
> That old pal of mine.[10]

This calypso, notes Kim Johnson, is the first celebration in song of a West Indies cricket hero.[11]

The 1950 West Indies tour of England was special in many ways. But the most significant feature was that thousands of West Indians had recently emigrated to England and represented for the first time a significant 'home crowd' within the English crowd cheering on the West Indies. The vocal support they offered the West Indies team during Tests strengthened its resolve to the same degree as it disturbed English supporters now faced with a new and novel circumstance. The tensions of race relations in England, and the 'blues' of the migrant communities, meant that the psychological profiles of West Indian spectators had also been reconfigured. Anti-black racism has long been an endemic feature of West Indian societies, but there was something different and unfamiliar about the English contexts of racism. Perhaps it was the absence of cultural space that prevented West Indian migrants from creating their own world, in spite of racism, that heightened anxieties and produced the besieged consciousness.

The first Test was played at Old Trafford, and England won by 202 runs. The second Test at Lord's, however, produced the long sought after result – West Indies won by 326 runs on account of the brilliance of young mystery spinners Sonny Ramadhin and Alf Valentine. England received a thrashing that broke their resolve, and the West Indies romped home to a 3–1 historic Test victory after winning the third and fourth Tests by 10 wickets and an innings and 56 runs respectively.

The Lord's Test was the scene of the first 'cricket carnival' in England. The ground exploded in dance, song and bacchanal, West Indian style, and signalled the beginning of a process that was to refashion the culture of cricket crowds in England. Lord Kitchener and Lord Beginner were at Lord's for the pivotal Test, and already known as legendary artists, led jubilant West Indians across the field in a procession of improvised singing. The well known photograph of these two Lords of calypso at Lord's, surrounded by chanting melody makers, says more about that moment in the hearts of West Indians than match reports ever could. Kitchener, with guitar in hand, and Beginner leading the vocals, produced for the cricket world the song "Cricket, Lovely Cricket":[12]

Cricket, lovely cricket
At Lord's where I saw it
(repeat)
Yardley tried his best
But Goddard won the Test
They gave the crowd plenty fun
Second Test and
West Indies won
With those two little pals of mine
Ramadhin and Valentine
The King was well attired
So they started with Rae and Stollmeyer
Stolly was hitting balls around the boundary

But Wardle stopped him at twenty
Rae had confidence
So he put up a strong defence
He saw the King was waiting
to see
So he gave him a century

For West Indians, even those who came of age (in a cricketing sense) after the 1950 Test, this was their redemption song.

Lord Beginner, then, was critical in the establishment of a literary and musical tradition that is, ironically, perhaps more West Indian than the cricket itself. Kitchener, notes Kim Johnson, built upon and deepened this art form in ways that enhanced the standing of cricket for West Indians as "de Lord's game". According to Johnson, Kitchener sang "The Cricket Song" about the 1964 series, telling the story in his beautiful couplets alongside an old-time call-and-response chorus:

(Bowl Griffith) Bowl, don't
stop at all
(Bowl Griffith) Give him back the ball
(Bowl Griffith) Sobers and Hall
(Bowl Griffith) Bring Gibbs and all.

And then in 1967 he sang "Cricket Champions" about the 1966 series in England when West Indies, led by Sobers, won three, drew one and lost one Test:

England must understand
We are the champions
Sobers carray and hit them
potow! potow! – two four
Holford come back and hit
them bodow! bodow! – two more.

But in between these two gems by Kitchener something had changed; Sparrow sang "Sir Garfield Sobers" (1966) about "the greatest cricketer on Earth, or Mars" and the victory over Australia, and narrative ball-by-ball calypso commentaries went out of fashion.

Thereafter, in the 1970s, Relator penned the marvellous 'Gavaskar'. Although this was structured in an old-time narrative mode and made fun of the names of the Indian cricketers, Relator was not only singing humorously about series cricket – not no Chinese match – but also commenting on the first West Indian Test defeat at the hands of India:

and its Gavaskar
We real master
Just like a wall
We couldn't out Gavaskar at all.

Short Shirt sent "Viv Richards" from Antigua in 1975, Maestro gave us "World Cup", and Sparrow sang "Kerry Packer" which in 1978 savagely tore down the final myth of cricketing heroism:

I eh negotiating ah told them
If they got money we can't control them
A West Indian cricketer must always be broke
Is then he does bowl fast and make pretty stroke.[13]

These songs reflect both the celebratory and commemorative values of the wider society, and are rooted in the cultural bedrock of their 'call-and-response', 'praise song' and 'judgemental' oral traditions. They also chronicle the history of West Indies cricket, the successes and failures. But, more importantly, they articulate national political concerns and popular ideologies.

David Rudder's "Rally Round the West Indies" calls for firm support for the West Indies team during the difficult years that followed the retirement of several players from the extraordinarily victorious Clive Lloyd team. But Rudder is also concerned with the wider geopolitical issues involved in West Indies survival when he beckons:

Soon we must take a side or be left in the rubble
In a divided world that don't need islands no more
Are we doomed for ever to be at somebody's mercy
Little keys can open up mighty doors
Rally round the West Indies now and forever.

The West Indies cricket crowd, of course, provides the inspiration and ideological parameters for this musical tradition. It is common indeed for the crowd to call upon known musical talents to take the lead and improvise songs to suit the occasion and mood of the game. What happens in the recording studios is but a refashioning of forms and ideas already ventilated by the cricket crowd. It is the crowd that provides the interpretation of events to which the artist responds, and within the creativity of the moment history is preserved in sound.

A classic 'character' in the musical tradition of the West Indies cricket crowd is the Barbadian calypsonian, Mac Fingall , a schoolteacher by profession, and also popular comedian. He loves cricket as much as he cares for the popular theatre, and blends the two to magical effect much to the delight of spectators at Kensington Oval. Fingall enters the Oval with his trumpet under his arm, and big bass drum around his neck. Soon he is accompanied by persons unknown to himself who arrive with conch shells, kettle drums, flutes, fifes and other instruments. The 'band', somehow, is assembled, the crowd calls the tune, and Fingall's trumpet rings out. By this time, 8,000 people within the stand are rocking, swaying and nodding to the pulsating song.

The music, of course, reflects the mood of the moment. When West Indies batsmen are in trouble, the music ceases. When West Indies batsmen are punishing the opposition's bowlers, the silence erupts into carnival. When, however, West Indies fast bowlers are not making the required impression on the oppositions' batsmen, Fingall puts away the trumpet and seeks to inspire them with a drumming solo that heats the blood, quickens the heartbeat, and energizes the muscles. The quickening rhythmic sound of drums drives the fast bowlers on, unnerves the batsman, and often wickets begin to tumble.

During the recent tours of England and Australia to the West Indies, complaints were lodged to West Indian officials by the tourists with respect to the musical scores of crowds. In response, an attempt was made in Barbados to outlaw the taking of musical instruments, the drum in particular, into the Oval. This resulted in a heated national debate in which spectators vowed to boycott 'matches' unless the 'sounds' were allowed. References were made to the persistent attempts, before and after slavery, by white colonials and their black allies, to criminalize the drum, star of the African musical cosmology. Any attack upon the drum, they said, is an attack upon the "souls of black folks".

Viv Richards, West Indies captain, responded to a decision of the Barbados cricket authorities to ban the drum by stating that it was shortsighted, antisocial and disrespectful of black people whose cricket culture has long been characterized by the presence of sound. The drums, he said in addition, had inspired his bowlers and fieldsmen, and should be treated with respect. The crowd would have none of it. They won this battle, and officials were left to plead for a sound level consistent with the cultural norms of tourists.

Playing Mas' and the Crowd

Familiarity with the display of West Indian social culture, furthermore, would indicate that wherever there is 'sound', there are sights to behold. It is here that we enter the psychological world of the saturnalia, mask, masquerade and make-believe of everyday life. The two 'theatrical' 'crowd' characters of the postcolonial era carry the names King Dyall (Barbados) and Gravey (Antigua). King Dyall, as his alias indicated, was assumed to derive his royal bearing from an ancient pedigree. He was the most well-known member of the Barbados cricket crowd, and announced his arrival at the gates with the waving of his walking cane, the tipping of his derby, and the installation of his pipe. A tailor by trade, he wore brightly coloured three-piece suits, with matching shoes, hat and gloves, and rode an old bicycle which had been variously painted yellow, white and pink. As a member of the inner city black working class, the 'King' as he was known, had no time for black people and preached at cricket his love for all things white and English. He was not a supporter of the West Indies team, and made much of his preference for the English team. For him, the 'greats' of cricket were Peter May, Colin Cowdrey and Len Hutton. Black spectators around him he described as 'monkey', 'ignorant sheep' and 'primitives'.

The King of the Oval verbally abusing his subjects with language not far removed from that used by Kipling brought tremendous comic relief to spectators during less exciting cricket moments. The King represented the imperial mask that upwardly mobile blacks were forced to wear during the colonial regime. The mask in time became a cultural norm which now stands in a dichotomous relation to the liberating cricket culture. While the King at the Oval was symbolic of the nineteenth century white, colonial gentleman spectator, the tackiness of his attire portrayed his class position, and revealed the self-contemptuousness endemic to the colonized mind. The 'King', therefore, in his masquerade, was a reminder of the values and practices black cricketers fought against, and at the same time his presence represented a confirmation of popular admiration for the pomp and regalia of graceful gait and carriage.

Antigua's Gravey is a different kind of cricket character. His is the masquerade associated with dance, song and flamboyant costume. He dresses, more often that not, in women's clothing – wigs, earrings, make-up and handbag included – and dances, some would say immorally, throughout the game in front of amused crowds. The sexual connotations of his dances entertain spectators who call upon him to show them what he can 'do'. His dances and other athletic antics are popular with the Antiguan cricket crowd, which has developed a reputation in the region for its musical character. Gravey's intention is to mock the ascribed weaknesses and effeminacy of opposing cricketers, and his dance suggests that they are being assaulted by West

Indian machismo. It is a dance of triumph and conquest, well understood by the West Indian masses, particularly in terms of the subliminal sexuality of the experience.

The West Indian cricket aesthetic, then, is shaped fundamentally by cultural expression in the form of colour, song and dance, which dictate that cricket looks best if played on a clear bright day. Fielders, of course, ought to be clothed in sparkling white flannels and the field should be green with a pitch Barbadian fans would refer to as "shining like dog stones", meaning flat, shiny and glasslike. This is the perfect setting for the first day of a Test match. The requirements for the spectators are largely visual, in terms of mass and colour, and the pleasures are maximized when moments of tension and tautness are mixed with periods of relaxation.

This is the cricket arena of action, the perfect theatrical environment. The centre of good theatre is conflict and this begins long before the first ball is delivered. The objectives of the opposing teams are clear. Bat must dominate ball or vice versa; and after five days only West Indian cricket can end in the fashion Paul Keens-Douglas describes in his 'performance' poem "Tanti [Auntie] at the Oval":

Islands need seven runs with nine balls to bowl an' one wicket to fall.
Dis time I forget 'bout Tanti Merle,
Excitement in de Oval like you never seen in ya life,
Gore come into bat an' is den de action start
Nine balls seven runs to go . . . noise in de place
Eight balls six runs to go . . . Tanti start waving de basket
Seven balls six runs to go . . . Tanti on top de seat
Six balls five runs to go . . . Tanti fall off de seat
Five balls five runs to go . . . Tanti wavin' de parasol
Four balls four runs to go . . . Police cautionin' Tanti
Three balls three runs to go . . . I can't see Tanti
Two balls three runs to go . . . Tanti climbing de fence
One ball three runs to go. . . Tanti on the field
Gore hit de ball an' Finlay pelt down de wicket for two runs
And is then de bachanal start.[14]

West Indian masses also demand from cricket what they seek in every form of art – a sense of style. This special quality cannot be defined. It can be perceived by senses well trained for the task, and the sensation is unmistakable. Quality drama must promote high art, and in West Indian society an important cultural residue of the African ancestry is the centrality of style to all ontological expressions. Some batsmen can be very prolific, consistent and reliable, but are never in the West Indies defined as 'great' unless they meet the popular criterion of style. This special quality – essence if you like – is considered endemic to West Indian cricket culture, and does not occupy centre stage in other cultures. As Sobers walked to the wicket, the evidence of this 'thing' is witnessed and celebrated. Something in the way he moved satisfied some spectators who readily confess that they paid to 'see' Sobers, not to watch him score runs.

The question of cricket style, or 'class', has occupied literary aestheticists for some time. V.S. Naipaul in a letter to C.L.R. James indicated that cricket in the West Indies "represents style, grace and other elements of culture in a society which had little else of the kind".[15] This quality which is celebrated and deified by West Indians within the cricket culture is defended in the most uncompromising manner, and is indicative of the popular refusal to be liberal on the matter of 'artistic purity'. C.L.R. James concludes:

I submit finally that without the intervention of any artist the spectator at cricket extracts the significance of movement and of tactile values. He experiences the heightened sense of capacity. Furthermore, however, the purely human element, the literature, the frustration, in cricket may enhance the purely artistic appeal, the significant form at its most unadulterated is permanently present. It is known, expected, recognized and enjoyed by tens of thousands of spectators. Cricketers call it style.[16]

This visual impression, West Indians would suggest, is expressive of individual confidence that by extension indicates a mastery of form that allows the game to transcend the mundane and to be elevated into the category of art. And, it is this rare quality that occasionally solicits from West Indian crowds another kind of 'sound' – that of stone silence – which indicates a sudden neutralization of the central nervous system. Extreme beauty, they say, can only be understood, experienced and appreciated within the total freedom of a vacuum or the cluttered anarchy of sensual abandonment and madness.

The West Indian cricket crowd, then, has made its distinctive contribution to the artistic tradition in the forms of music, dance, theatre, and oral and scribal literature. It is a special contribution that requires careful attention lest its value be lost within a haze of élitist assumptions about the culture of the 'lower orders'. This, of course can easily happen in the West Indies where such groups who attend cricket matches dressed in jacket and tie in spite of the heat (96 °F in the shade) commonly refer to popular culture as expressions of the 'mob' or 'rabble'. The 'sounds' of the crowd, they consider, are the result of a lack of domestic manners and breeding, an attitude that reflects the traditional world view of the colonial white community.

But the redemption 'sounds' of the crowd are indicative of a deeper cultural search for authenticity and nationalist cultural freedom. That you must make your own distinct sound in order to have an independent voice is pretty well understood. What needs to be further understood is the relationship between social life as 'activated' consciousness and the reproduction of the creative process. Understanding how social attitudes and mentalities are translated into performing art – on the field in the case of players – and 'sounds' in the case of the crowd cannot be fully understood in the absence of an indigenous anthropology. What seems clear, furthermore, is the manner in which the cricket crowd continues to be both transmitter and receiver of artistic forms and practices that go to the centre of any definition of the term 'West Indian'.

NOTES

1. Aspinall, *The British West Indies: Their History, Resources and Progress*, (London: Pitman, 1912), 153–54.
2. Ibid.
3. Ibid., 154.
4. Edward Brathwaite, *The Arrivants: A New World Trilogy* (London: Oxford University Press, 1981), 200.
5. Errol John, *Moon on a Rainbow Shawl* (London: Faber, 1958) 61–62.
6. Ibid.
7. Bruce St John, "Cricket", in *Bumbatuk* 1 (Bridgetown: Cedar Press, 1982), 17, 19.
8. Brathwaite, *The Arrivants*, 198.
9. V.S. Naipaul, "England v. West Indies (1963)", *The Faber Book of Cricket*, edited by M. and S. Davie (London: Faber, 1987), 187.
10. Cited in Kim Johnson, "Calypso cricket", *Sunday Express* (Trinidad and Tobago) 4 April 1993.
11. Johnson, "Calypso Cricket".
12. Ibid.
13. Ibid.
14. Paul Keens-Douglas, "Tanti Merle".
15. Anna Grimshaw (ed.), *C.L.R. James: Cricket* (London: Allison & Busby, 1986) 131.
16. C.L.R. James, *Beyond a Boundary* (London: Hutchinson, 1963), 198.

6

Gender Order and the Women's Game

Attitudes to Women in West Indian Cricket

Neither colonialism nor nationalism sought to problematize the principle of patriarchy upon which their cultural values rested. The nation building project, and the 'independence' politics of 'founding fathers', were inherently gendered enterprises that excluded women as equal, privileged partners. The masculinist culture of the military-plantation complex within which cricket was imported and developed, had also settled at the outset its gender agenda. As an element in the cultural expression of the nineteenth century ruling class, organized cricket took social divisiveness and inequality to the extreme with respect to gender relations.

While as a popular institution cricket sought mediation of race and class inequalities, it stood firm and unmoved in its encounter with gender. While black men, and poor men of all races, were gradually included, women remained excluded from the mainstream throughout colonialism, and indeed into the nationalist period. While women also played competitive cricket up to the Test level, the social ostracism of their game indicates more the presence of hostility than indifference. Gender, therefore, has proven the stickiest of cricket wickets, and the politics of female exclusion remain active and potent into postcolonialism. The nationalist agenda did not include gender exclusion in any systematic way but fundamental continuity rather than change on this issue remains the order of things.

Viv Richards, West Indian cricket megastar and legend within the global sports culture, described West Indies women's cricket as a "purely natural extension" of the men's game. Rachel Heyhoe, captain of the 1970 England touring team to the West Indies, identified with this conceptualization by stating that Jamaican women cricketers, such as Vivalyn Latty-Scott and Dorothy Hobson, have the "same inborn quality of being natural game play-

117

ers as their male counterparts". Richards, however, recognized that this 'natural' phenomenon has not found popular acceptance within contemporary West Indian nor English ideological conditions. As a result, he called for the removal of discriminatory attitudes and practices against women's cricket by means of the adoption of innovative strategies and nonsexist attitudes.[1]

Such emphasis upon the alleged 'natural' ability of women cricketers and their 'natural' relation to the dominant male cricket culture provides a valuable instance within which the social consequences and ideological effects of patriarchy in West Indian society can be examined. Certainly, women cricketers in the West Indies have long been popularly received as most 'unnatural' persons. They have evoked responses at different levels of communities that suggest their reception as being exotic and spectacular, raising questions concerning their sexual ideologies and proclivities. The popular imagination has not been respectful of their organized activities, which continue to raise eyebrows rather than sponsors and spectators.

These attitudes have contributed to the suppression, textual trivialization, and gendered distortion of information concerning women's cricket in the region. While being stereotyped as cricket fanatics, West Indian male 'sportists', for example, whose encyclopaedic grasp of cricket matters is well known, are generally lacking in basic and rudimentary knowledge about the women's game. While information relevant to the hegemonic men's game has transcended the sports sections of the regional media, competing favourably for prime time and space with corporate and political issues, women's cricket continues to fight for minimal, nonsexist coverage.

While these circumstances provide yet another arena within which the gender consciousness of empowered West Indian males can be explored, they also indicate the degree to which the marginalization of women in colonial and national society has been effected through the ideological environment of popular institutions.[2] Since the nineteenth century, West Indian males have seen cricket as an exclusive manifestation of their world view. The social consumption and reproduction of its practice is guarded by gendered ideological boundaries that indicate the limits and nature of female involvement. In spite of significant encouragement in recent years by corporate sponsors, women cricketers throughout the region continue to share emotional experiences not dissimilar to those of black male players in the early decades of the twentieth century. Treated as girls playing a man's game, women cricketers are, at best, 'tolerated' in their protest against marginalization by officialdom, which is generally seen as the correct 'political' approach in an increasingly gender sensitive social culture.

So settled within contemporary West Indian male consciousness is the view that the social possession of cricket is maintained by their gender enterprise that discourse in relation to ownership patterns has centred exclusively around race and class issues. While black men and white men jostled for position in relation to the historic rights of ownership, women have remained silent with respect to their rights after several decades of spectator and playing participation. For example, a letter entitled "Away with cricket" published in the *Dominica Star*, 17 May 1969, stated that Black Power leaders have urged West Indians to "throw off the white Imperialist culture and adopt Black African ways", and made reference to the disgrace involved in "young men who ape their white masters by playing cricket – a truly white man's game". The question which followed is even more indicative of the gendered West Indian view: "Isn't there a good African game our young men could play in the Botanical Gardens on Sundays?" The voice of women with respect to this discourse is not heard though by this time their cricket activity was an established part of popular culture.

The postmodern discourse, within which the colonized 'other' has had new conceptual images of itself thrust upon it, emphasizes the superordinate degree to which colonial cultural formations have reflected the liberated consciousness of the European male. The subordination of the white female to the male perception and general objectives of the colonizing mission, and the allocation of specific supportive roles to her within the imperium, suggest her overall powerlessness with respect to defining and participating autonomously in the social process of institutional formation.[4]

In the realm of organized cricket leisure, the white woman's role was defined within patriarchal ideology as that of facilitating the building of a family approach to participation which would ensure its popular legitimacy. Cricket was the game of her husband, father and sons; she was expected to support the moral claims and virtues of the activity, accept her roles as domestic organizer and passive consumer. Furthermore, she was required to surround the game with an aura of respectability that represented a barricade designed to exclude men of other races whose 'hidden' claim to participation was understood by white males as directed at her sexuality. The location of the woman, then, within the early ideological formation of cricket, was understood to be well 'beyond the boundary'.

The domestication of cricket within the sociopolitical context of the nineteenth century plantation society, however, provided a politicized arena within which coloured and black men could challenge within the limits of civic society the monopolistic authority of a white planter–merchant oligarchy. The struggle for the democratization of this élite institution within the undoubtedly superordinate patriarchal colonial West Indian world, therefore, was socially understood as characterized by rivalry between two categories of men – the politically enfranchised of European descent and the dispossessed of African and Asian descent.

Those who observed the nineteenth century formation understood this competitive encounter, furthermore, as one between men of varying socioeconomic standing and ideological interests, and conceived it as consistent with and supportive of, the uncompromising maleness of the plantation mode of production. In addition to all its supposedly moral expressions, cricket embraced the ideological construct of 'manliness' as central to its very essence and meaning. It tolerated, however, with great difficulty and pain, those males who were socially constructed as 'less than men', since it symbolized within the colonial mind the refinement and sophistication of male power and consciousness. Giving support to these ideological forms were concepts of muscular beauty, gentlemanly pride and honour and, most critically, notions of civic duty and social respectability.[5]

Nineteenth century West Indian cricket, then, by virtue of its location within the matured, creole plantation culture was a formidable gendered creation. Like other activities in which empowered white males invested considerable social revenue, such as political leadership, corporate management, and intellectual creativity, competitive cricket was promoted as unsuited to women. West Indian men, furthermore, more than other men within the nineteenth century cricket world, were able to enforce their monopoly of the cricket culture, and in so doing they mirrored the ideological circumstances of the plantation system in which they were bound together as owners, managers and agents.

It should not be considered phenomenal, then, that white women in the nineteenth century West Indies did not establish a cricketing culture of their own. While they were often described as colourful spectators at cricket matches, no evidence exists so far to indicate that they ever did play among themselves in an organized fashion. Their English 'cousins', however, were active in this regard since the late eighteenth century. Certainly, the evidence shows that by the 1830s matches were played frequently between 'single' women and 'married' women, and in 1840 the 'Original English Lady Cricketers', two professional teams, the Reds and Blues, toured the country playing exhibition matches.

In spite of some exposure to cricket within the curricula of West Indian élite schools, white women of propertied families, unlike their male counterparts, did not emulate the cricketing culture of their English 'cousins'. Not much had changed in the West Indies up to the 1930s, despite major developments in women's cricket throughout the empire. In 1886, for example, New Zealand women were playing organized matches in the Nelson province, and in 1931 the well developed Australian women's cricket culture witnessed the foundation of the Australian Women's Cricket Council. New Zealand followed with the establishment of their cricket council in 1934.[6]

The year 1934 was an eventful one in other respects. Dutch women, long involved in the fledgling cricket culture of continental Europe, moved to establish the All Holland Women's Cricket Association (Nederlandse Dames-Cricket Bond). Their 'sistren' in the West Indies did not follow, and the Dutch colonies of Aruba, Curaçao and Suriname experienced no organized women's cricket. Also, in 1934 the first English women's team toured Australia, captained by Betty Archdale, and the first ever Women's Test Match, Australia vs England, was played at Brisbane. In 1935, England toured New Zealand, and in 1937 an Australian touring team visited Holland. In 1952, white women in South Africa and Rhodesia also established cricket associations, leaving West Indies women very much an uncounted element within the imperial cricket culture.

By the 1940s, West Indies white male cricket, after a century of dominance, was on the retreat. Blacks had become the main numerical force in both the intercolonial contests and the West Indies team. The shifting demographics of West Indies men's cricket undoubtedly had a dampening effect upon whatever initiatives white women would have wished for, and certainly by the end of World War II it was clear that the further expansion of West Indies cricket required the social democratization of its culture. It was at this historical juncture that black and coloured women began to discuss plans for the autonomous organization of their cricket.

Organized Women's Cricket in the West Indies

Organized women's cricket in the West Indies, then, awaited the transformative years of the postwar era when the black nationalist and socialist movements finally broke the constitutional power of the ancient imperialism, seized political office, and established the social ethos necessary for a democratizing political culture. It was during this period that blacks finally attained leadership of the West Indies men's cricket team, an achievement that required a high profile regional political campaign that insisted upon selection based upon merit rather than criteria of race and class.

It was also a period in which official efforts were made to legitimize and institutionalize the popular culture of the masses. The 'living' culture of the oppressed working people was appropriated and refashioned into something called 'the national identity' – the possession of which was a requirement of all new nation states. Alongside the dance, song, storytelling and street drama of the communities, in town and country, cricket as a social practice among women was caught in the upsurge of 'recognition' politics. It was now politically right for women's cricket to enter the field.

Jamaica as Trailblazer

Though women's cricket had been visible throughout the West Indies at an earlier period, it was not until 1966 that Jamaican women, who had already established a reputation as leaders in the regional anticolonial and nationalist movements, took the initiative and established a women's cricket association. This was a critical movement in the social history of West Indies cricket culture. No longer was women's cricket confined to the leisurely pastime within rural villages and urban slums, or seen exclusively as a diversion for middle class women on the grounds of private clubs. It had now moved to secure for itself a reputation of competitive organization and professionalism. The specific circumstances that informed the Jamaican case have not been fully documented, but some important things are known. By 1965 there were about 30 to 40 women who displayed interest in the game as a profession and a series of friendly matches were arranged on a fairly regular basis. The popularity of these games became so evident that the suggestion was put to Johnny Wong Sam, cricketer–coach–umpire, to facilitate the formation of an association. The result of the meeting was the establishment of the Jamaican Women's Cricket Association (JWCA) on 26 January 1966. The objects of the association were outlined clearly in the constitution:

(a) To preserve, foster and promulgate the game of Ladies Cricket throughout the Island of Jamaica and to improve the standard of Ladies Cricket in the Island of Jamaica;
(b) To promote and conduct Ladies Cricket in and over the Island of Jamaica;
(c) To prescribe rules of eligibility of participation in games under its own auspices;
(d) To consider and pass upon reports of dishonest, unethical or improper conduct of participants in games and to bar or suspend persons guilty of such conduct from further participation;
(e) To conduct such other activities as may be in keeping with its principal objectives.[7]

MONICA TAYLOR

First president of the JWCA was Monica Taylor, an established player, and a prominent upper class 'coloured' businesswoman. Taylor was an aggressive and determined campaigner who immediately went about the task of putting in place a national infrastructure for women's cricket. In addition, she saw the need for regional organization and established contacts with women's groups in Trinidad and Tobago and in Barbados. At the end of the 1967 national season, Taylor had secured arrangements for a Jamaica tour to Trinidad, which took place between 4 and 21 February 1967. Three 'Test' and three second-class matches, were played over the 17-day tour. The 'Test' series resulted in a draw.

Meanwhile, still in Jamaica, through the efforts of Sally Kennedy, the Diamond Mineral Water Company and the Canada Dry Bottling Company donated trophies – the Ferdie Yap Sam Trophy for the league competition, and the Canada Dry Trophy for the knockout competition. These trophies were competed for in 1968 by teams that took the names of their corporate sponsors.[8] Five teams entered the league competition: Kilowatts, Waterwell, Kingston and St Andrew Council (KSAC), Canada Dry, and Diamonds. It was the first showing for the rural team, Waterwell, which nonetheless gave the more experienced Kingston teams a hard fight, and was in fact the only team to beat Canada Dry, the trophy winners. Immediately after the league competition the teams competed for the Canada Dry Knockout Cup and this time the Diamond Team was able to take revenge for their defeat in the league by knocking out both Canada Dry and Waterwell. Bowling and batting averages for the season were dominated by V. Latty and S. Kennedy respectively (see Tables 6 and 7).

Jamaica, furthermore, under the leadership of Taylor, led West Indies women's cricket into another era – that of the extraregional and international game. By 1970, while women in Barbados, Grenada, St Vincent, Guyana and St Lucia were making efforts to put their own game on a similar organizational standard to Jamaica and Trinidad and Tobago, the JWCA had already finalized plans for an inaugural 'Test' series against England in Jamaica. The English team, led by Rachel Heyhoe, and managed by Derrief Taylor, a former Jamaican/West Indian player who coached youth players at Warwickshire County in England, arrived in Jamaica on 15 January 1970, to play in three two-day 'Test' matches. Arrangements were also made for the visitors to play one-day games against established league teams at 'rural' venues.[9]

The first 'Test' at Sabina Park was attended by some 6,000 spectators on the second day. Among these was the legendary West Indies star of the interwar era, George Headley, who told the *Sunday Gleaner* that "if women's cricket continues in the same trend then there is every indication that not only the West Indies but Jamaica will have people who love cricket flocking the cricket grounds of the world". 'Strebor' Roberts, the sports columnist for the *Sunday Gleaner*, reported:

Some of the catching I have seen by the women of both sides should be an object lesson for the butter-fingered male cricketers. Another lesson for the men was the use of the feet in getting to the pitch of the ball. It was nice to watch the women as they danced down the wicket to make their shots.[11]

Rachel Heyhoe, the England captain (who brought the experience of 15 Tests with her) commented in describing the tour:

It was such a delight to play in front of such fanatical crowds. At Test matches in England we often struggle to get 1,000 spectators to the series. I can honestly say that I have never played in front of such a large crowd as the 6,000 fans who greeted us all at Sabina Park. It was marvelous to be accepted as an international cricket team rather than a team of peculiar women playing cricket, which is so often the reaction of the public in the other countries, which I have toured.[12]

Heyhoe, however, would have recognized that both teams did attract a different set of responses 'beyond the boundary'. On Saturday, 17 January, for example, the teams paid a courtesy visit to a KSAC Public Health Department.

TABLE 6 AVERAGES FOR THE 1968 JWCA SEASON, BATTING

Names	Team	No. Innings	Times not out	Total runs	Highest score	Ave.
S. Kennedy	Diamond	8	3	180	45*	36.0
A. Brown	Canada Dry	7	3	116	34	29.0
Z. Plummer	Waterwell	6	1	125	40*	25.0
M. Powell	Canada Dry	5	1	95	52	23.5
A. Innis	Canada Dry	6	1	90	54*	18.0
M. Taylor	Kilowatts	7	1	105	32*	17.5
I. Morgan	Diamond	3	–	48	25	16.0
J. Cadogan	Diamond	7	2	83	30*	16.6
B. Williams	Canada Dry	6	–	84	25	14.0
V. Latty	Canada Dry	7	1	85	33	14.8

Note: * denotes 'not out'.

Source: The *West Indian Sportsman*, December-January 1969/70

TABLE 7 AVERAGES FOR THE 1968 JWCA SEASON, BOWLING

Names	Team	Overs	Runs	Wickets	Ave.
V. Latty	Canada Dry	67.4	96	29	3.3
B. Alexander	Canada Dry	12	44	8	5.5
M. Diah	Diamond	100.5	141	24	5.8
L. Noble	Waterwell	95	143	22	6.5
M. Laurence	Diamond	63	150	21	7.1
Y. McLean	Canada Dry	42.2	76	10	7.6
N. Wright	Waterwell	35	48	6	8.0
E. Boyle	Kilowatts	23	63	7	9.0
M. McCalla	Waterwell	43	103	11	9.4
A. Brown	Canada Dry	53.1	125	13	9.6

Source: The *West Indian Sportsman*, December-January 1969/70

A sports reporter for the Saturday *Star* described the experience as follows:

Male attention was distracted when the girls . . . walked into the Council Chambers. The girls showed that their shapely legs were not only to be seen on the cricket field but even in ordinary clothes. Their mini and near micro-mini skirts were to be thanked for this. Councillor Rose Leon, perhaps sensing that her male counterparts were too tongue-tied and spellbound to say anything, welcomed the cricketers.[13]

Councillor Leon expressed her admiration for the women in "taking up the difficult task of cricket" and indicated her respect for their 'courage' in doing so. Though England were the clear favourites to win the series, all three Test matches were drawn. The Jamaican team, however, seemed ready for further 'Test' status contests.

The next opportunity for a 'Test' encounter came the following year with another visit from the English team. This time the English won the three-match series 1–0, taking the Pearl and Dean trophy. On this tour the English team also visited Bermuda and the Bahamas before moving on to Trinidad (with the Jamaica team) to take part in a triangular tournament for the Jack Hayward trophy. This contest was won by Trinidad.

In May 1973, the Australian team, on its way to England for the first Women's World Cup championship, in which Jamaica was also a participant, stopped off in Jamaica to play a three-match series with the national team. Both teams used the opportunity to get into shape for the pioneering inter-national event. Playing for the World Cup, which started on 20 June, were teams drawn from Jamaica, Australia, Trinidad and Tobago, New Zealand, England and an Invitation team that consisted of two players from each of the competing countries. In addition to the 'A' team of England, a Young

England XI also contested (see Table 8). The declared favourites to enter the finals of the World Cup were England and Australia. This perception proved correct, and England succeeded in defeating the Aussies in the final at Edgbaston. The two teams from the West Indies were not very highly rated.

Regional Expansion of Women's Cricket

Of more importance, however, for the spread of women's cricket throughout the region, was the first ever Caribbean double-wicket competition which was played in November 1973 at the Kensington Oval and Carlton Cricket Club in Barbados. These contests were part of the country's seventh independence anniversary celebration.[14] Five countries, Jamaica, Guyana, St Lucia, Trinidad (excluding Tobago) and Barbados, guests of the Barbados Women's Cricket Association, met to compete in the historic contest. Two teams from Barbados were declared and the 'A' team won the championship from the 'B' team in a four-over play-off final after both teams tied at the top of the points

TABLE 8 WORLD CUP 1973: RESULTS OF MATCHES PLAYED BY JAMAICA AND TRINIDAD AND TOBAGO

Date	Teams	Result	Venue
23.6.73	Jamaica vs New Zealand	No play – rain	Hove
23.6.73	Trinidad & Tobago vs New Zealand	New Zealand won by 136 runs	St Albans
30.6.73	Jamaica vs Young England	Jamaica won by 23 runs	Sittingbourne
30.6.73	Trinidad & Tobago vs Australia	Australia won by 7 wickets	Tring
4.7.73	Trinidad & Tobago vs Jamaica	Jamaica won by 2 wickets	Ealing
7.7.73	Jamaica vs England	England won by 63 runs	Bradford
11.7.73	Jamaica vs Australia	Australia won by 77 runs	York
14.7.73	Jamaica vs International XI	International XI won by 5 wickets	Leicester
14.7.73	Trinidad & Tobago vs Young England	Trinidad & Tobago won by 5 wickets	Cambridge
18.7.73	Trinidad & Tobago vs International XI	International XI won by 7 wickets	Liverpool
20.7.73	Trinidad & Tobago vs England	England won by 8 wickets	Wolverhampton

Source: England Women's Cricket Association, World Cup Competition 1973: Official Report

chart with eight points at the end of the fifth and final round. Jamaica finished in third place with six points, while Guyana collected four. Trinidad and St Lucia failed to score any points (see Table 9).

With Jamaica and Trinidad and Tobago operating at the international level as separate teams, West Indies cricket was unable to impose its authority on the playing field. Opinion in the region, as a result, moved in favour of a united West Indies team as a remedial measure. Before such an institution could be established, however, it was necessary to put in place a vibrant regional competition in order to expand the catchment and make meaningful selections.

Jamaica and Trinidad and Tobago became members of the International Women's Cricket Council (IWCC) in 1973 in order to participate in the World Cup that year, but as the game grew in popularity so did the cost of hosting tours and sending teams abroad. Against this background a meeting was held in St Lucia on 25 May 1973, with representatives from Barbados, Grenada, Jamaica, St Lucia and Trinidad and Tobago, in order to establish a regional framework for women's cricket. In 1975 the Caribbean Women's Cricket Federation (CWCF) was formed as the vehicle on which women's cricket would travel into the future.[15]

At the 1973 meeting, the opinions and visions of veterans and newcomers alike were discussed. From Jamaica, the now legendary Monica Taylor, the distinguished Vivalyn Latty-Scott and Dorothy Hobson, were prime movers in this organizational development. The objectives of the CWCF were

TABLE 9 PARTICIPANTS IN THE 1973 DOUBLE-WICKET CONTEST
HELD IN BARBADOS

Country		Players
Barbados	A-team	Angela Harris
		Pat Whittaker
	B-team	Janet Selman
		Janet Mitchell
Jamaica		Vivalyn Latty-Scott
		Evelyn Boyle
Guyana		Fay Cadogan
		Daphne Batson
Trinidad		Florence Woods
		Menolta Teekah
St Lucia		Francisca Didier
		Priscilla Phillip

specified: to make tours more affordable by sharing costs; to develop a West Indies team; and to promote more interesting cricket.

It was a meeting of historical significance. Delegates decided that the body would become affiliated to the IWCC as a group, host regional competitions between countries every two years, and select a West Indies team, based on the results of each competition. Monica Taylor was elected president and served until 1982. It was also agreed to have tournaments at the following venues: 1975 Barbados, Grenada, and Trinidad and Tobago; 1977 Grenada; 1980 Guyana; 1982 Jamaica; and 1988 Trinidad and Tobago. Barbados won the first encounter, and held proud the Monica Taylor Trophy. Trinidad and Tobago won the four subsequent encounters.[16]

The leadership of the CWCF showed both vision and determination. At the Second Conference of Delegates held in Port of Spain on 12 July 1975, involving member countries Barbados, Jamaica, Trinidad and Tobago, and Grenada, the decision was taken to select the first West Indies women's cricket team for international competition in 1976 (see Table 10). The final selection was made on 27 October 1975, after the Jamaica vs Barbados match at Kensington Oval.

The executive of the federation knew of Australia's intention to visit England during 1976 to participate in England's women's cricket jubilee celebrations, and immediately extended an invitation to them, to travel to England by way of the Caribbean, and engage the West Indies Team in three two-day 'Tests'. It was agreed that the series would take place in Jamaica during April in order to facilitate the travel plans of the Australian visitors. In a keenly contested series, all three matches were drawn – largely on account of insufficient time.

Confronting Institutional Bias in Women's Cricket

By 1976, then, the organizational infrastructure had reached a level of sophistication, and presented players and spectators alike with opportunities to promote the culture of women's cricket. The West Indies Cricket Ladies Team, playing under the auspices of the CWCF, was now in place. Tours were arranged to India at the end of 1976, and to England in 1979. An earlier series which was scheduled against England was cancelled because of the participation of some of the English players in South Africa. They drew the 1976 six-Test series against India 1–1, and lost the 1979 three-Test tour against England 1–0. Since then the West Indies women's team has become a regional institution, though not reaching anywhere near the popularity or international standing of its male counterpart.

The considerable achievements of women's cricket administrators and players have not brought them into a close, supportive relationship with their counterparts in the men's game. Only since 1994 have they been satisfied with the progress made in relating to the WICB. Neither has the WICB formulated a strategic plan with regard to the serious promotion of women's cricket. In individual territories, officials of men's cricket have expressed irritation over adjustment in competition schedules resulting from women's request for the use of first class grounds and other facilities.

Women cricketers, in addition, have good reason to see the existing WICB as a bastion of unsupportive male power within the region's cricket culture, a perception that has not elicited any denials from executive officers. Indeed, when, a few years ago, the WICBC advertised a vacancy in the regional press for a public relations administrator the wording of the job description was made explicitly male centred. This raised some critical comments from a woman's action group in Trinidad, but the WICBC saw no need to explain an already clear position. In addition, since the 1970s women players throughout the region have protested the practice of not inviting females to the prestigious annual dinner function of the WICBC.

The institutional discrimination against women cricketers, furthermore, is deeply ingrained within the culture of club cricket. For some players, it has been accepted as a way of life rather than an area of social exchange desperately in need of political struggle and social redress. This can be identified at both the level of the village club and the international Test venues. In Jamaica, for instance, the Kingston Cricket Club that manages Sabina Park, the well-known cricket venue, has maintained the century-old policy of not allowing women to use as equals the facilities of the members' pavilion. The members' bar, for instance, is considered off limits to women, even though they may be West Indies players. The same is true also for Queen's Park Cricket Club in Trinidad. Indeed, it was only in the 1980s that this policy, or custom, was removed fully from the Pickwick Cricket Club that manages the members' facilities at Kensington Oval in Barbados.

Though many former West Indies men players, such as Allan Rae, Jackie Hendriks, Michael Holding, Viv Richards and Gordon Greenidge have taken time out to support and encourage women's cricket, thereby seeking to gain greater official and governmental support for it, the evidence continues to indicate general lack of male interest. When, for example, in 1989 Barbados lost the charismatic energy of cricketing star Angela Harris, the national

TABLE 10 FIRST SELECTED WEST INDIES WOMEN'S CRICKET TEAM 1976

Name	Country	Description
Beverly Brown	Trinidad & Tobago	Middle order bat, medium pacer
Dorothy Hobson	Jamaica	Leg spinner, middle order bat
Gloria Gill	Barbados	Opening bat, reserve keeper
Louise Brown (captain)	Trinidad & Tobago	Opening bat
Sherill Bayley	Barbados	Front line bat, leg spinner
Jasmine Sammy	Trinidad and Tobago	Opening bat
Grace Williams	Jamaica	Pace bowler, middle order bat
Janet Mitchell	Barbados	Allrounder
Peggy Fairweather	Jamaica	Pace bowler
Angela Harris	Barbados	Right arm medium pacer, left hand bat
Nora St Rose	Trinidad & Tobago	Pace bowler
Vivalyn Latty-Scott	Jamaica	Allrounder
Pat Whittaker (vice captain)	Barbados	Pace bowler, lower order bat
Yolande Hall	Jamaica	Wicketkeeper/bat
Joan Alexander	Grenada	Wicketkeeper/bat
Menolta Teekah	Trinidad & Tobago	Allrounder

game sank into disrepair, and has not recovered sufficiently to supply players to recent West Indies teams. The Barbados government, well known for its generous contribution to men's cricket, has made no significant investments towards its revival. It is not seen, according to a government official, as a priority area within the promotion of sport; more media and resource attention being given to golf, surfing, tennis, motor racing and soccer.

Starved of adequate financial resources and denied honourable access to first-class institutional facilities, West Indies women cricketers are asked, nonetheless, to perform within the international arena at the level now expected of their male counterparts. That West Indies men cricketers dominated the international game during the 1980s and early 1990s has therefore placed considerable pressure upon the women's team. Dorothy Hobson, manager of the West Indies team during the 1993 World Cup championship in England, indicated that spectators, particularly West Indians, found it difficult to accept their defeats in matches against England and Australia. Their attitudes, she surmised, were informed from experiences and observations derived from the men's game. Indeed, she stated, the media and English cricket officials expected the West Indies women to be a team of superstars by virtue of their being West Indian. It is noteworthy, furthermore, that as West

Indies women suffered a series of defeats they became the 'darlings' of the section of the same British press that has long questioned the professional ethics of West Indies male stars and teams.

West Indies female stars, while cognizant of the inadequacy of professional relations with their male counterparts, have had no difficulty in admitting that their role models are more male than female. They speak more passionately of the exploits of male players than their own, indicative of the effect of popular culture upon subjective consciousness. Grace Williams, the legendary Jamaican/West Indies fast bowler of the 1970s, for example, admits that as a young girl she was "hypnotized" by the fast bowling skills of West Indies stars, Wes Hall and Charlie Griffith. She sought to model her style upon Griffith, and even to "part" her hair in the middle to "resemble" him. He was her hero, and fast bowling became her love on account of the artistic beauty of the physical explosion involved.[17] She admits to learning her cricket within the social context of the male game, and as a result identification with its heroes seemed inevitable – the ultimate ideological success of male hegemony.

The Media and Women's Cricket

To some extent, the resource insufficiency and media indifference that contribute towards the suppression of West Indies women's cricket have to do with its class characteristics. The administration of West Indies men's cricket has remained within the hands of the professional men in the business community. Women cricketers and administrators, however (since the pioneering years of Monica Taylor), have been drawn predominantly from the working class and lower middle class. The administration of women's cricket, therefore, represents a more democratic and egalitarian institutional culture, and is not haunted by the class and race considerations that continue to feature so prominently in the ideological discourse and social practices of men's cricket. These sociological processes within women's cricket culture have problematized easy access to large-scale corporate funding, state resources, and supportive media attention. It is particularly striking in small West Indian societies the manner in which access to institutional power and media support vary in direct proportion to relation and proximity to élite groups.

The overtly gendered responses of men, particularly sports journalists, have also had a telling effect upon the emotional and professional attitudes of women cricketers. C.L.R. James, who chronicled in several texts the ideological revolution of cricket culture, offered no opinions on and concepts of women's intervention and contribution, essentially because his vision was 'seduced' by the ideological maleness of early Victorian cricket philosophy. The social elements within this scholarship are the curricula of élite boys grammar schools, English literature within which the gentleman-scholar-sportsman concept was constructed, the impact of the Adamite image of W.G. Grace, and the politics of the struggle to liberate the black male player from a bankrupt planter-merchant managerial authority. Tony Becca, for example, a leading regional sports writer, while reporting the performance of Trinidad and Tobago's Shirley Bonaparte (in a championship game against Jamaica) described her as "a confident player who bats with the skill of many men". Ironically, the 1973 Women's World Cup brochure which was produced in England carried an advertisement by Kendall Travel Services with a picture of little boys (not girls) playing cricket, under the caption: "Another Gary Sobers/Given Time He Could Well Be – We All Have to Start at the Bottom before We Can Get to the Top".

The bottom, for women, historically, has been those 'special' places where social services are rendered with little or no social honour and financial remuneration. Not surprisingly, the 'bottom' within the cricket culture has been disproportionately inhabited by women. The tea ladies, the nut sellers, the honorary treasurers or secretaries, scorers, commentators and, more recently, second-class match umpires are now established female icons within the cricket world. Often the view is expressed that club members should elect or select female secretaries or treasurers on the basis that they are less likely than men to raid, or disappear with, club revenues. On the other hand, the view is seldom expressed that women should be elected presidents and managers of these institutions. The number of women's roles, then, has increased considerably, but their general locations remain the same.

In addition to these popular social consequences of patriarchal consciousness, the ideological effects within the public media have been overtly hostile to women's search for institutional respectability. The definition and categorization of women's discourse as devoid of vigour, ideological clarity, and internal intellectual integrity, present the context for the denigration of its subtext. In 1973, for example, on the eve of Jamaica's departure to the World Cup, difficulties erupted within the executive of the JWCA. Board discussions over the resolution of these difficulties were reported in the *Daily Gleaner* by Baz Freckleton under a headline "Women's Cricket Cas Cas". Here, Freckleton referred to the debate as "cas cas" and "su su", which in national parlance means gossip, malicious slander, loud invective and quarrelling – all supportive evidence, he states, that "Hell hath no fury like a woman's scorn [sic]".

The Struggle for Legitimacy Continues

West Indies colonial cricket, then, originated and matured within the context of a white, male-dominated plantation society. In this ideological world all women, especially those of African and Asian ancestry, were socially ostracized from autonomous involvement in civic institutions through which the values of élitism, public authority and respectability were transmitted and represented. Cricket in the nationalist era was conceived by all empowered élite males as a principal instrument of their dominance within the sphere of leisure or social recreation. Nationalism, then, did not rupture the gender order of cricket.

Colonial white women, unlike those elsewhere in the empire, did not, or could not, challenge the right of white males to monopolize such a universally respected institution. Organized women's cricket, then, emerged within the West Indies as a social expression of African and Asian communities during the postwar years. African and Asian men had challenged white men to democratize the structures of the organized game since the late nineteenth century, creating the context within which the community as a whole could embrace and promote it as popular culture. In spite of their own struggle for participation, African and Asian men came to consider cricket as a principal index of their own achievements, and have enforced gender values and attitudes designed to marginalize the autonomous women's game. Women, then, are involved in a struggle to legitimize their activity within a male-centred social world that sees them as competitors.

NOTES

1. Viv Richards, *Hitting Across the Line*, 198; Rachel Heyhoe, "A magical mystery cricket tour", in the *West Indian Sportsman* March–April 1970.
2. See Stephanie L. Twin, "Women in sport", in *Sport in America: New Historical Perspectives*, ed. D. Sivey, 193–219 (New York: Greenwood Press, 1985); Jack Scott, "A radical ethics for sports", *Intellectual Digest* 2, no. 11 (July 1992) 49–50; Darlene Kelly, "Women in sports", *Women: A Journal of Liberation* 3, no. 2, 16.
3. *Dominica Star*, 17 May 1969.
4. See Bill Ashcroft et al. (eds.) *The Empire Writes Back: Theory and Practice in Post-colonial Literature* (London: Routledge, 1989), 2–15; Richard Holt, *Sport and the British: A Modern History* (Oxford: Clarendon Press, 1989), 204–23.

5. See Jennifer Hargreaves, "Where's the virtue? Where is the grace? A discussion of the social production of gender through sport", *Theory, Culture and Society* 3, no. 1 (1986): 16; J.A. Mangan, "Gentlemen galore", *Immigrants and Minorities* (July 1982): 154–55; K.A. Sandiford, "Cricket and the Barbadian society", *Canadian Journal of History* (December 1986): 367–68; K. Moore, "Sport, politics and imperialism", Proceedings of the Fourth Annual Conference of the British Society of Sports History (1986), 46–57; C.L.R. James, *Beyond a Boundary* (London: Hutchinson, 1963).

6. See K.E. McCrone, "Play up! Play up! And play the game! Sport at the late Victorian girl's public school", *Journal of British Studies* 23 (Spring 1984); K.E. McCrone, "The 'Lady Blue': sport at the Oxbridge women's colleges from their foundation to 1914", *British Journal of Sport History* (*BJSH*), 3 (September 1986); Jennifer Hargreaves, "Playing like gentlemen while behaving like ladies: contradictory features of the formative years of women's sport", *BJSH* 2 (May 1985).

7. "History of women's cricket in Jamaica", Official brochure, *Jamaica v. Australia; Women's Cricket Series 29 May–5 June 1973*.

8. "History of women's cricket in Jamaica", in *Inaugural International Women's Cricket Series: Souvenir Programme, January 1970*; "1968 women's cricket: Ferdie Yap Sam trophy", *West Indian Sportsman* (December–January 1969–70).

9. *Daily Gleaner* (Jamaica), 16 January 1970; see also, *West Indian Sportsman*, March–April 1970.

10. *Daily Gleaner*, 18 January 1970.

11. Ibid.

12. *West Indian Sportsman*, March–April 1970.

13. *Star* (Jamaica), 17 January 1970.

14. *Advocate News* (Barbados), 30 November 1973.

15. "Caribbean women's cricket federation", in Caribbean Women's Cricket Federation (CWCF): *Inaugural Test Series, West Indies vs Australia, 1–17 May 1976 (official brochure)*.

16. "Background on the Jamaica Women's Cricket Association", CWCF brochure, *Caribbean Women's Cricket Competition, 1989*.

17. "Grace Williams", in CWCF brochure, *Women's Cricket Competition, 1989*.

Denis Atkinson, Barbados, born 7 August 1926.
Photo taken on 1957 tour of England

Frank M.M. 'Tai' Worrell (later Sir Frank), Barbados, born 1 August 1924.
Here, at age 19, he was already batting for Barbados

Everton D. Weekes
(later Sir Everton),
Barbados, born 26
February 1925

Frank Worrell, at left, and Everton Weekes go out to resume a long partnership at
Trent Bridge during the 1957 tour of England

Franz Alexander, Jamaica, born 2 November 1928. Photo taken on 1957 tour to England

West Indies team on the inaugural Test tour of England, 1928. *Left to right, standing:* J.E. Scheult, W. St Hill, A. Rae, E.L. Hoad, J. Small, F. Martin, L.N. Constantine, H.C. Griffith, O.C. Scott; *sitting, left to right*: E.L. Bartlett, M.P. Fernandes, C.V. Weight (vice-captain), K. Nunes (captain, G. C. Challenor, C.R. Browne. Played 36, Won 7, Drawn 17

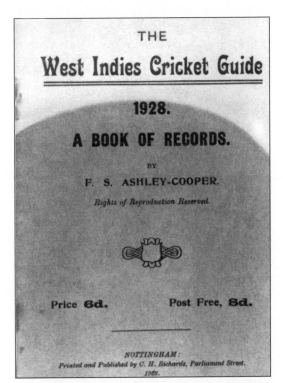

The West Indies cricket team in England, 1933. *Left to right, standing*: E. Martindale, F.R. Martin, C. Merry, V.A. Valentine, I. Barrow, O. DaCosta, E. Achong; *sitting*: H.C. Griffith, E.L.G. Hoad, J.M. Kidney (manager), G.C. Grant (captain), C.A. Wiles, C.A. Roach; *front*: B. Sealy, C.M. Christiani, G. Headley

Roy Gilchrist, Jamaica, born 26 June 1934. Photo taken on 1957 tour to England

Sir Donald Bradman (left) receiving a demonstration of spin from 'Sonny' Ramadhin. Photo taken on the West Indies' 1957 tour of England

At left: Garfield Sobers (later Sir Gary), Barbados, born 28 July 1936. Photo taken on the 1957 tour of England

Rohan B. Kanhai, Berbice, Guyana, born 26 December 1935. Photo taken on 1957 tour to England

A souvenir programme from the
first tour to England on which
the West Indies registered a win
over England

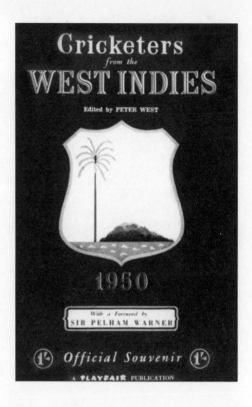

West Indies cricket team to England, 1957. *Standing*: A.G. Ganteaume, R. Kanhai,
N. Asgarali, F.C.M. Alexander, D. Atkinson, T. Dewdney, W. Hall, G. Sobers,
B.H. Pairaudeau, R. Gilchrist, O.G. Smith; seated, K.T. Ramadhin, F.M. Worrell,
J.D.C. Goddard (captain), C.L. Walcott (vice captain), E.D. Weekes, A.L. Valentine

Women cricketers start early, too. Here women and girls are involved in a game in the backyard

143

West Indies women's cricket Test team, 1979

7

The Anti-apartheid Struggle at Home and Abroad 1893–1993

Improved Attitudes to Race in West Indies Cricket

With the 1900 West Indies tour to England, the concept of a representative multiracial West Indies team seemed irretrievably established. The West Indies Cricket Board of Control (WICBC) was formed in 1927 with a mandate to promote an 'international' first-class cricket culture. The West Indies team was elevated to Test status in 1928, just in time that year for a three-Test tour to England. People of African and Asian descent, therefore, had brought their cricket to the international stage. The West Indian team impressed wherever it went as attractive ambassadors of the socially modernized game. In so doing, blacks had broken down parts of the outer barriers of institutionalized racism in the West Indies and advanced the wider democratic discourse.

But, as was to be expected, the movement of the democratic process towards nationalist agenda was not linear or predictable. This is always the case within the historical context of a dying colonialism. More often than not, one step forward is accompanied by two sideways and the threat of as many backwards. Marcus Garvey knew this in 1928 when the West Indies set out on its Test career. It was a graduation in more ways than one. It was, in fact, a test of the effectiveness, or long-term possibilities, of multiracialism as the organizing principle of colonial institutional life. Furthermore, it was a test of the patience and judgement of Africans and Asians who, now partly admitted, would have to decide on the extent to which they would submit to the enduring legacy of white supremacy ideology and praxis. Learie Constantine, superstar of the team and leading theoretician and activist of the nationalist agenda, was on board to root the political discourse in the culture of day-to-day cricketing encounters.[1]

The entry of blacks in the West Indies team, and the Test arena, effectively highlighted the peculiar legacies of a home-grown apartheid system that seemed on the retreat and therefore not as crude as its counterpart in South Africa and in other areas of the colonized world. Racism in sport was not distinguishable from racism in life, and cricket had already made its bid for an ideological association with the very principles of social being. White players continued to lead West Indies teams, as they expected to rule beyond the boundary. It was only 'natural' that men of property with European ancestry in colonized societies would expect to provide the leadership of the premier cultural institution of empire. Blacks, such as Constantine, disagreed, and to the extent that they did, were prepared to push forward a movement towards decolonization. It was all interlinked; the collapse of colonialism could only lead to a nationalist agenda, and already in 1928 the programme was articulated and understood clearly by Constantine.[2]

In this process of political struggle and social transformation 1948 was seminal. It was the moment that witnessed simultaneously on both sides of the Atlantic both great achievement and deep despair for colonized communities. The WICBC, under 20 years of persistent pressure from a fractured but deepening democratic agenda, and fueled by players such as Herman Griffith (Barbados), Learie Constantine (Trinidad), administrators such as Mitchie Hewitt (Barbados), and political activists such as Marcus Garvey and C.L.R. James, succumbed and appointed George Headley, arguably the greatest player of his time, to captain the West Indies cricket team for part of a Test series. Headley's tenure lasted for just one Test match. It was, nonetheless, another significant breach in the walls of the plantation-based West Indian apartheid in cricket culture. That a black man from the lower orders of colonial society could lead a prestigious public institution, and direct the cultural activities of white men of property, seemed more than ordinary within the ideological context of these societies.[3]

Apartheid and Cricket in South Africa

While, however, West Indians had made this crab-like advance, 1948 witnessed the constitutional imposition in South Africa of apartheid – a social system already established in custom, if not in legislation, and publicly demanded by whites. What had transpired prior to 1948 was the preparation of the social prerequisites for the formal institutionalization of white supremacy.[4] South African apartheid required, as West Indian chattel slavery did, a judicial framework within which social life could be regulated and controlled. This was systematically constructed over time as follows:

1949 – mixed marriages illegalized
1950 – racial classification of all inhabitants made statutory by the Population Regulation Act
1950 – Suppression of Communism Act: allowed the state to suppress any political or civic organization that questioned or opposed apartheid
1950 – Group Areas Act mandated the spatial segregation of races
1953 – Primary and secondary schools racially segregated by law
1953 – Reservation of Separate Amenities Act imposed racial segregation in public places
1957 – Native Laws Amendment Act: regulated racial segregation of civic organizations, sports clubs, schools, churches, etc.
1965 – Group Areas Act: amendments R. 26/R. 228 banned black crowds from white games

Finally, starting first in 1952, Pass Laws were codified, with amendments in 1956, 1957, 1959, 1963, 1964, 1966, 1967, 1968, 1969, and 1970. These laws obliged every African over 16 years of age to carry on his or her person at all times a pass book which could be demanded by security forces at any moment, and which indicated whether or not he or she was entitled to be present in a white zone.[5]

The objectives of these legislative developments, according to the Minister of Interior, Dr Donges, were that whites, blacks and coloureds were required to organize their sports separately: no mixed sports would be allowed within the borders of South Africa; no mixed teams could represent South Africa, at home or abroad; international teams playing against South Africa at home or abroad should be all-white.[6] With respect to the relationship between sports and education, the South African government was direct and destructive. Cricket, especially, had been closely related to educational development. The terms of the separation were made public policy. In 1954, Dr Verwoerd, then Minister of Native Affairs, declared to the Senate:

There is no place [for the Bantu] in the European community above the level of certain forms of labour ... For that reason it is of no avail to him to receive a training which has as its main aim absorption into the European community ... Education must train and teach people in accordance with their opportunities in life ... It is therefore necessary that native education be controlled in such a way that it should be in accordance with the policy of the State.[7]

Within a decade the black population of South Africa, 80 percent of the inhabitants, was stripped of access to adequate education and completely politically disenfranchised. Cricket culture in the universities and secondary schools was strengthened for whites and undermined for blacks. The objective was to drive black proficiency in cricket to a level far inferior to that of whites. The 1981 report of the main committee of the Human Science Research Council shows that white schools had 88.6 percent of the cricket pitches in the country (79.9 percent of athletic tracks, 87.7 percent of rugby fields).[8]

On the ideology of merit, as a criterion of social engagement, Prime Minister John Vorster, in an address to Parliament on 11 April 1967, said: "I, therefore, want to make it quite clear that from South Africa's point of view no mixed sports between whites and non-whites will be practised locally, irrespective of the standard of proficiency of participants. We do not apply that as a criterion because our policy has nothing to do with proficiency or lack of proficiency."[9] The logic of history and the course of social change, then, were moving in the opposite directions within the Caribbean and South Africa in 1948.

Up to 1948, however, the black struggle against racist exclusion in South African cricket had taken shape in ways similar to the West Indies experience. During the late nineteenth century, cricket was played popularly by all social groups, including Africans and coloureds. As in the West Indies, blacks were alienated from the established formal game, and denied entry to the élite schools where it was entrenched in the curricula. The black middle class was attracted to the game for the same reasons their counterparts in the West Indies were; it provided access to respectability, upward social mobility, and financial reward, no matter how small.

The game was widely played by educated blacks throughout the Cape Colony. In the mining town of Kimberley, for instance, two black clubs (with several teams each), the Duke of Wellington Cricket Club and the Eccentrics Cricket Club, say Archer and Bouillon, symbolized the social and political qualities upon which the British Empire was built. During the 1890s these two clubs competed with eight other (Indian, Malay and coloured) teams, first in the Griqualand West Coloured Cricketers Union (1892–95) and thereafter in the Griqualand West Colonial Union.[10]

As with the Challenge Cup in the West Indies, whites in South Africa during the 1890s generally refused to play with blacks in the same team or against them. In 1894, for example, the coloured cricketer, T. Hendricks, one of South Africa's best players at the time, was not included in the party that toured Britain; nor was he included in the 'Colonial Born' side that played the 'Mother Country XI' in 1894–95. He was ruled ineligible on account of his 'race'. C.B. Llewellyn, the first coloured cricketer to play for South Africa, while touring Australia in 1910–11, was "ostracized and bullied by his team mates". Furthermore, when the South African team visited England in 1929, they objected to playing against Sussex's distinguished Indian captain, K. S. Duleepsinghji.[11]

Blacks, however, did not play as much cricket as the coloureds during the late nineteenth century and early twentieth century. Records of organized black cricket go back to 1876, at which time coloured cricketers already predominated in South Africa. Cape Town, Port Elizabeth, Johannesburg, and Claremont had several coloured clubs that competed in a tournament. In 1902, the first national cricket association was formed, the South African Coloured Cricket Board (SACCB). In 1926 a rival organization split off and formed the South African Independent Coloured Cricket Board; this group was renamed the Coloured Cricket Association in 1948. Neither the black nor coloured teams played against whites up to the 1930s. In 1932, the black teams pulled out of the Coloured Union and formed the South African Bantu Cricket Board, centred around the high quality game played in the Transvaal. In this period, South Africa produced its greatest ever black cricketer, Frank Koro, who scored over 20 centuries in the 1930s and 1940s.[12]

On the whole, white cricketers and the white cricket establishment were "overwhelmingly responsible for the racism and racist practices which characterized the game".[13] When the Nationalists took power in 1948, cricket was already racially segregated, and formal competitions organized along apartheid lines. Customs and traditions were established in ways that excluded blacks and coloureds from the leagues managed by white businesses and social organizations. Racial segregation meant that the West Indies Test team did not engage the South Africans in the 20 years leading up to formally established apartheid. South Africans played their ethnic cousins, England and Australia, but showed no interest in engaging India or the West Indies.

White nationalism in South Africa, therefore, had tried but failed to exclude non-white cricketers completely from colonial representation; it succeeded, however, in designing a cricket culture in which blacks and coloureds did not feel welcome. In the West Indies, on the other hand, black nationalism sought to put an end to racism in cricket, and pursued an aggressive democratic agenda. In West Indies Test teams after 1928, as well as in colony teams, blacks, Indians, Chinese and whites played together. Up to 1960, when Sir Frank Worrell emerged as the first full-time, long-term black captain, all ethnicities had formed a working agenda of racial co-existence. Multiracialism became a reality in West Indies cricket in the years building up to the 'first rising' under Sir Frank's successor, Sir Gary Sobers. In South Africa, on the other hand, blacks played among themselves, and occasionally with the coloureds.

How, therefore, would it be possible to interface these ideologically contradictory worlds at the rendezvous of a celebratory cricket culture? Under what political banner, and to what end, could the galloping pace of West Indian nationalist democracy come to terms with a society that represented anathema for those involved in the popular struggle? The entire world, it seemed, and particularly South Africa, knew that cricket was serious business. Indeed, everywhere it was recognized that sport, in general, was no 'sporting matter', but a foundation stone of modern political discourse that sought to give meaning and life to political concepts such as national identity, nationhood, and social justice.

International Opposition

The first signal of opposition to South African apartheid in sport within the international community came from the British Empire Games Federation (BEGF). In 1934, shortly after Learie Constantine had published his now classic book, *Cricket and I*, in which he called for the removal of the last vestiges of institutional racism in West Indies cricket, the BEGF decided not to award its next games to South Africa. The reason advanced was that the government there had indicated that non-white athletes would not be welcome. The Canadians led the protest, inspired in part because their black long-jump star, Sam Richardson, would have been debarred. Richardson went on to win a gold medal when the games were held in London.[14]

The international attempt to reject South Africa for its racist policy, however, moved slowly after 1934. The cricket fraternities, of the major sporting bodies, were perhaps slowest. In 1956, the International Table Tennis Federation expelled South Africa's all-white team; the government had refused passports to black and coloured players. In 1964, South Africa was barred from the Tokyo Olympics as well as the World Fencing Federation Games. Closer to the Caribbean, Mexico in 1967 refused entry visas to the South African white team for the Mini Olympics, and the following year South Africa was expelled from world boxing by the International Amateur Boxing Association.[15]

Finally, at the end of 1968, 20 years after the establishment of constitutional apartheid, a scheduled cricket tour to South Africa by the English team was cancelled by the organizers, the MCC. Coloured England player, Basil D'Oliveira, who was born in South Africa, was declared unacceptable on racial grounds by the South Africans. The MCC objected to the attempt to determine the combination of its team, but was not explicit in opposition to the all-white policy of South African cricket authorities. In 1970, the Australians took a stance specifically against apartheid and cancelled their 1971–72 tour to South Africa.[16]

The West Indian Response

West Indian cricket institutions, however, long before the MCC took their decisions, had problematic relations with South African apartheid. It should be noted, however, that South Africa was a founding member of the Imperial Cricket Conference (ICC – later renamed the International Cricket Conference and in the early 1990s chaired by former West Indian Test player Sir Clyde Walcott). During the 1950s there was no organized attempt to expel South Africa from the ICC. In fact, the South Africans were never kicked out; they merely lost membership when the Pretoria government withdrew from the Commonwealth in 1961. The WICBC, considerably marginalized within the ICC, and led by white men, some of whom seemed indifferent to the South African question, was divided on the adoption of a firm policy. It is true to say, however, that after 1961 West Indian cricketers, and the WICBC, played a major role in ensuring South Africa's ostracism.[17]

In spite of formal opposition by the WICBC to South African apartheid, many West Indian cricketers held the view that they could make critical anti-apartheid contributions through the direct interface of the two cricket cultures. Those who articulated this opinion recognized and accepted that their ideas were cast in terms of a moral contest between political good and evil, social progress and reaction, and were confident with respect to the inevitable triumph of the good and progressive – altogether a perspective on social change that is intrinsic to a particular theory or philosophy of history.

Evidence of this perspective could be seen at home in the bitter but successful campaign to secure for Frank Worrell the captaincy with tenure of the Test team, thus putting to an end the traditional assumption of white leadership. Worrell's appointment by the WICBC in 1959 represented the completion of a political and social process that had begun with the 1900 tour to England. Furthermore, it signalled a structural advance towards full internal democratic governance and constitutional independence. It symbolized dramatically the final collapse of racist ideology in West Indies cricket, and the triumph of merit as the dominant organizing principle.[18]

As was the case in 1948, 1959 carried within its bosom a complex and seemingly contradictory set of ideological possibilities. Mass celebration soon turned to private reflection when it was announced that Worrell, triumphant hero of the crowd, had agreed to lead a goodwill West Indies team to South Africa in order to play eight matches, not against the white national side, but against black and coloured teams, though under the auspices of the South African Cricket Union (SACU).

Public opinion in the region was deeply divided; those who argued in support of Worrell stated that any West Indies cricket tour to South Africa would give encouragement and support to black and coloured players in spite of apartheid, a process that could only strengthen domestic anti-apartheid consciousness. Persons in opposition to this view suggested that such a tour would constitute a victory for apartheid in that it would legitimize an inter-black cricket culture, leaving whites to chart a separate, privileged course. They argued, furthermore, that it would suggest to the world that black West Indians, despite their domestic struggles against racism, had no deep seated revulsion to a legal definition of themselves as second or third class citizens.

Learie Constantine, wrote C.L.R. James, quarrelled with him and opposed the tour. James supported Worrell and argued that the team should go. Apartheid, James argued, "sought the isolation of the Africans not only from whites but from progressive black voices in the diaspora". The tour would have had worldwide publicity, he continued, and the "African cricketers and the African crowds would have made contact with world-famous West Indian cricketers who had played in England and Australia. There might have been incidents", he said, "so much the better. A pitiless light would have been thrown on the irrationality and stupidity of apartheid."[19] The proposed tour was cancelled as a result of "wide and acute" public controversy, and Worrell, it has been said, subsequently agreed that this was a good thing because the project was premised on faulty and unconvincing political assumptions.

Worrell's reconsideration had much to do with personal experiences with persistent racist attitudes in Barbados domestic cricket. Too often he expressed disgust with traditional "whites only" clubs that continued to defend a policy of black exclusion despite the presence on the island of internationally respected black Test players. His decision to settle in Jamaica at the height of his career was in part a reaction to Barbadian white racism, and a refusal to accept the patronizing social politics of élite society.

In the immediate aftermath of the Worrell discourse, West Indians went about the negotiation of their constitutional independence at Lancaster House in London, divided with respect to their support of the anti-apartheid struggle. That Nelson Mandela, and many of his African National Congress (ANC) colleagues, were thrown into jail in 1963, while Trinidad and Tobago,

Jamaica, and Guyana were breathing the fresh air of constitutional freedom, had no pressing political significance for most West Indian politicians. Identification with the criminalized ANC–Mandela vanguard was not publicly stated by the West Indian nationalist leadership, though support for trade embargoes against Pretoria was uniformly adopted. As a result most West Indian cricketers, and spectators, unexposed to information on the anti-apartheid struggles, had no clear political understanding of what was going on in Southern Africa.

In 1967, the year after Barbados, according to Prime Minister Errol Barrow, had ceased to "loiter on colonial premises", and had severed constitutional links with 341 years of unbroken British rule, the BCA, still under the management of the merchant–planter white élite, fired the first salvo against the numbed ideological sensibility of black political governance. It extended an invitation to three white South African players, Colin Bland, Peter Pollock, and Graeme Pollock, to join a Rest of the World Team to play a match against Barbados at the Kensington Oval, as part of a public celebration of independence. The Barbadian community, divided on the politics of this invitation, argued the case from all sides.

The spirit of the 1959 debate was revived, but Sir Frank Worrell, clearer on the issue this time, opposed the game on the grounds that it was sheer nonsense for Barbados rather than the West Indies to take on the world. For him Barbados was seeking to establish for itself a prestige greater than the West Indies – the arrogance of the part considering itself larger than the whole. Popular debate, however, focused on the invitation of the three South Africans who were described as supporters of apartheid, on account of their refusal to denounce the system publicly. Demonstrators attacked E.D. Inniss' leadership of the BCA in the press, and claimed that as a member of the merchant–planter élite he was generally politically insensitive to black suffering in South Africa. The debate, in addition, indicated considerable ideological divisions along lines of race and class on the question of apartheid. After three weeks of public protest, the BCA withdrew the invitation.[20]

THE 'SOBERS AFFAIR'

The publication two years later in 1969 of Walter Rodney's seminal work, *The Groundings with my Brothers*, a statement that encapsulated his intense ideological work and struggle against racial and class injustice in the Caribbean and Africa, foretold what was perhaps the major postcolonial regional political crisis. Described as the 'Sobers Affair', the crisis occupied West Indian popular attention during most of September and October 1970. As an event it took credit for, among other things, establishing focused political discussions between Fidel Castro and many Commonwealth West Indian leaders who, for the first time, seemed prepared to express public support for the overthrow of South African apartheid.[21]

On 7 September 1970, news originating in London swept through the Caribbean, and over the world, that Gary Sobers, the West Indies cricket captain, had accepted an invitation to play in a double-wicket weekend competition in Ian Smith's apartheid Rhodesia. No other matter, since the collapse of the British West Indies Federation, had mobilized regional public opinion in this way. The debate took place in the press, on the streets, in parliaments, within trade union congresses and cricket organizations.[22]

Persons defined as 'Black Power' nationalists provided a compelling local framework within which sections of society understood and judged this event. Revolutionary movements throughout Africa provided the global context, while the intensification of the civil rights movement in the United States energized them both. The American Olympic basketball team in Mexico had already provided West Indian youths with an iconography of struggle with the 'high fist'; Mandela was languishing in jail, but Steve Biko was not; Malcolm X and Martin Luther King were murdered but Stokely Carmichael and the Black Panthers were trying to hold it together; Mohammed Ali had declared his hand and Fidel Castro's Cuba was defiant in the face of American counter-revolution intentions; Angela Davis had emerged the rebel woman of black America and Winnie Mandela was 'Queen Mother' of African liberation. Within the ideological and political circumstances of this pan-African upsurge, West Indian cricket, forged in a crucible of anti-apartheid and resistance, seemed fractured in terms of its mandate and moral sensibility. Once again, however, it provided West Indians with an opportunity to examine themselves, to look into their history, and to choose a path.

West Indians reacted as if their cricket culture had met its nemesis. Frank Walcott, head of the Barbados Workers' Union, and a former first-class cricket umpire, condemned the decision of Sobers on the grounds that he "is an international personality and represents the heart and soul of millions of people in the West Indies who see their national identity manifested in cricket".[23] Next door to Rhodesia, Forbes Burnham, president of Guyana, also a 'son' of Barbadian lineage, was visiting Zambia to attend the Conference of the Non-Aligned Nations. Burnham pledged $50,000 to Zimbabwe's Freedom Fighters and stated that unless "Sobers recants and apologizes for this foolish and ill-advised stand", he would in future be unwelcome in

Guyana. The West Indies were scheduled to play a Test match in Georgetown during the 1971 Indian tour.[24]

On 15 September, Sobers returned to Barbados and indicated publicly that only good could come of his visit to Rhodesia, and that he had received an open invitation to return. He stated also that he had met Premier Ian Smith and found him less sanguine than represented by the press. Joshua Nkomo, a senior leader of the Zimbabwe Liberation forces in combat with the Smith regime, expressed disappointment with Sobers. He stated that Frank Worrell, whom he knew and respected, had spoken highly of Sobers. The *Workers' Voice*, a newspaper in Antigua, reported that Sobers had abdicated his loyalty to Africans everywhere, and described him as "a white-black man". It went on to say that Sobers' "deed was the unkindest cut to all those dedicated to the struggle against racism in all its forms".[25]

In Barbados, the issue assumed an importance of the highest political nature, and dominated parliamentary debates for three consecutive days. Deputy Prime Minister Cameron Tudor, declared that much of the criticism levelled at Sobers had been out of proportion to the offence, and said that "the people of Barbados will not even for friendship's sake countenance the implied denigration of Mr Sobers by those who now choose to divorce politics from common sense". On 21 October, Lionel Craig, opposition member of parliament, tabled a resolution calling on the House to deplore Burnham's statement, and the *Barbados Advocate-News* in an editorial asked West Indian political leaders to "cool it". The prime minister of Trinidad and Tobago, Dr Eric Williams, sent for Wes Hall, who had been employed by his government in Port of Spain as a sports commissioner. He instructed Hall to go to Barbados, meet with Sobers, and report back to him on the discussion.[26]

Dr Williams had been in touch with Fidel Castro on the issue, and had also asked Indian prime minister, Indira Gandhi, not to cancel the forthcoming Indian tour to the West Indies. Williams needed information and guidance, and Hall functioned as his advisor. The WICBC, meanwhile, had asked Guyana for a "clarification" of the president's statement. Kenny Wishart, president of the Guyana Cricket Board of Control, said that it called for an "apology" from Sobers. A Guyana Sunday paper on 18 October also called for an apology from Sobers. In response to these published positions in Guyana, Vernon Jamadar, leader of the opposition in the Trinidad and Tobago House of Representatives, praised Sobers on 20 October for his "calm dignity in response to the savagery of West Indian gutter politicians".[27]

Prime minister of Barbados, Errol Barrow, in New York to address the UN General Assembly, telephoned Sobers and asked him to do nothing until his return. After close consultations between Sobers, Dr Williams, and Barrow, a letter was prepared clarifying Sobers' position to a specially called meeting of the WICBC. It was issued on 25 October. Those in Sobers' corner insisted that his letter to the WICBC was a statement of 'regret' rather than an apology. The statement said:

Dear Mr President

When I accepted an invitation to take part in a two day, double-wicket competition in Rhodesia I was assured that there was no segregation in sport in that country but I was not made aware of the deep feeling of the West Indian people. I have since learnt of this feeling and the wider international issues involved. I am naturally deeply distressed by and concerned over the tremendous controversy and bitterness which have arisen after my return from Salisbury. As I was not aware of the serious repercussions I may have expressed myself in such a way as to create the impression for indifference to these issues. Mr President, I wish to inform you that in all sincerity that is far from my true feelings as the prestige of West Indian cricket and the unity and dignity of West Indian and African people are interests I have always served. I therefore wish to convey to you and the members of the Board my sincere regrets for any embarrassment which my action may have caused and to assure you of my unqualified dedication whenever I may be called upon to represent my country – the West Indies – and my people.

G. St A. Sobers[28]

Two days later, President Burnham welcomed Sobers' statement, and said that the West Indies captain was now assured of a "great welcome in Guyana". Prime Minister Barrow insisted that no apology was given anyone, and certainly not to persons who seemed keen on African redemption mainly as an instrument to suppress popular aspirations in their own front yards. It was, however, a moment that indicated West Indian determination to oppose cricket links with Southern African apartheid, and to set its face against all those who supported it.

Other Incidents

No sooner had West Indians adjusted to the political crisis that had tarnished the public reputation of Sobers, their greatest ever cricketer, than the issue of apartheid and West Indies cricket resurfaced. In 1974, a tour of the West Indies by an International Wanderers team, organized by British entrepreneur, Derrick Robbins, had to be rescheduled because President Burnham and Prime Minister Williams refused it entry into their respective countries. Robbins had carried a similar team to South Africa the previous year, and news of this preceded their visit to the West Indies. The team, however, was permitted entry to Barbados, Grenada, Antigua, St Kitts, Dominica, and St

Lucia. Lester Bird, then prime minister of Antigua, and later president of the Antigua Cricket Association, argued Robbins' case. He stated that philosophically Robbins was no supporter of apartheid, and that by taking multi-racial teams to South Africa he was contributing to the "breaking down of apartheid".[29]

Two years later, in 1976, a Shell Shield match between Barbados and Guyana scheduled for Bourda (Guyana) was cancelled when President Burnham refused entry to Barbados batsman, Geoffrey Greenidge, who had toured South Africa the previous year with an international team. The BCA recalled the national team, and the incident represented the first occasion that political intervention had led to the abandonment of a first-class regional cricket match in the West Indies. This event placed the issue of the relations between West Indies and South African cricket or, more generally, West Indies sports and apartheid, firmly at the top of the regional political agenda.[30]

The Guyana government, unlike others in the region, was unequivocal in its support for the United Nations' resolution on nondiscrimination in sport. President Burnham went further, however, when he declared that "no South African who supports apartheid, and no non-Guyanese who participates in sports in South Africa, shall be allowed to enter Guyana". Guyana, the president argued, could not accept any compromise or assault from that quarter upon the historic dignity of citizens of African descent. Guyana joined Jamaica in spearheading an effort to arrive at a common position among Caricom member states. In 1977 the governments of Barbados, Guyana, Trinidad and Tobago, and Jamaica – the traditional 'big four' in cricketing terms – succeeded in sketching the parameters of a framework for a national, regional, and international anti-apartheid policy.[31]

In this development, Michael Manley's hand was evident everywhere. His anti-apartheid politics, consistent with his father's, had provided global leadership, and his love of cricket rivalled only his commitment to political decolonization. His task was to bring along reluctant West Indian nationalists, and hold them in alliance with a Guyanese position that seemed by global standards extreme and inflexible. When the policy framework was finally enunciated, Barbados had adopted what appeared to be a conservative approach, which fell short of the Jamaican and Guyanese provisions. The core of the Barbadian position was that it would: disapprove, and not support, any Barbadian, or Barbadian team, visiting South Africa; support a decision by sporting bodies that did not consider eligible for selection any player in future who went to South Africa; but would not ban a national of any other country who had previously played in South Africa from entering

Barbados to play if they were part of a country with which Barbados had sporting links.[32]

Jamaica accepted these points but qualified the latter with a ban on national teams who played in South Africa. With respect to the ban, Guyana went further and extended it to all individuals, including journalists, coaches, and administrators. The WICBC was ahead with regards to these policy positions. After its annual general meeting, 13–15 May 1976, in Port of Spain, the secretary of the WICBC issued the following statement:

The West Indies Cricket Board of Control wishes to reiterate its total opposition to the system of apartheid as obtains in South Africa and Rhodesia and advises that all players from Caribbean territories under its jurisdiction who play cricket or coach in South Africa or Rhodesia will not be permitted to participate in matches organized under the auspices of the Board at home or abroad. In addition, the Board reaffirms that no official team from any country which tours South Africa or Rhodesia will be welcome in the West Indies and until there is complete multiracial cricket and teams are selected solely on merit in those countries.[33]

Within the context of anti-apartheid policies enunciated by governments, and the declaration of the WICBC, the 1976 England young cricketers tour proved to be divisive. The team was debarred from Guyana, since many of its members had played in South Africa. Games were rescheduled, however, for Dominica, Barbados, Montserrat, St Kitts, and Grenada, where anti-apartheid provisions were less penetrative.

In June of 1977, Commonwealth Heads of Government, meeting in the United Kingdom, signed the Gleneagles Agreement which aimed at establishing further guidelines for determining steps by the Commonwealth to isolate South Africa in sports. The structure of the agreement reflected many of the opinions of West Indian political leaders, and the views of the WICBC were integrated into its ideological spirit and language.[34]

Official opposition to apartheid by West Indian governments, argued Hall, Favier and Thomas, was insufficient when viewed from the perspective of the West Indian cricketer whose economic future always appeared insecure. What was required, as a measure of nationalist commitment to players, was for governments to support a development fund through which players could be assured of income when the local season was over, and in the early aftermath of their Test careers. According to Hall et al.:

The failure of Caricom Member States, to date, to develop harmonious and co-ordinated postures and actions on the question of combating apartheid in sports could possibly have its impact first of all on individual players or athletes. This is most easily seen in the field of cricket where, in the words of the West Indies Cricket Board of Control, "the prowess of our citizens at the game has earned for them a world-wide reputation for being among the best players in the international field and as sportsmen par excellence".[35]

Furthermore, they added:

At the level of the individual a major concern deriving from pursuit of the anti-apartheid campaign is the 'income effect' which is most obvious in the field of cricket. The search to develop and perfect cricketing skills has often been at the expense of higher studies at professional and technical levels for the Caribbean cricketer. Income-earning skills of cricketing 'heroes' of the West Indies have in the main been confined to the cricket game. Moreover the capacity of the West Indian cricketer to earn a reasonable standard of living, now that cricket has been 'democratized', is attached to his being outside the West Indies and performing under contract with clubs in either the United Kingdom or Australia. The up-shot of this situation is that, for the individual cricketer, there could be a pretty wide gap between earning a livelihood and adhering to a political line where offsetting income benefits are not attached as incentives to following the political line. While his income-earning skills are sharpened by competing with some of the best players in the field (a number of whom might be from apartheid countries or might have played there) the cricketer's contractual obligations could easily reinforce the urgency to isolate cricket from politics. Indeed in the present circumstances, the pursuit of cricket as a career has meant West Indian professionals playing in parts of the world against South Africans as well as against many who have gone to South Africa.[36]

This situation of financial uncertainty no doubt was a major factor in many West Indian players' decision to oppose government policy and develop careers in South Africa under apartheid. But there were other factors, including the unsupportive policies of the WICBC towards players.

The centre stage of West Indies opposition to South African apartheid, however, was not completely dominated by men's cricket culture. The West Indies Cricket Women's Team, playing under the auspices of the CWCF, which had participated in staging the first ever Cricket World Cup in 1973, cancelled a Test tour by England because some of the English women had played in South Africa. Vivalyn Latty-Scott and Dorothy Hobson, veteran Jamaica and West Indies stars, supported the stance against apartheid even though their team was just coming on stream and desperately needed the international experience and exposure.[37]

West Indians, then, had no reason to be surprised when in 1981 the second Test against the touring England team scheduled for Guyana was cancelled. Robin Jackman, a member of the English team, was refused permission by the Guyana government on account of his having played and coached in South Africa. The tour, however, went ahead; matches were played in Jamaica, Barbados, Trinidad and Tobago, and Antigua. It was no surprise, furthermore, when the WICBC, also in 1981, informed former West Indies captain, Alvin Kallicharran of Guyana, that he was debarred from all cricket organized under its auspices, on account of his signing a contract to play Currie Cup cricket in South Africa. Kallicharran had followed in the footsteps of Barbadian and West Indian allrounder John Shepherd who held the record for being the first black man to play Currie Cup cricket in South Africa, an achievement for which he was vilified by the anti-apartheid movement in England and branded a traitor of the black cause and a self-hater.[38]

The murder of Walter Rodney in Guyana took place at a time when the free Mandela campaign was gaining international momentum and respectability. Under political pressure globally, as well as at home, from a cricket or sports crazy white populace, the apartheid government in South Africa was forced into a position of mediation. The murder, by the state, of Steve Biko accelerated the militancy of black youth in the townships, and the SACU, playing its part in the defence of apartheid, went on the offensive and targeted West Indies cricket with a razzmatazz of political and ideological propaganda that stunned the world.

A West Indies Team in South Africa?

While the bloodstained apartheid state insisted to the world that racial barriers were being removed, and that liberal reforms were taking place, the SACU planned a daring raid upon West Indies cricket in much the same way that the Cuban army was demolishing South African military strongholds in support of liberation struggles in Angola, Mozambique and Namibia. It was a torrid time for the West Indian mind; what greater political coup for the South Africans than a black West Indies team playing against white teams in South Africa while the system of apartheid remained intact? President of the WICBC, Allan Rae, had spoken of such a threat to West Indies cricket by money offers from South Africa as early as 1982, and had referred to it as a "policy of piracy".[39]

The man who led the raiding party on West Indies cricket was Dr Ali Bacher, director of the Transvaal Cricket Union; his agents in the West Indies were Barbadian cricketers Sylvester Clarke and Gregory Armstrong. On 4 January 1983, news broke of a proposed tour of West Indies cricketers to South Africa. Names called in this first report were Sylvester Clarke, Wayne

Daniel, Collis King, Lawrence Rowe, Faoud Bacchus, Albert Padmore, Richard Austin, Jim Allen, and Emmerson Trotman. The Caribbean News Agency (CANA) listed Sir Gary Sobers as manager and Padmore as assistant manager, and gave the team as Lawrence Rowe (captain), Everton Mattis, Collis King, Sylvester Clarke, Desmond Haynes, Hartley Alleyne, David Murray, Alvin Greenidge, Emmerson Trotman, Malcolm Marshall, Colin Croft, Alvin Kallicharran, Derek Parry and Winston Davis.[40]

Panic broke out in the camp of West Indies cricket, expressed in a rash of allegations and accusations. It was clear that a sick and insidious hand had gripped West Indian cricket by the throat. Secrecy and distrust pervaded the air. Padmore, Davis, and Clarke issued denials; Sir Gary was in Australia, and his wife, Lady Prue, said she was "surprised and shocked" at the report. In a release to the press she stated: "I am sure Gary would want me to let all West Indians know that he would not be engaged in any such tour." On 5 January, the Barbados *Daily Nation* carried a front page report in which a "former Barbados cricketer", who claimed to be the West Indies agent for the South African organizers, stated that the tour was planned for December 1985, and that players would receive up to Bds$250,000.[42]

South African officials confirmed that some West Indies stars were scared off by the leaked report, but remained confident of attracting top players. Insights into the nature of behind the scenes negotiations between Ali Bacher and West Indian stars can be found in the recent biography of Desmond Haynes, *Lion of Barbados*. What Haynes tells us is that many West Indian players were open and vulnerable as far as making a deal with Bacher was concerned, and that they weighed potential financial benefits with contractual terms offered by the WICBC.[42]

The WICBC, though not surprised, seemed caught off-guard by the depth of the South African penetration, but did very little to secure the loyalty of targeted players. President Rae, after receiving personal assurances from Jamaica captain, Lawrence Rowe, and West Indies fast bowler Colin Croft, praised them publicly for their principled stand in rejecting South African offers. Rae, speaking at a function in Kingston, stated: "I believe the cricketing fraternity of the West Indies ought to say a big thank you to those gentlemen who have put the temptation behind them. It is something in their favour that their pride is bigger than their right hands."[43] Four days later, WICBC secretary, Steve Camacho learnt in Kingston that Rowe and Croft were booked to fly out to Johannesburg. In Barbados, the airlines confirmed that Clarke, Greenidge, King, Moseley, Padmore, Trotman and Armstrong, all distinguished national players, were booked for the same destination.

While the sense of implosion within West Indies cricket magnified under the heat of public debate, the centre received a significant strengthening when news circulated that Viv Richards, still considered the best batsman in the world, was offered EC$1 million to play in South Africa and that he had refused, describing the financial offer as "blood money". The provision of firm anti-apartheid leadership by Richards further polarized public opinion, and the weakness of political leadership seemed the more treacherous.

Richards received a message from Mandela's ANC thanking him for his vision and solidarity. He was not alone, however, in making firm ideological statements in response to the South African offensive. Michael Holding, front line West Indies fast bowler, in reacting to an offer received, said he could not sell his birthright for a "mess of porridge" [sic]; furthermore, he added, with respect to those who had accepted: "These men are selling themselves. If they were offered enough money they would probably agree to wear chains. They would do anything for money." Clive Lloyd, West Indies captain, seeing the reserve players of his dream-team being spirited away by the rand, told the press: "I know that some of them are out of work and the money is very tempting, but that is not all in life".[44]

West Indian cricketers knew very little of South African society, despite some exposure to South African cricketers through contact in the English county circuit. On arrival in South Africa Captain Rowe declared: "we feel a bit jittery, but we are professionals, and we are here to do a job". Everton Mattis, the young, promising stroke player from Jamaica, and still a West Indian Test prospect, told the Jamaica *Daily News* before departure from Kingston: "I am a Rastaman. That is my philosophy. I am not supporting apartheid. I am dealing with survival. At one stage I did not want to go, but I had to think about my family."[45]

Rowe's team was dubbed by the local and international media as 'rebels'; some were banned for life, others for short terms, by clubs, countries, and the WICBC. They were labelled 'cricket outcasts' and 'mercenaries', and described as traitors to the cause of African liberation. In Barbados, Minister of Sport Vic Johnson told a press conference:

. . . there is no price for which self-respect or human integrity can ever be bought. Those who did not go upheld the honour of the whole region and signalled to the rest of the world that human dignity is not a commodity to be traded in the market place of expediency.[46]

Veteran Barbados journalist, Al Gilkes, writing in the *Daily Nation*, disagreed. He stated:

Lawrence Rowe and his rebel team had become, not the mercenaries they were labelled outside South Africa, but 18 black missionaries converting and baptizing thousands and thousands of whites to the religion of black acceptance and respect from Capetown to Johannesburg, from Durban and right into the throne room of Afrikanerdom itself, Pretoria.[47]

In South Africa, where cricket had been cultivated as a sport for whites, and the small but important coloured and black professional élite, responses to the arrival of West Indian cricketers were mixed. West Indians were classified by the state, and welcomed by whites for the purposes of the project, as temporary 'honorary whites'. In the black townships, however, they were hailed as villains, and graffiti, saying "West Indies traitors go home" was common enough. Their presence was interpreted as part of a strategic political move by the government to counter mounting global criticisms of apartheid. West Indians, once again, were divided in their opinions, but the clandestine manner in which the entire operation was conducted drew disgust even from those who seemed willing to give players the most liberal consideration.

In his autobiography, Gladstone Mills, Jamaican cricket administrator, and professor of public administration, records a discussion between President Rae and Jamaica's batting star, Herbert Chang. News had broken in the Jamaican press that Chang had signed a contract to join the 'rebel' party in South Africa. Rae sought clarification of the matter. Mills wrote:

Rae: Mr Chang, there is a rumour that you are going to South Africa to play cricket. If this is not true, let us know, and we will assist you in scotching it.
Chang: Mr Rae, I have no contract to play in South Africa.
Rae: I did not ask you if you have a contract. Are you going to South Africa?
Chang: Me going to South Africa. No Sir![48]

The next day Chang was on his way to South Africa. As a result of these events, West Indians were called upon by forces within their cricket culture to examine themselves and to see what C.L.R. James meant when he stated that cricket beyond the boundary is but a manifestation of the state of political consciousness. The debate over 'rebel teams' was recorded in every village, town, and city of the region. In every workplace and public institution everyone had a view, and cricket, quite clearly, functioned as a mirror that reflected attitudes within the fragmented but hopeful West Indian nation.

South African Cricket Regains Legitimacy

In 1991, when West Indians rose in spontaneous celebration of Nelson Mandela strolling out of prison, as if he had gone there to pay someone a visit, they had no way of knowing that he, with apartheid still intact, would soon be asking them to accept and embrace Afrikaner cricketers as their newest 'Test mates'. Was the nightmare really over? Were West Indians waking up to a re-engineered, but even more obnoxious reality? All eyes in the West Indies opened as the WICBC announced that the South African cricket team would tour the West Indies in early 1992 and play a Test in Barbados.

Political leaders declared that ideally they had hoped the matter of democratic elections would be settled before such an enterprise was launched, but the WICBC, which claimed extensive consultation with the ANC, boasted evidence of Mandela's support. Mandela's superlative credibility in the world arena had tilted the balance of opinion in favour of readmission; certainly, it was this factor that led India to propose the resolution at the ICC. Mike Proctor, veteran South African cricketer, acknowledged this much in his book which outlines the torrid experience of his country's cricket:

The ANC's vital input confirmed that our return was a political issue. In the past we had been rather naive as we kept on about the fact that we had done everything in cricket terms, and that it was therefore wrong to keep denying us. I hope that frustration is understandable, because we did feel we were just being fobbed off by the ICC, year after year. But eventually it dawned on us that the ICC was just the medium by which we could get back: the outside political world had to accept us as well. Until other countries could see that the political structure in our country was going to change irrevocably, and that multiracialism was squarely on the agenda, then we were going to stay in isolation. The cricket administrators at the ICC were just rubber-stamping what their governments were making of the current situation. South Africa had laws on the statute book which were offensive to sections of the human race; those laws had to go before we could be accepted by the politicians of the countries we wanted to play in the Test arena. It's not as if we had enjoyed a packed international programme when we were still in that arena. A series against Australia or England at two-year intervals wasn't exactly a schedule designed to burn out our top players, who have always thrived on competition. Now we could think about playing the West Indies, Pakistan, India and Sri Lanka on an official basis for the first time. Apart from the cricketing benefits, it would be a thrill to visit those countries which had always barred us because of politics.[49]

In all of this, the West Indies occupied centre stage. The apartheid system had been most punishing of the black race, and West Indies cricket was stocked largely with such people. With considerable skill Birbalsingh has shown also that the Indian community in the West Indies that had produced cricket stalwarts such as Rohan Kanhai, Joe Solomon, Sonny Ramadhin and Alvin Kallicharran, had also taken a positive stand against apartheid, reinforced by their own ancestral, antiracist, ideological traditions that had propelled Mahatma Gandhi into deep oppositional politics during his early adult years in South Africa.[50]

The first encounter between the two teams took place during the 1991–92 World Cup in Australia/New Zealand. The moment was at best a test of West Indian sentiment. The West Indies were defeated by South Africa, and Captain Richie Richardson incurred, perhaps forever, the wrath of the West Indies public who, he lamented, had misunderstood his meaning when he said that the defeat was "just another match". Would Viv Richards have said that, they asked? Was Richards not selected by the WICBC for the World Cup because his presence would have given a combative ideological texture to the historic match?

The Barbados Test vs South Africa

South African cricketers, however, fresh from their success against the West Indies in limited overs cricket, were on their way to Barbados for the grand 'inaugural' Test. The front page of the Barbados *Daily Nation*, 17 April 1992, carried the bold caption "Out of Africa" over a picture of Gary Sobers embracing Ali Bacher and Mike Proctor, manager and coach, respectively, of the visiting South African team. Next to the headline, a smaller caption says, "Traitors: pan-Africans come out against cricket tour". While declaring themselves united in opposition to South Africa's visit to the West Indies before the system of apartheid was fully disbanded, Barbadian pan-Africans were divided on the tactics necessary to effectively represent their position. Some were prepared to carry into the stands placards and banners that denounced apartheid while watching the game. Others were prepared to keep vigil outside under the watchful eyes of well armed police contingents.

Against the background of this proposed visit to the West Indies, South African cricket had been receiving considerable assistance in their development programme from West Indian stars. No longer branded as 'rebels', West Indians travelled to South Africa, with Mandela's blessing as part of a supportive mission in the quest for a democratic cricket culture. Multiracial cricket in South Africa was seen as a seminal development in the world game, and West Indians were there supporting the trend with as much passion as in the days when they opposed the apartheid system. Proctor commented on this process, and recognized in particular the efforts of Clive Lloyd and Conrad Hunte:

During our years of isolation the West Indies had been one of South Africa's sternest critics and it was hard to take issue with Clive's observations on our political structure. If we could manage to win over admired figures such as he, then we were definitely on the move. Clive came over as ICC referee for the India tour in 1992 and we were delighted that he wanted to go to the townships to measure the strength of our development programme. He was impressed by the sight of black kids enjoying their cricket, and at the improving facilities. He thought it was crucial that the country's youth were being encouraged to mix in multiracial sport, and that at last youngsters of all races had a chance to play for South Africa. But he was right to underline that a great deal of social deprivation still existed. Clive said that there was a life beyond the boundary rope, that decent accommodation tended to produce decent human beings. He praised Ali Bacher and the other administrators who had done so much to bring the races together in cricket, but warned that the pace of reform mustn't slow down. Mixing at school and in the workplace was as important as mixing in the cricket arena. Clive pointed out that sport was a stepping-stone to a fairer society but it couldn't divorce itself from that society.[51]

Hunte moved to Johannesburg with his family in 1992 to help coach promising black youngsters. He coached the Soweto Under-19 team that did so well against the best schoolboys in Transvaal, and two of those he had tutored made it to the South African Schools squad.

THE 'ANDY CUMMINS AFFAIR'

The Test match was played at Kensington Oval, 18–22 April 1992. From the first week of the month pan-Africanists led the campaign against the event, but the effects of their protest were overtaken by a larger community effort fuelled by the belief and allegation that the exclusion of Barbadian player Anderson Cummins from the West Indies team for the match was a blatant injustice, constituting evidence of yet another strike against Barbadian cricketers by WICBC selectors. Protest action that started as a limited anti-apartheid campaign was soon transformed into the popular 'Andy Cummins Affair'. Those at the vanguard of the Cummins campaign called for a national boycott of the Test. Cummins, they said, had performed well in the prior World Cup and did not deserve to be abandoned. His nonselection, they said, was the result of discriminatory regional politics that had taken root within the WICBC. Cummins' replacement, Antigua's Kenneth Benjamin, they claimed, was less tried and tested, and universally considered more unreliable.

After 40 years of trying to stage a successful boycott of a Test match, a West Indian community had succeeded. The Barbados boycott was almost total. Rumour circulated that on the first day the Kensington Oval was inhabited by two teams, two stray dogs, two umpires and a depressed groundsman. Some blamed the success of the boycott on Prime Minister Erskine Sandiford's structural adjustment programme with the International Monetary Fund and the World Bank; others said it was a strike against the arrogance and unaccountability of the WICBC. Few, however, reported that success was due to the pervasiveness of ideological opposition to apartheid.

Newspapers in neighbouring Trinidad and Tobago screamed denouncements of Barbadian boycotters with the following headlines during the week of the Test: "Bumptious Bajan Boycott"; "Insularity May Again Be Stepping into West Indies Cricket"; "God Don't Like Ugly"; "Bajan Boycott Opens New Wounds in West Indies Cricket"; "Destroying the Single Bond that Unites Us"; "WICBC Lose over $1 Million". One only headline echoed a different note. It called upon readers to "Praise Barbadians for South Africa Boycott."[52] Over a letter in support of the anti-apartheid movement in Barbados by Dr James Millette, lecturer in history at the UWI, this headline stood in naked isolation during a time when West Indians were shocked by the sight of empty seats at a Barbados Test match.

Consequently, popular interpretations of the event revolved around what became the 'Cummins thesis'. Media debates, therefore, were conducted in terms of its validity as an explanatory model, and no alternative accounts were offered. Boycotters were lumped together as a homogeneous group of reactionaries acting to the detriment of West Indies cricket. Former Barbados ambassador, Oliver Jackman, writing in the Barbados *Sunday Sun*, 22 January 1993, stated that "the boycott of West Indies-South Africa was a national disgrace fomented by a bunch of chauvinistic, small minded people, including the media".

The 'Cummins thesis', however, seems flawed against the background of the traditional behaviour of Barbados cricket crowds, their accumulated knowledge with respect to the eligibility of competing players, and the general ideological contexts of the encounter. Many questions can be asked, but one that seems compelling is this: Would Barbadians, who have accumulated a respected understanding of cricket, even within the context of a prior disenchantment with selectors, have boycotted a match in protest over a player whose selection was far from obvious?

In recent years many Barbadian players with considerable merit 'died on the vine' of nonselection. Would Barbadians have boycotted the Test if it had been staged against respected adversaries such as England, Australia, Pakistan and India? Were Barbadians not showing deep disrespect for an encounter against a team for whom they were not ideologically prepared?

Were they reluctant to offer respectability to South Africa before the advent of universal adult suffrage and democratic governance? Where were the hundreds of non-Barbadian West Indians who usually visited Kensington Oval? Did not the players themselves signal to the public their own reluctance to play the Test at that particular political moment?

In 1994, England visited the West Indies for a five-Test series. Students at the CCR, Cave Hill campus, UWI, took the opportunity of the Barbados Test to conduct a limited survey of opinion among regular cricket spectators. Of the 343 respondents, 325, stated that they had taken a conscious decision not to attend the match; 18 stated that they attended the match at various stages. An analysis of the reasons offered by boycotters indicates considerable diversity in motivational factors: 34 percent explained their action in terms of their disenchantment with the WICBC for its maltreatment of outgoing stars, and for not appointing Desmond Haynes as captain following Viv Richards' retirement; 26 percent stated their objection to the timing of South African Test which they considered a premature project; 8 percent offered miscellaneous reasons; such as the high cost of tickets in the relation to the quality of opposition, falling interest in cricket, and the general contentious mood that surrounded the game.[53]

While these data are at best crude aggregates, and are offered with no pretence to scientific validity, they do indicate the need to question the accuracy of explanations that surround the 'Cummins thesis'. Furthermore, they suggest that wider issues beyond and within the boundaries of cricket were at play, and should be taken on board if the historic moment is to be adequately scrutinized and properly understood. What the event indicates for sure is that after 50 years efforts to interface these cricket cultures that symbolized opposing ideological currents were still considered problematical in the West Indies. Barbadian spectators, looking at their cricket through the lens of past history and future expectations, were dissatisfied and stayed at home. The social and political price of attendance was too high; no one should have been shocked by these developments.

An Emerging Cricket Democracy

West Indies cricket culture, then, constituted the main theatre within which an intense and transformative democratizing discourse developed with respect to the politics of anti-apartheid. The dialogue took place first within the context of the anticolonial movement in which white supremacy ideologies and practices were targeted by an aggressive political philosophy that located meritocracy at the vanguard of an egalitarian, pluralist, ethnic culture. At once a class and a race struggle for justice, the opposition to élite domination in cricket culture sustained the democratic movement, and widened the base of the challenge to traditions of colonial governance.

The political and social results of this process by the 1950s constitute a significant part of empirical evidence that validated the call for nationhood as a project whose time had come. Between 1948 and 1958, when the leadership of West Indies cricket moved slowly and painfully from George Headley to Frank Worrell, it was understood that social apartheid in the West Indies was no longer a viable public institution. The weight of this understanding, and the momentum it gathered, meant that West Indian society was fractured in an attempt to come to terms with global apartheid. South African cricket was encountered after the 1950s as a test of the depths of West Indian public opinion and political consciousness. As governments, seeking to reflect rather than lead opinion on this issue, slowly turned their faces against South African cricket, persons who considered themselves economically disenfranchised and socially marginalized as citizens challenged the meaning and significance of official nationalism by participating in cricket encounters with apartheid regimes.

Cricket, during the 1980s, therefore, presented a new context for sustained democratic discourse that focused on class alienation within the postcolonial dispensation. Conflicting understandings of social freedom emerged, with some working class black West Indians considering themselves no more privileged than their counterparts in South Africa. The nationalist project had left most of them behind, particularly those in the working class whose parents had risen up during the 1930s in defiance of colonialism and in support of political freedom. By the 1980s, cricket culture was assuming new and contradictory characteristics, influenced by the blurred vision of the discredited postcolonialism political leadership. The attempt, however, to achieve rationalization between the democratizing inner logic and moral impulses of the game, and the social dislocations and crises beyond the boundary, continues to constitute a site for political tension and ideological display.

NOTES

1. See C.L.R. James, *Cricket* (London: Allison and Busby, 1989), 12–39.
2. See Brian Stoddart, "Caribbean cricket: the role of sport in emerging small nation politics", *International Journal* 43, no. 3 (1981); Frank E. Manning, "Celebrating cricket: the symbolic construction of Caribbean politics", *American*

Ethnologist 8, no. 3 (1981); Helen Tiffin, "Cricket, literature, and the politics of decolonization: the case of C.L.R. James", in *Liberation Cricket*, ed. H. Beckles and B. Stoddart (Kingston: Ian Randle Publishers, 1995), 356–70.

3. Richard E. Lapchick, "South Africa: Sport and apartheid politics", *Annals 445* (Sept. 1979): 155–60.
4. Ibid., 162–63.
5. Robert Archer and Antoine Bouillon, *The South African Game: Sport and Racism* (London: Zed Books, 1983), 29–45.
6. Ibid., 46.
7. Ibid., 47.
8. *Report of the Main Committee of the Human Sciences Research Council: Investigation into Education* (Pretoria: HSRC), 33.
9. Cited in *Report of the International Olympic Committee* (Lausanne: IOC, 1967), 68.
10. Archer and Bouillon, *The South African Game*, 88–89.
11. Ibid., 90.
12. Ibid., 93.
13. Ibid., 94.
14. Bruce Kidd, "The campaign against sport in South Africa", *International Journal* 43, no. 4, (1988): 648–49.
15. Kidd, 650–52.
16. See Lapchick, "South Africa", 156; Archer and Bouillon, *The South African Game*, 93–94.
17. John Davies, "Politics, sport and education in South Africa", *African Affairs* 85, no. 340 (1986): 351–63.
18. James, *Cricket*, 255–70; 278–80, 291–95.
19. Quotations from C.L.R. James, *Beyond a Boundary* (Duke University Press, 1993), 237.
20. See "The South African connection: the latest crises", *West Indies Cricket Annual* (1986): 19.
21. Ibid., 19.
22. "Sobers in Rhodesia: a crisis for cricket and the Caribbean", *West Indies Cricket Annual* (1976), 14–21.
23. Ibid., 14.
24. Ibid., 14.
25. Ibid., 14.
26. Ibid., 15.
27. Ibid., 16.
28. Ibid., 21.
29. "The South African connection", 19.
30. "Guyana bars anyone who has played sport in South Africa: another political threat to cricket", *West Indies Cricket Annual* (1976), 13; "The Gleneagles Agreement", *Sunday Sun* (Barbados), 1 March 1981, 10.
31. "Guyana bars anyone".
32. See Ken Hall, Joe Favier, and Arnold Thomas, "The anti-apartheid campaign in the Caribbean: the case of sport", *Caribbean Journal of African Studies* 1

(1978): 48–50. Also, "Hints of new UK Gleneagles look", *Advocate* (Barbados), 10 March 1981; "Cricket and our fight against apartheid", *Caribbean Contact*, editorial, April 1981, 3.

33. West Indies Cricket Board of Control, Press release, 15 May 1976 (mimeo).
34. The Gleneagles Agreement on Sporting Contacts with South Africa, Commonwealth Heads of Government, Scotland, 1977. See also, "The South African connection: the latest crisis", *West Indies Cricket Annual* (1986), 16–20.
35. Hall et al., "The anti-apartheid campaign", 61.
36. Ibid.
37. See Hilary Beckles, "A purely natural extension: women's cricket in West Indies cricket culture", in *Liberation Cricket*, ed. H. Beckles and B. Stoddart (Kingston: Ian Randle Publishers, 1995), 232.
38. See Neville Linton, "Boycotts and international relations", The *Nation* (Barbados) 12 March 1981, 5; also, Caribbean News Agency (CANA) release, "Grenada backs Guyana ban on Robin Jackman", *Advocate* (Barbados), 21 March 1981; "Guyana ban on Jackman ironic", *Advocate*, 28 February 1981; "Jackman's visa is revoked", *Guyana Chronicle*, 27 February 1981; "Hector hits at Burnham on Jackman decision", *Advocate*, 28 February 1981; "Jackman affair: good booting by Guyana", *Guyana Chronicle*, 7 March 1981. Joan French, "A principled stand", *Daily Gleaner*, 2 March 1981; "Southern Africa Liberation Committee backs Guyana move", *Advocate*, 2 March 1981; "Gleneagles and the Jackman affair: Ramphal slaps down Maggie Thatcher", *Guyana Chronicle*, 9 March 1981; "Ramphal: contacts hostile to Gleneagles", *Advocate*, 9 March 1981; "Loophole saves the cricket", *Advocate*, 5 March 1981; Lakshmi Persaud, "Why the spirit of Gleneagles must survive", *Advocate*, 4 March 1981.
39. Quoted by Tony Cozier, "Another crisis for West Indian cricket: South African tour controversy", *West Indies Cricket Annual* (1983): 9.
40. Ibid., 13.
41. Ibid.
42. Rob Steen, *Desmond Haynes: Lion of Barbados* (London: Witherby, 1993), 99–105.
43. Cozier, "Another crisis", 13.
44. See Viv Richards, *Hitting Across the Line* (London: Headline Books, 1991), 187; also Cozier, "Another crisis", 15.
45. Ibid., 14.
46. Ibid.
47. Ibid., 15.
48. Gladstone Mills, *Grist for the Mills: Reflections on a Life* (Kingston: Ian Randle Publishers, 1994), 177.
49. Mike Proctor, *South Africa: The Years of Isolation and Return to International Cricket* (London: Queen Anne Press, 1994), 127.
50. Frank Birbalsingh and Clem Shiwcharan, *Indo-West Indian Cricket* (London: Hansib, 1988).

51. Proctor, *South Africa*, 113.
52. See *Sunday Express*, 26 April 1992; *Express*, 10 April 1992; *Guardian*, 11, 15, 22 April 1992; 15, 19, 22 May 1992; 18 June 1992.
53. *Research Survey on Boycott of South African Test in Barbados 1992* (Barbados: CCR, UWI).

Appendix I

Tribute to Sir Gary Sobers

The author delivered this tribute in London on 21 May 1995 to the Barbados Youth and Friends Association

The facts, Kwame Nkrumah, once said, constitute no more than the tyranny of commonsense, and should often be ignored.

The truth, however, is seldom found in that quarter, and should be pursued relentlessly, particularly while invoking the deeds of those who are still placed to participate in a response to the invocation.

This reference, Mr Chairman, to Nkrumah's juxtaposition of facts (or commonsense) and truth, is not intended to provoke anyone into a philosophical discourse on the subject of collective wisdom vs subjective perception, but merely to indicate that the subject of cricket and great cricketers will inevitably be a contentious one, and so I am merely seeking to prepare myself by laying before you my terms of reference.

It is indeed an honour, and more importantly a challenge, to make this intervention with respect to the legacy of a truly great and immensely important West Indian.

While ideally I would have preferred if a West Indian, rather than a Barbadian, organization had sponsored this celebration, I concede that there is nothing wrong when a village within a nation stands up on a point of local order, since such an action enriches rather than impoverishes the collective well being.

It is my duty, then, as an academic worker, to identify the bridges that connect the local to the national, and to place Sir Gary Sobers, a Barbadian, firmly within his West Indian context, by demonstrating the specific West Indian nature of his contents.

Just a month ago I was in Trinidad, called upon by the Hon. Michael Manley, to deliver the feature address at the official launch of the revised second edition of his *History of West Indian Cricket*. Inevitably, the subject of Lara's genius came to the fore, and participants in the discussion admitted to finding young Lara quite a phenomenon – a freak of local history, so to speak.

The basis of their confusion had to do with an admission that Trinidad has a proud record with respect to producing competent players, but no claim to greatness at the Test level, and therefore, it seemed, logically Lara fell from the skies or, better yet, like Barbadian flying fish, he found himself mysteriously conceived and born in Trinidad – just waiting to be reclaimed, as George Headley was in the 1930s, by Barbadians, as a native son.

None of this, of course, makes sense, given our understanding of what is West Indian society, how it works, and how it is driven by historical forces, but I will return to this!

But for now, allow me to pose my two fundamental questions? One, *What* is Gary Sobers? Two, What is the meaning of *a* Gary Sobers? The issue of *who* is Gary Sobers is not relevant to any serious discussion about the nature of the West Indian condition.

Great men, we are told, make history, but only that amount that history allows them to make, and so we should begin by looking at history in the search for the 'what'– the 'who' will follow from our discoveries.

At this stage it would be improper, if not sacrilegious, to proceed without calling my first and primary witness – the greatest philosopher of cricket culture – the late C.L.R. James whose spirit remains our guiding star in all our intellectual deliberations.

No one, it seems to me, understood how Gary Sobers was manufactured by historical and social circumstances in the way that James did. As always, he initiated his enquiries with an assumption of data deficiency, then with the posing of questions, through which he moved to historical analysis and ideological assertion. I will give you an example of James at his best – and most provoking. This is a letter written to his friend, hero and ally, Sir Frank Worrell in 1963.

Staverton Rd.
Lon. NW2
July 12, 1963:

My Dear Frank,
I have nothing to write, except that I perpetually wonder that a little scrap of West Indian territory has produced Gary Sobers and you. Anything you feel I can do, or may be able to do, just let me know.
C.L.R. James

Six years later, he had ceased to wonder. He examined Sobers closely, studied his Barbadian roots and personal circumstances, and came up with the following statement:

The pundits colossally misunderstand Garfield Sobers – perhaps the word should be misinterpret, not misunderstand. Garfield Sobers, I shall show, is a West Indian cricketer, not merely a cricketer from the West Indies. He is the most typical West Indian cricketer that it is possible to imagine.

That he is a genius is now a cliché for children, but, "geniuses are only persons who carry to an extreme definitive the characteristics of the unit of civilization to which they belong. Therefore to understand Sobers is to understand the West Indies, and to misunderstand him is to misunderstand the West Indies."

Here, then, is part of the answer to my first question, "What is Gary Sobers?" The answer – the person in whose being is manifested to the logical extreme the potential and capability of a people at a given moment in time.

James says the same of Michelangelo and Picasso, but in the specific case of Sobers he adds a qualifying term that speaks directly to a wider agenda and his view of history – "the masses of people". What then about Sobers, the masses of people, the small scrap of land in the Caribbean, and the creation of genius? We have some prior examples of such vision in other spheres of Caribbean life.

Take for example Toussaint. Toussaint L'Ouverture was born into slavery, but organized his people, abolished slavery, freed his people, and built the first society in the modern world based on universal recognition of liberty, social justice, and constitutional freedom. That we cannot forget. Another example is J.J. Thomas. Marcus Garvey hailed from the most oppressed section of Jamaican colonial society, but succeeded in building the largest anti-colonial and socially liberating movement the world has ever seen. What of Sobers and all of this? Where does this history locate him in its relentless flow?

We do not need James at this stage because as natives from that part of the West Indian nation, we have a little direct knowledge of the physical and social environment that produced Sobers. We know that he came from that section of Barbadian colonial society that was most materially impoverished – the economically alienated urban working class. We also know that such a circumstance placed him in an unfavourable relationship with educational facilities, and therefore the poverty was endemic, and perhaps seemed inescapable.

We also know that like most families in this structural condition, there existed no relationship between material poverty and intellectual capability. The 'respectable poor' has never admitted its intellectual defeat – but speaks of defiance. This fact, I think, is key to understanding West Indian history, and the development of Sobers' enormous mathematical competencies. It is the kicking away of the scaffold, and the liberation of the emerging edifice, that speaks to the question of the human essence in search for freedom. It has allowed the world's oppressed from Calcutta to London, Capetown to Sidney, to claim Sobers as a man "sprung from among the masses", sending a signal of hope for collective redemption.

This is no ordinary fact of history. Neither is it to be submerged in the foot-notes of historical narratives. Here was a young man in his early thirties, born and raised in what we may now call an inner-city depressed area, captain of a victorious West Indies team, leader of a Rest of the World team, without the benefit of a solid secondary education, no university exposure, standing before the world as the 'Greatest Cricketer of All Time' – the world's greatest, produced in a West Indian urban village not yet independent, colonial. This brings me to my second question – What does it all mean?

We must begin, I think, at the beginning, somewhere during the early nineteenth century, when this most English of games was introduced into the West Indies. It is important to note that cricket made its West Indian début during the final stages of the collapse of the slave system. The extraordinary build-up of military forces in the region by England to keep the rebellious slaves in subjection, to prevent other European powers from 'stealing' their colonies, created a new circumstance in the islands. The imperial soldiers started playing organized cricket among themselves first, and later against resident white planters and merchants. Records from Antigua, 1790s, and Barbados, 1810s, illustrate this quite clearly.

By the end of slavery in the 1830s, West Indian whites embraced and domesticized this cricket culture, started playing amongst themselves, and in the process established a new system of cultural apartheid by denying blacks and coloureds access to cricket institutions which were now blessed by the colonial establishment. The majority community, however, did not see the cricket culture in the same way. In the hands of whites, it was an instrument of class élitism, social exclusion, racial segregation, and general ideological conservatism. For the blacks, however, it was a cultural space, an institution to be desegregated, democratized, and liberated as a symbol of the rising democratizing ethos that had been unleashed by emancipation and marked by the struggles of J.J. Thomas, Paul Bogle, Samuel Jackman Prescod, Frederick Douglas, and many others. It was in fact this tradition that produced radical cricketers in the democratic progressive movement such as Learie Constantine, Herman Griffith, George John, George Headley and organizations like the Barbados Cricket League.

By the 1950s this struggle had swept aside racial privilege as the basis of selection, allowing merit to rise in the form of the 'Three Ws' and of course the juvenile Gary Sobers. This cricket revolution was a principal part of the wider democratic movement, articulated and organized by men like C.L.R. James, and finding concrete focus in the rise of Sir Frank Worrell in 1958–59 as the first black man to be appointed captain with tenure of the West Indies cricket team. It was a long struggle indeed. It took over 100 years to complete this process, and Sir Frank Worrell stood at what seemed then to be the end of history.

But it is what Sir Frank Worrell said and did at that historical moment that indicates what C.L.R. James meant when he said that a genius is merely a person who gives extreme logical definition to a historical process that is endemic to a people. James recalled a discussion between Sir Frank and himself in 1961 about who would replace him as a West Indies captain. He wrote:

We talked about the future captaincy of the West Indies. Worrell was as usual cautious and non-committal. He said, yes, so-and-so is a good man, capable, and so on. Then, when that stage of the conversation was practically at an end, he suddenly threw in: 'I know that in Australia whenever I had to leave the field, I was glad when I was able to leave Sobers in charge'. 'He knows everything?' I asked. 'Everything,' Worrell replied.

We are therefore speaking about something much more than what is now called in the fancy language of economists, "sustainable development" – though that is part of what we speak. When at age 28 a man can be described as acquiring the entire stock of wisdom and knowledge accumulated by four past generations, we are speaking of the very steep learning curve that constitutes the signs of genius.

The record then speaks for itself. I do not need to speak of it, because you all know it much better than I do: The record 365 at age 21; the record 6 sixes in county cricket; the record Test centuries for the West Indies; other countless extraordinary achievements; the artistry, dignity, and high-cultured performance, the celebration of excellence and humility, all wrapped up in a personality that represents a humanism at its finest.

But there is more – not only documented by the statistics and supported by the memories of spectators, but underlying the process of political development generally referred to as the 'independence movement'.

Sobers represented not only the ultimate triumph of the ideology of merit as the sole principle of social organization in a democracy, but a symbol of what the independence movement was all about. Before him there were great bowlers, great batsmen, great fielders and great captains. It was a division of labour that was promoted by the colonial regime, and used as evidence in the argument that West Indians were not ready to rule themselves or to take their place with dignity in global affairs.

In Sobers, history brought together the fragments of a disintegrated consciousness and culture, and said to the world, here is proof that the West Indian can master all aspects of an enterprise, redefine its standards, and establish new rules and levels of operation. Sobers the allrounder – Jack of all trades and master of all. We therefore went to the Colonial Office to demand our independence invested with this example of pride, loaded with self-confidence, and optimistic of the future. James knew this. He told Frank Worrell this in 1960. By 1963, it was commonsense. Yes, the little scrap of land that had produced the greatest, was now saying to the imperial ruler, we are perfectly able to manage our own affairs, thank you, and if you have doubts, look at Gary Sobers the next time he steps out at Lord's. He gave us a new sense of completeness and readiness that no other individual could in that way.

This is what in turn we West Indians gave back to English cricket, and to cricket in general. We said to the English, thank you for the gift of this remarkable game, now take in return these new standards of excellence by which to judge your own performance culture. My belief is that the greatest gift you can possibly give is the gift of high standards.

Outside of his own personal heroic achievements, it was under Sobers' leadership that it can be said that the West Indian team became, for the first time, the world champions – having defeated the Australians in the West Indies in 1965, 2:1, England here in 1966, 3:1, and India in India in 1966, 2:0. As leader he placed our team where his own personal reputation resided – at the top, and this to my mind is where Sobers' greatness truly lies – in his ability to place his personal genius at the disposal of his nation, and to inspire it collectively to global leadership. It is this bond between self and society that was affirmed and canonized, passed on to Lloyd and Richards, and is now awaiting reaffirmation from the Lara generation.

The thesis, of course, which this generation will have to study, is that Sobers was not only a master of the game in its various departments, but master of his mind within the context of the game. There was with him no abandonment of mind, as is now the case with today's team, but an application of mental power which you have all seen, and for which he became well known. For James, he was the "living embodiment of centuries of a tortured history". For me, he is further social evidence of the internal integrity of a philosophical discourse that promotes mind over matter, consciousness over constraints, as demonstrated once again in the second journey of Nelson Mandela.

Each generation has a mission with which to come to terms. It can either fulfil that mission or betray it – but never compromise it. Sir Gary did the best he could, and fulfilled his mission. I now wish him a long life and good health.

Appendix II

On Michael Manley's *A History of West Indies Cricket*

Speech delivered at Queen's Park Cricket Club, Trinidad on the occasion of the launching of Michael Manley's A History of West Indies Cricket, *second edition (André Deutsch, London, 1995) on 20 April 1995.*

I would like to thank my friend Michael Manley for bestowing on me this honour of speaking at his book launch in this historic and distinguished cricket facility. It is also a special pleasure for me because Michael has succeeded in doing, with his familiar eloquence and conceptual rigour, something that now occupies my own academic attention. I refer to the project of combining an incisive reading of Caribbean history with a clear understanding of political process in order to penetrate the inner cultural logic and deepest social meaning of cricket as a popular institution.

The arrival of a literary text into a West Indian world once typecast by one of its own acclaimed artistic sons as an "intellectual wasteland", is always good cause for celebration, particularly by those who disagree or disapprove of such a description of our 'living' space. The fact that this book is a revised and enlarged second edition is particularly exciting, especially for those of us who proclaim an evangelical Christianity in which a special place is assigned for a *second* coming. It is also good cause for celebration in solidarity with the author because this text constitutes not only a labour of love, but a monumental effort at historical construction.

There are certain things that should be said at the outset about this text. It is necessary to say these things before we place ourselves between the covers in search of elements to be used in the design of a critical review. Michael's book, by all criteria, is a seminal articulation of innovative concepts and accumulated knowledge. It is revolutionary in that it has no peer nor recognizable parentage within the context of West Indies cricket historiography. These two features tell us that the book belongs to no established literary tradition, and represents a beginning rather than a departure – a responsibility Michael will have to bear as a new canon takes shape in years to come.

Let us examine, then, what currently constitutes the tradition of West Indian cricket historiography. We need to do this in order to understand the literary world into which this text has arrived, and how it will live with its neighbours while redefining conditions of existence for all inhabitants. Three elements within the tradition are immediately recognizable.

First, there is a very exciting and rich legacy of the cricketer's autobiography, produced by our distinguished players who recall and reflect upon experiences and achievements. Trinidad can rightly claim a first lien upon this legacy. It was from here that we received pioneering work by the legendary Pelham 'Plum' Warner at the end of the nineteenth century, and our first classic, Learie Constantine's *Cricket and I* which was published in 1933.

Secondly, we have also produced a substantial body of fine, descriptive literature – mostly semi-biographical narratives – that details the lives and deeds of great players, reliving exciting and tragic moments, but which professes no concern with analytical discourse, sociological meaning, or scientific significance. It is the tradition of the 'cultured' raconteurs who have gained much respect in a social world that continues to value highly the oral and the folk as communicative technologies.

Finally, there is a less expansive but already rich literature that seeks to untangle and define the philosophical and cultural meaning of cricket within West Indies civilization. Trinidad, again, can also claim a first lien on this tradition. This island gave us George John's classic theatrical play, *Moon on a Rainbow Shawl* in which Charlie Adams, the pivotal figure, accounts for his tragic interface with pre-Williams' colonial society in terms of relations of class and race power within the cricket establishment. In addition, it gave us C.L.R. James's 'biblical' text, *Beyond a Boundary*, that represents a set of principles by which we now organize our thoughts and seek explanatory instruction.

This book belongs to none of these traditions. What distinguishes its structure is the way the author liberates and empowers the subjective voice as the narrative and analytical key to a storeroom of historical evidence. These data are marshalled by a chronology of historical meaning within which stages in the development of a West Indian cricket ideology are detailed with intellectual incisiveness and empirical depth. Personal performances of cricketers take on meaning within the political process, which in turn is woven into a social matrix that reveals the torn and tortured history of a people frantically seeking release from a colonial world that used cricket as a metaphor for structured social exclusion.

None of this should surprise any of us. Manley has enlivened Jamesian concepts in new and radical ways by placing the dialectical forces in West Indian history at the centre of the narrative. The book, then, is a history of West Indies cricket both within and beyond the boundary. It is a tribute to a social history methodology that excavates the cultural foundations of a nation at various levels of organized social consciousness. Planter and peasant, merchant and menials, sentinels of empire and soldiers of nationhood, are thrown together at the politicized centre of a game that rejects any narrow self-description and sees itself as a mirror of diverse social meaning.

These are the reasons why none of us has reason to take the wrong guard before facing up to this text. It emerges from the mind of the quintessential political philosopher of the postindependence era. It bears the deep marks of a mind that has been close to the stresses, strains, struggles, and successes of a people. In addition, it is a celebration of West Indian culture by one who as a political manager and theoretician led a process of cultural decolonization and popular empowerment that now threatens to Jamaicanize – hence West Indianize – the entire world with its cultural iconography.

These 706 pages are therefore not written for the 'one-dayers'. This is Test! They require a careful and cautious approach. The longer you stay in occupation, the greater will be your aggregate. The accumulation of knowledge is what we are gathered here for. But the seminal nature of the work, I suggest, is to be found in the subtext in which it is argued, as Kamau Brathwaite says in the poem "Rites" "This is cricket, this ain't no time for making sport". The journey begins with the late Victorian founding fathers – both 'foreigners' and creoles. Colonial aristocrats such as Pelham Warner are placed in ideological context and credited for laying the foundations on which the first great West Indian batsmen, white Barbadians such as George Challenor and Harold Austin, built a dynamic, indigenous, performance culture.

The decade of the 1930s has gained acceptance by historians and social scientists as a watershed in the struggle for West Indian democracy. Manley discusses the revolutionary impact of the Learie Constantine–George Headley generation of cricketers upon this political process and indicates the ways in which they in turn were social products of the turbulent era. The anticolonial political activities of Captain Cipriani here in Trinidad, and the phenomenal organizational work of Marcus Garvey everywhere, inform the meaning of this eruption within the boundary. For Manley, Headley is the seminal figure, and also the missile aimed at oppressive colonizing targets – the shining star of an anticolonial labour movement closing in upon a retreating, discredited, and dying colonialism.

This fascinating analytical flow spills out into a comprehensive account of the strategic politicking aimed at securing Frank Worrell the West Indies captaincy with tenure – again starting here in Trinidad under the visionary guidance of C.L.R. James. We know, Manley tells us, that until we had won that battle in which merit triumphed over racial privilege as the basis of social organization, no one could legitimately go to London to demand constitutional independence.

The Worrell–Sobers axis is then used as a metaphor for the deepening of the democratic process and working class empowerment via the popular franchise. That Sobers by 1960 is described by Worrell as "knowing everything" is just further evidence of why the 1960s political generation seemed ready to assume full leadership of West Indian affairs and to take a place with dignity in world affairs. Viv Richards constituted a subsequent political argument that in spite of constitutional independence and decades of social agitation, blacks had good cause to protest their institutional and economic marginalization relative to other historically privileged ethnic groups. He placed his genius at the disposal of this struggle and, according to Manley, emerged by the late 1970s as the standard bearer of a very relevant pan-Africanism.

Finally, we are treated to an assessment of the Lara intervention. This is where, to my mind, Manley drops his guard, but only to send home the final punch of an analysis that signifies, in a personal sort of way, a convergence of everything he believes and represents. It is the kind of punch, however, whose trajectory only intuition could track. In fact he sends it, as Michael Holding's autobiography states, in a "whispering and deadly fashion". I deduce from his final missile, the following message: in spite of structural adjustment, the IMF, World Bank and now NAFTA, we have produced this man-child of genius, product of the irrepressible people finding liberation in an area they know best.

This book, then, is really an analysis of the origins and maturity of the modern democratic movement within which the West Indian nation has been forged. It is a window through which to view the making of a distinct identity and the formation of a personality. For me it represents the finest statement of the view that from the 1920s West Indians have infused the ideologically sterile Victorian game with an intense sense of progressive purpose, and given it a new democratic mandate and philosophical vision. West Indians have raised the standards of performance and social expectation, redefined its context, and returned it across the Atlantic divide to the English as our gift. What greater gift can one receive than the gift of higher standards?

The book, furthermore, is the manifesto of a movement which says, as Constantine did in his 1933 text, *Cricket and I*, that the triumph of merit and the celebration of collective efforts, are the sharpened instruments of an authentic pursuit of cutting edge excellence. This is why I support Michael's compelling logic that Lara represents the crystallization of a long heroic mentality and the consolidation of a truly West Indian method. So here we have it. A text within which can be found the current statement of accounts of a national portfolio. Whose duty is it to protect and expand this investment? In whose hands should we place this most precious asset?

Appendix III

An Interview with Sir Clyde Walcott

This interview with Sir Clyde Walcott on his appointment as chairman of the International Cricket Conference (ICC) was first published in Caricom Perspectives, *1994*

BECKLES: Sir Clyde, congratulations on both your appointment to the chairmanship of the International Cricket Conference and on the honour the government and people of Barbados bestowed on you with the conferment of a knighthood.

WALCOTT: Thank you, Hilary.

BECKLES: Sir Clyde, you have had a most distinguished career as a cricket player and administrator. You have dedicated your entire adult life to the furtherance of our cricket culture, and this is universally recognized. Were you at all surprised by your election to the ICC chair?

WALCOTT: I would say that surprise is not the most precise term to describe my response. In recent years it was clear to many people that the time had come for the chairmanship to move away from the MCC group. I had received some indication from many members that my name was under consideration on account of my contributions. It was recognized that my role in securing the abolition of the veto vote, for example, was significant, and that I had further contributions to make in guiding the new dispensation.

BECKLES: Recently, Sir Clyde, in a televised discussion on West Indies cricket with the Hon. Michael Manley, he stated that he "walked tall" when he heard of your election. Did you feel at once the historical magnitude and significance of the development?

WALCOTT: Yes, because of my cricket background as a West Indies player and administrator I have a profound sense of the position West Indies cricket should have within the global arena. I know the distance we have travelled, and the contributions we have made. I think that the cricket public appreciates our value, and understands the direction we have taken.

BECKLES: You obviously brought much value to the boardroom of the ICC.

WALCOTT: Over the years my colleagues respected the experience I have accumulated, and as a result I had a sense of being listened to on critical matters. In the banning of players on the South African issue subsequent to the Gleneagles Agreement, for example, my position was clear, and my judgement was considered reasonable and in the interest of cricket.

BECKLES: That was a highly contentious time, and very testing for leadership.

WALCOTT: It was indeed, especially since opinions varied between countries. On the question of South Africa's readmission, West Indies stood firm against, and insisted upon the coming into being of a nonracial cricket culture there as a condition for admission. I stuck to the issues of the debate, not leaning to any political pressure, and colleagues recognized that my position had nothing to do with race, but with what was right for cricket in the short and long term.

BECKLES: It must have been a very difficult task, since for most cricket lovers the game is quasi-religious and definitely political. How did you handle the pressure of political expectations? Are we on the threshold of a breakthrough?

WALCOTT: Yes, in the decision of the Asian venue for the World Cup I played a major role in negotiating the deal and this was recognized. I think that my work background of industrial relations with unions helped. When I left that meeting I felt I had a great chance of being ICC president. The question was whether Sir Colin Cowdrey would do one more year.

BECKLES: Did you feel that with your reputation as a distinguished player and with management skills you could have been there earlier?

WALCOTT: No, the structure called for an English president of MCC to be chairman of ICC.

BECKLES: Pressure from countries, mainly foundation members; the maturity of cricketing countries on and off the field; now, for the first time MCC would not be administering cricket. The ICC is an independent body set up at Lord's. Offices are rented at Lord's with a full-time chief executive which means that because MCC is not responsible for the administration, we now have to set up our own structure and have a complete legal overhaul. Has this reform created a greater sense of international brotherhood within the cricketing cultures of the world?

WALCOTT: Yes, I think it has. The decision was accepted in other countries. Australia and England had reservations. All were in agreement that this was a necessary departure, and that ICC should not become political. We do not say that MCC would not have a role. MCC can continue to play a role in the development of cricket in the countries of the association.

BECKLES: Do you feel history in the making?

WALCOTT: I do. It is part of a big change. West Indies Cricket Board has tried to get this change. People still felt that MCC controlled cricket in a imperial sort of way and this was not good for the game.

BECKLES: Sir Clyde, when you look at West Indies cricket history and reflect on it, how do you explain why the greater skills of your day did not yield results as impressive as those of the last fifteen years?

WALCOTT: I am not one to say that skills were better in the fifties and sixties. There were certain individuals who were better players. There is now more team spirit and unity in West Indies cricket. The fitness of players and the team unity would compensate more. For example in the late seventies and eighties, Larry Gomes batted at No. 3. You cannot compare him with Rohan Kanhai or Frank Worrell, but he got runs and was backed up by players, and he was critical to West Indies' success.

BECKLES: Are there any other factors you would mention by way of comparison?

WALCOTT: There were territorial cliques in the early period. The team was not as united. The game itself has changed, especially with the introduction of 'limited over' cricket. The techniques in fielding have changed – for example, catches which Sobers took he would not be able to take now. In the days of the Three Ws, batsmen used to take more chances. Maybe the balls have changed also. Players may be studying cricket more – old players did not do this.

BECKLES: During the time of Lloyd as captain there seemed to be a strong sense of playing for the 'nation'.

WALCOTT: Yes, the administrative structure did not encourage this in the earlier period. There was one selector from each territory, and his job, he felt, was to get as many of his men on the team as possible. You still get some parochialism, but because selectors are now mostly ex-players they think more in West Indian terms.

BECKLES: On the matter of the outcry concerning the Board's decision to appoint Richardson as captain instead of Haynes, did you make the decision and hope for the best?

WALCOTT: Generally speaking, the Board knows more about the individual player than the public thinks and can therefore identify more readily the leadership and other competencies of individuals.

BECKLES: There is a view that the West Indies team does better when the captain is significantly older than his players, and that this has to do with the nature of the West Indian personality. For example, the cases of Worrell, Lloyd and then Richards.

WALCOTT: I don't go along with that. It depends on the individual. Richardson is 'one of the boys' so to speak, but still gets respect from the team. Many other factors should be considered with respect to the question of discipline and team solidarity. The whole image of West Indian cricket is high. Richardson handles the team well.

BECKLES: Richardson was invited to speak to the students enrolled in the "West Indies Cricket History" course at the University of the West Indies' Cave Hill campus. The students were very impressed with his clear ideas about leadership styles. Were you aware that he has developed his own concept of leadership?

WALCOTT: I am not surprised to hear this. The difference between the teams of today and past teams is that past teams just played. Today, teams discuss play before hand. Everything is planned, examined, and strategies discussed. The captain is required to have a clear mind, and to think in management terms.

BECKLES: Would you say that cricket is not 'fun' for players anymore?

WALCOTT: There are a few exceptions. Past players, however, enjoyed themselves more.

BECKLES: The professional movement within the game is a critical issue. Umpires have had to become very professional. Careers are at stake. Has the player's business ethic gone too far?

WALCOTT: Competitive sport is big business: Players are capital resources. Decision making is under scrutiny. Players are conscious of the fact of losing jobs because of bad decisions. The more we train umpires and use better techniques, the better for the game.

BECKLES: Is it unreasonable to expect an umpire to preside for six hours of a game? What is your view on the changing of umpires during a game?

WALCOTT: Up to now players are not for it because if one umpire, for example, is perceived as a 'batsmen' umpire one may feel that there is preference. Players prefer consistency and uniformity. The proposal was therefore turned down by players.

BECKLES: What are the WICBC's plans for dealing with massive West Indies crowds in England? Have we done enough to reach out to them? Can we ask for specific programmes for them?

WALCOTT: Nothing detailed has yet been done. In the past when the West Indies team was playing in England, efforts were made for players to attend functions in the West Indian communities. Periodically, players attend functions and give a few lectures; but today it is difficult to get players involved outside of the actual cricket games.

BECKLES: When the West Indies team is preparing for tours, are young players especially exposed to seminars/lectures and other contacts in order to explain the role of cricket in West Indian nation-building and civilization in general?

WALCOTT: We have attempted on a few occasions to do this, but the feedback is that the majority of players say it is of little direct value. We have organized lectures/seminars on topics such as (i) leadership concepts, (ii) sports nutrition (iii) the player as an ambassador, (iv) financial management, (v) West Indies cricket administration. The majority said they need to know more about the strategic aspects of the game. The Board, I think, should continue. The younger players especially would have to be targeted.

BECKLES: You have stressed the need to keep former players at the centre of the game's management structure. Why the emphasis?

WALCOTT: I would like to see more ex-cricketers getting involved in administration rather than coaching and assisting in the general development of cricket. They bring to the table a particular kind of value that non-cricket managers do not possess. This is vital.

BECKLES: We have had a lot of extraordinary players over the last 50 years but to date we have no monument to cricket on the West Indies landscape. There is no statue in a square, roundabout, or park, symbolic of our cricket genius and leadership. Politicians are everywhere. What is your view?

WALCOTT: The cricketing body cannot do these things alone. The community has to act. Symbols should come from the people who need them. But I agree that cricket should be recognized more as culture and something that is valuable to society.

BECKLES: Barbados is known globally more for its cricketers than its beaches. Why, therefore, not represent that fame with symbolic recognition?

WALCOTT: Twenty years ago the chairman of the National Sports Council was speaking about a Frank Worrell memorial, but it is not up yet.

BECKLES: The University of the West Indies, Cave Hill (History department) is having an inaugural Sir Frank Worrell Memorial Lecture on the 8 April 1994. It is hoped that this will develop into a major annual event. What more can we do?

WALCOTT: There is much more to be done. Of course we have several pavilions named after players all over the West Indies. This is a start; we need to build on this.

BECKLES: Students have asked me to find out from you whether there are any items on the agenda for the development of women's cricket.

WALCOTT: It is noted that only three West Indian countries were represented on our women's team in the last Test tour. The WICBC has not concentrated on or showed an aggressive interest in our women's cricket. I myself have never been invited to watch a game of women's cricket. They have had some resource problems, but I understand that progress is being made.

BECKLES: Has an attempt been made to affiliate the Confederation of West Indies Women's cricketers to the WICBC?

WALCOTT: No, the Board was never approached. When the West Indies women's team was at Lord's recently I did not know about it.

BECKLES: I understand from the women cricketers that women cannot become members of some major West Indian cricket clubs. When the WICBC holds its annual dinner are women ever invited?

WALCOTT: At Sabina Park I understand that women are now allowed to be members. At Queen's Park no women are allowed. Because of this my wife has never been to watch a match there. She says that until she can sit with her husband to watch cricket there she will not go. In Guyana and Barbados it was the same thing until recently. When the question of the dinner was raised numbers rather than sex created a problem. The sponsors, Cable and Wireless, were paying for the dinner and of course wanted the press to be present. In Guyana, Georgetown, some of the paid administrators are female. In the outside world administrators are female at association and club level.

BECKLES: Is there the possibility of using female umpires in the future for Test matches?

WALCOTT: If they are good enough, I think so.

BECKLES: Are there any who are close now to qualification?

WALCOTT: I don't know at this time. In England they are receiving much exposure at the club level.

BECKLES: Having accepted the chairmanship of ICC, do you feel that you will be losing your grip on West Indies cricket?

WALCOTT: Yes, I feel sad that I will no longer have a direct say in West Indies cricket. I now have to think in wider and broader terms. As chairman of ICC I have to be careful not to refer to the West Indies Board as 'we'.

BECKLES: This is indeed a loss to the West Indies game. It is felt that you have an eye for spotting the talents of younger players, for example, Marshall and Holding.

WALCOTT: When I thought it was time to come out (1984–85) most of the senior players asked me to stay on for this reason. I did my best for them and they appreciated it.

BECKLES: That does indicate a vote of confidence. Sir Clyde, you are known to be hard- lined, frank, but fair. Is it true that your motto is "stick by the rules and principles and progress will be made"?

WALCOTT: Yes, some of the ex-players still refer to me as "Mr Manager".

BECKLES: In reflecting on your 50-odd years in cricket, what are the moments that leap to mind?

WALCOTT: Immediately, I would say that in an era of the new 'ball-game', I would like to preserve Test cricket. We are trying to commercialize the limited over cricket to assist in the development of cricket worldwide. There is now a proposal to move towards a six-a-side cricket in order to get Americans and Europeans interested. We have got to look at the commercial level of cricket at ICC level. The World Cup is now a big commercial venture. One would hope that by the year 2000 West Indies would be able to sponsor the World Cup with full television coverage. Once the West Indies targets the World Cup – it would be theirs. The West Indies is seen as leading in the cricket world. It is possible that ICC would try to develop cricket in North America. I do see the World Cup as a major instrument. Also some aspects of the game are getting out of hand. Conditions of play need to be standardized globally. Countries have different conditions and this is not right. We must also eradicate the indiscipline which is developing in the field of play.

BECKLES: Do you think there will be a move towards drug testing of cricketers?

WALCOTT: Yes, but it would be useful to know precisely whether drugs can enhance the players' performance. In England already there is some drug testing done. Yes it will come eventually.

BECKLES: What about 'neutral' umpires?

WALCOTT: ICC is hoping to have a sponsor for an international panel of umpires. From February 1994 ICC will be using one visiting umpire and one local umpire in every Test match in the world. The international panel is a step in the right direction. In terms of international cricket, I think we have made another step forward. We have appointed a cricket committee to deal with matters and to make recommendations.

BECKLES: Any sad moments on which you often reflect?

WALCOTT: As a player I enjoyed playing and making runs. I was not criticized often. It was more difficult when I moved to administration, because this affected a lot of people. I would say of my involvement in cricket I have always done all to the best of my ability. I would like to finish by saying that I can never do more for cricket than cricket has done for me. I can never put back what was given to me.

BECKLES: Sir Clyde, talking to you has been a wonderful experience. You have given your life to this aspect of West Indian culture, and you are a regional hero. I feel proud in knowing that at the height of our achievements as cricketers you were to be found steering things from behind with great care and vision. I wish you all the best in your chairmanship of the ICC, and hope that one day you can return to us with new perspectives. Sir Clyde, good luck, and God's blessing.

Appendix IV

Rejecting Women: Queen's Park Cricket Club, Trinidad

This article was first published by The Independent *on 10 May 1996*

Nowhere in the rules of the Queen's Park Cricket Club (QPCC) is there a line debarring women from membership. But a line exists nonetheless, and according to Club President, Gerry Gomez, no member has yet had the "temerity" to cross it.

The QPCC is celebrating its centenary at the Queen's Park Oval this year (the club was actually formed in 1891, when members occupied the Queen's Park Savannah) and one of its plans is to rewrite its constitution to take it into the next century. Already a proposal has been drawn up, and although Gomez is loath to make it public until the club's 2,800 members have had a chance to consider it; there is clearly no plan to include women in the membership.

"It is a gentleman's club," says Gomez. "It is regarded as a sort of man's sanctuary. Right off the top of my head, if we opened the club for female membership, it would transform the club physically . . . I think generally speaking, its history is as a man's club. Men come here to relax away from females."

Besides, he says, there isn't total exclusion of women, there are events like family days, football games, cocktail parties and the like, to which members are encouraged to bring along their "wives, girlfriends and families". There is also a gym which is available for use by members' families.

"Whatever facilities we have like that," says Gomez, "it's extended to women." But among the rules pertaining to visitors, one clause says, "A member shall not be permitted to introduce as a visitor to the club any of the following": and the second category (following rejected candidates) lists, "Ladies or children under the age of 14 years".

There are six categories for membership in the club: Ordinary, Life, Honorary, Temporary, Visiting and Associate. To be considered for membership, one must first be proposed by a member and seconded by another on a form requiring full name, address, profession or business at least 14 days before the candidate is eligible for ballot. After that, there is an entrance fee of $3,000 and annual subscription fees.

A ballot committee, consisting of the management committee (which currently comprises Gerry Gomez, president; Willie Rodriquez, vice-president; William Lucie-Smith, treasurer; Ian Stone, honorary secretary; Michael Joey Carew, executive manager; Bruce Annensen, Brian Stollmeyer, Nicky Inniss, Cecil Camacho and Michael Carew, cricket captain) and five other members elected at the annual general meeting, votes on applications. If there is a nay from one in every five members of this ballot committee, the candidate is rejected.

If a woman were to get to the ballot committee stage, says Gomez, "I don't think it will go down well with the members. They may feel so strongly about it, they may call a special meeting." His personal feeling is that, "having been a member for 64 years, I think it will alter the character of the club, and it's not like a country club; it's a sportsman's club". "I think if a female wanted to join the club it would be purely to score a point for suffrage", he says contemplatively.

A cursory look at the membership list reveals so many public figures who might want to support allowing women into what has been defined as one of the last male bastions in the country, that surely Gomez is misjudging his membership. Life members include well-known names such as: Dr Wahid Ali, Dr Michael Beaubrun, Ralph Armorer, C.J. [Chief Justice] Michael De La Bastide, Ken Gordon, Sydney Knox, David Lamy, Justice Ralph Narine, Dr John Neehall, Daniel Samaroo, Teasley Taitt, Audley Walker and Garvin M. Scott. Ordinary members include the likes of: Tajmool Hosein, Cecil Kelsick, Clive Pantin, Brigadier Carl Alfonso (well . . .), Desmond Allum, Oscar Alonzo, Robert Amar, Reginald Armour, Clinton Bernard, Ralph Brown, Kenneth Butcher, Alwin Chow, Gregory Delzin, Gordon Draper, Ameer Edoo, Joe Esau, Ishwar Galbaransingh, Dr Hamid Ghany, Dr Tim Gopeesingh, Dr Kusha Haracksingh, Justice Zainool Hosein-Russell Huggins, Brian Kuei Tung, Louis Lee Sing, Michael Mansoor, Professor Selwyn Ryan, Brian C. Lara, and several others who must surely have a casting ballot in the direction of the club. Gomez says that the other major cricket clubs in the region have similar policies, though expressed in varying degrees. The other clubs are the Kingston Cricket Club, which runs Sabina Park, the Georgetown Cricket Club, and the Pickwick Cricket Club, which has an "arrangement" with the Barbados Cricket Association over the Kensington Oval.

While the Queen's Park Cricket Club remains a club, and is thus entitled to the privileges of its status, the club's membership should be wary of going into the twenty-first century with an image of being a sportsman's retreat. The club's history alone, as rich as it is, follows an antiquated, colonial posture – which did not escape the eye of Chief Justice Michael De La Bastide when he addressed members at their annual dinner. De La Bastide also said that although he had never known the club to practise racial discrimination, maybe in the admissions process the ballots may have been influenced by "not so much racial, as what Lloyd Best calls tribal" prejudices. In any event, although the club is also home to other sports such as hockey, football, tennis, and cycling (which all have female participants), it is best known for its role in cricket. Indeed, the club had been the local cricket authority for decades until the effective establishment of the Trinidad and Tobago Cricket Board of Control in 1981.

It ought not to neglect the growing role of women in cricket. In his autobiography, *Hitting Across the Line*, Vivian Richards writes about his mixed feelings towards Lord's because of the rules debarring women from the Long Room. "Women have played a very important role in cricket, and for a long time, and deserve better rights of access to this place which is the very heart of cricket. It is a beautiful room and when you walk in there you are swamped with cricket history. We should not deny this pleasure to women along with the pleasure they would derive from being full members of the MCC", he writes, adding "I have seen quite a lot of women's cricket in England and the West Indies. There are some very good cricketers. I have certainly been entertained, on many occasions, by their skill and their talent has often surprised me."

In a loaded chapter called "Women's Cricket in West Indies Culture", in the book *Liberation Cricket*, historian Hilary Beckles traces the growth of women's cricket and complains that despite its steady and organized development, it has not brought them "into a close working relationship with their counterparts in the men's game". "They have never sat in session with the West Indies Cricket Board of Control to discuss matters of common interest. Neither has the WICBC expressed a policy position with regard to the active promotion of women's cricket. In individual territories, officials of men's cricket have expressed irritation over adjustment in competition schedules resulting from women's request for the use of first class grounds and other facilities."

Professor Beckles observes that the Kingston Cricket Club, "has maintained the century-old policy of not allowing women to use as equals the facilities of the members' pavilion. The members' bar, for instance, is considered off limits to women – even though they may be West Indies players. The same is true also for Queen's Park Cricket Club in Trinidad. Indeed, it was only in the 1980s that this policy, or custom, was fully removed from the Pickwick Cricket Club that manages the members' facilities at Kensington Oval in Barbados."

The Queen's Park Cricket Club has done a lot to develop cricket in the country, there is no denying that. The Oval grounds are beautiful, and the infrastructure itself, under the stewardship of the remarkable Gerry Gomez, has been modernized to keep up with changing needs. But while members celebrate their club's one hundredth anniversary at those lovely grounds, while they contemplate their constitution before the next annual general meeting in October, they might want to reconsider the value of going into the twenty-first century clad in eighteenth century garb.

Vaneisa Baksh

Appendix V

Gavaskar in the West Indies

This response by the author to Clifford Narinesingh's book Gavaskar: Portrait of a Hero *(Royards Publishing Co., Port of Spain, 1995) was delivered in Port of Spain at the Valley View Hotel in 1995*

Clifford Narinesingh's study of Sunil Gavaskar's life and career is part of a growing body of literature that challenges traditional approaches to analyses of West Indies cricket culture. It is an energetically written text that targets our understanding of why and how we have received cricket icons into our personal imagination and popular consciousness. It departs, therefore, from the main currents in West Indian cricket historiography, and sets us new conceptual agendas for our consideration. I can think of no West Indian cricket analyst who has produced a comprehensive, detailed, and philosophically meaningful account of a non-West Indian cricketer. There have been short narratives, and a few critical reflections, but nothing as major and important as this text. To my mind, it is an important and radical development which speaks to the growing maturity and universality of the West Indian literary vision. I am sure that with this lead we will be seeing more within this tradition in the future.

Important books in any field are usually characterized by an elegant display of a definite stamp of conceptual rigour and critical familiarity with the issues at hand. What Clifford has done here is to speak to the social history of cricket in the West Indies with a voice, and through vistas, that communicate a powerful sense of knowledge and feeling. For the first time, I am satisfied that Gavaskar's historic, liberating, and fulfilling intervention in the Caribbean mindscape and landscape is properly focused and understood. That it required a special investigation by an engaging mind is evident from the sociopolitical context and literary content of the intervention. Trinidad, and by extension, the West Indies cricket cultures, were changed for the better despite publicized views to the contrary. The calypsonians knew it; the public felt it, and Clifford to my satisfaction has documented and explained it.

Cricket books written by nonplayers are usually unbalanced celebrations of players, uncritical recollections of matches and events, viewed from the perspective of results and performance. What we have here, however, is something more sophisticated and valuable. Its centre stage is an historic moment, melodramatic in its theatrical content, and socially powerful in its ideological significance. Using cricket as a metaphor it invokes the history of East Indians in the West Indies and locates it at the centre of a narrative of contest and co-option that was not understood by the main actor, but which as we all know presented a complex political dilemma for all concerned. Could Gavaskar have done what he did on a debut tour of Australia or England? The counterfactual evidence suggests not. To what extent was he home away from home and received a welcome which only prodigals could understand? The evidence seems clear that he was claimed by Trinidad, and in a way, ironically, that Richards at a later date, against India, was not, or could not be claimed.

Clifford's language presumes the questions but takes the answers and deposits them at the back of the mind. It is clever, perhaps devious. But this book does not employ the language of the historian or the sports journalist. It is a magnetic language to which are attached a magnificent grasp of cricket detail and social reconstruction. Take for instance how he handles the John Snow incident at Lord's in 1971. I was there; I saw the event and read the press. I was a school boy who admired both men. I later met Snow when he joined Warwickshire and I was a youth player for the county. Clifford's language on pages 32–35 is poetic, befitting 'Snow', the accused, who I am sure you all know is an accomplished poet. Knowledge of events, processes, and contexts are conveyed with sensitivity, and Gavaskar will have to accept that his magic is now better understood. For this reason alone, it is a good book. The 'subject' of the text is opened to scrutiny, and the facts are enlivened by the power of sensitive, sincere social discourse. Many more questions can be asked. Could Clifford not take the thesis one step further and link Gavaskar's classical methodology and stoic manner to the scientific tenets and cultural history of the ancient civilization that threw him up, and across the oceans to its diaspora? Committed to a balanced analysis, he held his ground, and so he should, leaving the reader to dash down the wicket if so inclined. I am satisfied, that Gavaskar's method, his confidence, determination, and obsession with detail, has nothing to do with Hinduism, Brahminism, or his Bachelor's degree in Economics. Rohan Kanhai cannot be so described, but he possessed these skills of the artisan and artist in equal measure. That these men admire each other is not surprising; they are the two halves of the same process, separated by circumstances of history and social condition.

Clifford documents this relation between ancestral nation and emerging diaspora with considerable clarity. It's a dramatic and powerful history. That Gavaskar and Kanhai should lead their respective countries is significant in terms of the popular expectations of their respective political worlds; the movement from Kanhai to Jagan to Panday shows that the Caribbean circumstance is ultimately a liberating one, that can produce Sobers and Lara within a short time, and be modest enough to embrace and celebrate Gavaskar – an outsider – all at once. Watching Sunil bat always reminded me of my grandmother eating. Knife and fork gently held, every bone picked clean without noise, fuss or effort; a nerve racking, stomach heaving observation that disturbs the mind by its clinical efficiency, but pleases the spirit in its celebration of order, method, and purity.

I am not surprised that he chose to study microeconomics, while the results of his career indicate a preference for large numbers. It is the dialectics of the issue that constitute its gripping power. I welcome this contribution, therefore, for many reasons. It is a text that requires careful study and considerable reflection. There are many kites flown through its pages, and we now know what we have to do. The research process into cricket culture needs to be intensified, and those with clear vistas have responsibilities. This book tells all there is to know about runs, averages, and results. But that is only the necessary statistical scaffold for the great structure of sociological analysis and literary observations. Through Gavaskar's journey we come to learn much more about our own Caribbean world, the cricket culture we have democratized, redefined, and empowered, and how great men are elevated to excellence by circumstances beyond their comprehension.

Appendix VI

West Indies: Test Captains' Records

Complete up to and including Third Test vs Australia, January 1996

Captain	Tenure	Tests	Won	Lost	Drawn	Tied
Robert Nunes	1928–30	4	0	3	1	
Edward Hoad	1929–30	1	0	0	1	
Nelson Betancourt	1929–30	1	0	1	0	
Maurius Fernandes	1929–30	1	1	0	0	
George Grant	1930–35	12	3	7	2	
Rolph Grant	1939	3	0	1	2	
George Headley	1947–48	1	0	0	1	
Gerald Gomez	1947–48	1	0	0	1	
John Goddard	1947–57	22	8	7	7	
Jeffrey Stollmeyer	1951–55	13	3	4	6	
Denis Atkinson	1954–56	7	3	3	1	
Gerry Alexander	1957–60	18	7	4	7	
Frank Worrell	1960–63	15	9	3	2	1
Gary Sobers	1964–72	39	9	10	20	
Rohan Kanhai	1972–74	13	3	3	7	
Clive Lloyd	1974–85	74	36	12	26	
Alvin Kallicharran	1977–79	9	1	2	6	
Deryck Murray	1979–80	1	0	0	1	
Vivian Richards	1980–91	50	27	8	15	
Gordon Greenidge	1987–88	1	0	1	0	
Desmond Haynes	1989–91	4	1	1	2	
Richie Richardson	1991–95	24	11	6	7	
Courtney Walsh	1993–97	11	4	3	4	

DETAILS

Year	Opponent (HOME/AWAY)	Opposing captain	P	W	L	D	T
1. R.K. NUNES							
1928	Eng (A)	A.P.F. Chapman	3	0	3	0	

Year	Opponent (HOME/AWAY)	Opposing captain	P	W	L	D	T
R.K. NUNES cont'd							
1929–30	Eng (H)	F.S.G. Calthorpe	1	0	0	1	
	Total		4	0	3	1	
2. E.L.G. HOAD							
1929–30	Eng (H)	F.S.G. Calthorpe	1	0	0	1	
3. N. BETANCOURT							
1929–30	Eng (H)	F.S.G. Calthorpe	1	0	1	0	
4. M.P. FERNANDES							
1929–30	Eng (H)	F.S.G. Calthorpe	1	1	0	0	
5. G.C. GRANT							
1930–31	Aus (A)	W.M. Woodfull	5	1	4	0	
1933	Eng (A)	D.R. Jardine/ R.E.S. Wyatt	3	0	2	1	
1934–35	Eng (H)	R.E.S. Wyatt	4	2	1	1	
	Total		12	3	7	2	
6. R.S. GRANT							
1939	Eng (A)	W.R. Hammond	3	0	1	2	
7. G.A. HEADLEY							
1947–48	Eng (H)	K. Cranston	1	0	0	1	
8. G.E. GOMEZ							
1947–48	Eng (H)	G.O.B. Allen	1	0	0	1	
9. J.D.C. GODDARD							
1947–48	Eng (H)	G.O.B. Allen	2	2	0	0	
1948–49	Ind (A)	L. Armanath	5	1	0	4	
1950	Eng (A)	N.W.D. Yardley/ F. Brown	4	3	1	0	
1951–52	Aus (A)	A.L. Hassett/ A. Morris	4	1	3	0	
1951–52	NZ (A)	B. Sutcliffe	2	1	0	1	
1957	Eng (A)	P.B.H. May	5	0	3	2	
	Total		22	8	7	7	
10. J.B. STOLLMEYER							
1951–52	Aus (A)	A.L. Hassett	1	0	1	0	
1952–53	Ind (H)	V.S. Hazare	5	1	0	4	
1953–54	Eng (H)	L. Hutton	5	2	2	1	
1954–55	Aus (H)	I.W. Johnson	2	0	1	1	
	Total		13	3	4	6	

Year	Opponent (HOME/AWAY)	Opposing captain	P	W	L	D	T
11. D.S. ATKINSON							
1954–55	Aus (H)	I.W. Johnson	3	0	2	1	
1955–56	NZ (A)	J.R. Reid/					
		H.B. Cave	4	3	1	0	
	Total		7	3	3	1	
12. F.C.M. ALEXANDER							
1957–58	Pak (H)	A.H. Kardar	5	3	1	1	
1958–59	Ind (A)	P. Umrigar/Ghulam Ahmed/V. Mankad/ H.R. Adhikari	5	3	0	2	
1958–59	Pak (A)	Fazal Mahmood	3	1	2	0	
1959–60	Eng (H)	P.B.H. May/ M.C. Cowdrey	5	0	1	4	
	Total		18	7	4	7	
13. F.M.M. WORRELL							
1960–61	Aus (A)	R. Benaud	5	1	2	1	1
1961–62	Ind (H)	N.J. Contractor/ Nawab of Pataudi Jnr	5	5	0	0	
1963	Eng (A)	E.R. Dexter	5	3	1	1	
	Total		15	9	3	2	1
14. G.S. SOBERS							
1964–65	Aus (H)	R.B. Simpson	5	2	1	2	
1966	Eng (A)	M.C. Cowdrey/ M.J.K. Smith/ D.B. Close	5	3	1	1	
1966–67	Ind (A)	Nawab of Pataudi Jnr	3	2	0	1	
1967–68	Eng (H)	M.C. Cowdrey	5	0	1	4	
1968–69	Aus (A)	W.M. Lawry	5	1	3	1	
1968–69	NZ (A)	G.T. Dowling	3	1	1	1	
1969	Eng (A)	R. Illingworth	3	0	2	1	
1970–71	Ind (H)	A.L. Wadekar	5	0	1	4	
1971–72	NZ (H)	B.E. Congdon/ G. Dowling	5	0	0	5	
	Total		39	9	10	20	
15. R.B. KANHAI							
1972–73	Aus (H)	I.M. Chappell	5	0	2	3	
1973	Eng (A)	R. Illingworth	3	2	0	1	

Year	Opponent (HOME/AWAY)	Opposing captain	P	W	L	D	T
R.B. KANHAI cont'd							
1973–74	Eng (H)	M.H. Denness	5	1	1	3	
	Total		13	3	3	7	
16. C.H. LLOYD							
1974–75	Ind (A)	M.A.K. Pataudi/ S. Venkat	5	3	2	0	
1974–75	Pak (A)	Intikhab Alam	2	0	0	2	
1975–76	Ind (H)	B.S. Bedi	4	2	1	1	
1975–76	Aus (A)	G.S. Chappell	6	1	5	0	
1976	Eng (A)	A.W. Greig	5	3	0	2	
1976–77	Pak (H)	Mushtaq Mohammad	5	2	1	2	
1977–78	Aus (H)	R.B. Simpson	2	2	0	0	
1979–80	Aus (A)	G.S. Chappell	2	2	0	0	
1979–80	NZ (A)	G.P. Howarth	3	0	1	2	
1980	Eng (A)	I.T. Botham	4	1	0	3	
1980–81	Pak (A)	Javed Miandad	4	1	0	3	
1980–81	Eng (H)	I.T. Botham	4	2	0	2	
1981–82	Aus (A)	G.S. Chappell	3	1	1	1	
1982–83	Ind (H)	Kapil Dev	5	2	0	3	
1983–84	Ind (A)	Kapil Dev	6	3	0	3	
1983–84	Aus (H)	K.J. Hughes	4	3	0	1	
1984	Eng (A)	D.I. Gower	5	5	0	0	
1984–85	Aus (A)	A.R. Border/ K.J. Hughes	5	3	1	1	
	Total		74	36	12	26	
17. A.I. KALLICHARRAN							
1977–78	Aus (H)	R.B. Simpson	3	1	1	1	
1978–79	Ind (A)	S.M. Gavaskar	6	0	1	5	
	Total		9	1	2	6	
18. D.L. MURRAY							
1979–80	Aus (A)	G.S. Chappell	1	0	0	1	
19. I.V.A. RICHARDS							
1980	Eng (A)	I.T. Botham	1	0	0	1	
1983–84	Aus (H)	K.J.Hughes	1	0	0	1	
1984–85	NZ (H)	G.P. Howarth	4	2	0	2	
1985–86	Eng (H)	D.I. Gower	5	5	0	0	
1986–87	Pak (A)	Imran Khan	3	1	1	1	
1986–87	NZ (A)	J.V. Coney	3	1	1	1	

Year	Opponent (HOME/AWAY)	Opposing captain	P	W	L	D	T
I.V.A. RICHARDS cont'd							
1987–88	Ind (A)	D. Vengsarkar/ R. Shastri	4	1	1	2	
1987–88	Pak (H)	Imran Khan	2	1	0	1	
1988	Eng (A)	M.W. Gatting/ J.E. Emburey/ M.C. Cowdrey/ G.A. Gooch	5	4	0	1	
1988–89	Aus (A)	A.R. Border	5	3	1	1	
1988–89	Ind (H)	D.B. Vengsarkar	4	3	0	1	
1989–90	Eng (H)	G.A. Gooch/ A.J. Lamb	3	2	1	0	
1990–91	Aus (H)	A.R. Border	5	2	1	2	
1991	Eng (A)	G.A. Gooch	5	2	2	1	
	Total		50	27	8	15	
20. C.G. GREENIDGE							
1987–88	Pak (H)	Imran Khan	1	0	1	0	
21. D.L.HAYNES							
1989–90	Eng (H)	G.A. Gooch	1	0	0	1	
1990–91	Pak (A)	Imran Khan	3	1	1	1	
	Total		4	1	1	2	
22. R.B.RICHARDSON							
1991–92	RSA (H)	K.C. Wessels	1	1	0	0	
1992–93	Aus (A)	A.R. Border	5	2	1	2	
1992–93	Pak (H)	Wasim Akram	3	2	0	1	
1993–94	SL (A)	A. Ranatunga	1	0	0	1	
1993–94	Eng (H)	M.A. Atherton	4	3	1	0	
1994–95	Aus(H)	M.A. Taylor	4	1	2	1	
1995	Eng (A)	M.A. Atherton	6	2	2	2	
	Total		24	11	6	7	
23. C.A.WALSH							
1993–94	Eng (H)	M.A. Atherton	1	0	0	1	
1994–95	Ind (A)	M. Azharuddin	3	1	1	1	
1995–96	NZ (A)	K.R. Rutherford	2	1	0	1	
1995–96	NZ (H)	L.K. Germon	2	1	0	1	
1996–97	Aus (A)	M.A. Taylor	3	1	2	0	
	Total		11	4	3	4	

Amended slightly from an Internet contribution by Jeff Thomas
(jthomas@bmgtmail.umd.edu)

Appendix VII

Test Career Batting Averages for West Indian Players

Based on all matches up to and including Test #1391: Pakistan vs West Indies at Karachi, 3rd Test, 6 December 1997

Name	M	I	NO	Runs	HS	Ave	100	50	Ct	St
E.E. Achong	6	11	1	81	22	8.10	–	–	6	–
J.C. Adams	29	46	11	1991	208*	56.88	5	9	30	–
F.C.M. Alexander	25	38	6	961	108	30.03	1	7	85	5
Imtiaz Ali	1	1	1	1	1*	–	–	–	–	–
Inshan Ali	12	18	2	172	25	10.75	–	–	7	–
D.W. Allan	5	7	1	75	40*	12.50	–	–	15	3
I.B.A. Allen	2	2	2	5	4*	–	–	–	1	–
C.E.L. Ambrose	74	106	23	1105	53	13.31	–	1	14	–
K.L.T. Arthurton	33	50	5	1382	157*	30.71	2	8	22	–
N.S. Asgarali	2	4	0	62	29	15.50	–	–	–	–
D. St E. Atkinson	22	35	6	922	219	31.79	1	5	11	–
E. St E. Atkinson	8	9	1	126	37	15.75	–	–	2	–
R.A. Austin	2	2	0	22	20	11.00	–	–	2	–
S.F.A.F. Bacchus	19	30	0	782	250	26.06	1	3	17	–
L. Baichan	3	6	2	184	105*	46.00	1	–	2	–
E.A.E. Baptiste	10	11	1	233	87*	23.30	–	1	2	–
A.G. Barrett	6	7	1	40	19	6.66	–	–	–	–
I.M. Barrow	11	19	2	276	105	16.23	1	–	17	5
E.L. Bartlett	5	8	1	131	84	18.71	–	1	2	–
K.C.G. Benjamin	24	32	7	215	43*	8.60	–	–	2	–
W.K.M. Benjamin	21	26	1	470	85	18.80	–	2	12	–
C.A. Best	8	13	1	342	164	28.50	1	1	8	–
N. Betancourt	1	2	0	52	39	26.00	–	–	–	–
A.P. Binns	5	8	1	64	27	9.14	–	–	14	3
L.S. Birkett	4	8	0	136	64	17.00	–	1	4	–
I.R. Bishop	40	60	10	570	48	11.40	–	–	7	–
K.D. Boyce	21	30	3	657	95*	24.33	–	4	5	–

Name	M	I	NO	Runs	HS	Ave	100	50	Ct	St
C.O. Browne	13	20	6	250	39*	17.85	–	–	59	1
C.R. Browne	4	8	1	176	70*	25.14	–	1	1	–
B.F. Butcher	44	78	6	3104	209*	43.11	7	16	15	–
L.S. Butler	1	1	0	16	16	16.00	–	–	–	–
C.G. Butts	7	8	1	108	38	15.42	–	–	2	–
M.R. Bynoe	4	6	0	111	48	18.50	–	–	4	–
G.S. Camacho	11	22	0	640	87	29.09	–	4	4	–
F.J. Cameron	5	7	1	151	75*	25.16	–	1	–	–
J.H. Cameron	2	3	0	6	5	2.00	–	–	–	–
S.L. Campbell	26	45	2	1735	208	40.34	2	12	18	–
G.M. Carew	4	7	1	170	107	28.33	1	–	1	–
M.C. Carew	19	36	3	1127	109	34.15	1	5	13	–
G. Challenor	3	6	0	101	46	16.83	–	–	–	–
S. Chanderpaul	24	39	6	1607	137*	48.69	1	15	9	–
H.S. Chang	1	2	0	8	6	4.00	–	–	–	–
C.M. Christiani	4	7	2	98	32*	19.60	–	–	6	1
R.J. Christiani	22	37	3	896	107	26.35	1	4	19	2
C.B. Clarke	3	4	1	3	2	1.00	–	–	–	–
S.T. Clarke	11	16	5	172	35*	15.63	–	–	2	–
L.N. Constantine	18	33	0	635	90	19.24	–	4	28	–
C.E.H. Croft	27	37	22	158	33	10.53	–	–	8	–
C.E. Cuffy	3	5	2	6	3*	2.00	–	–	1	–
A.C. Cummins	5	6	1	98	50	19.60	–	1	1	–
O.C. DaCosta	5	9	1	153	39	19.12	–	–	5	–
W.W. Daniel	10	11	4	46	11	6.57	–	–	4	–
B.A. Davis	4	8	0	245	68	30.62	–	3	1	–
C.A. Davis	15	29	5	1301	183	54.20	4	4	4	–
W.W. Davis	15	17	4	202	77	15.53	–	1	10	–
F.I. deCaires	3	6	0	232	80	38.66	–	2	1	–
C.C. Depeiza	5	8	2	187	122	31.16	1	–	7	4
D.T. Dewdney	9	12	5	17	5*	2.42	–	–	–	–
R. Dhanraj	4	4	0	17	9	4.25	–	–	1	–
M.V. Dillon	3	5	1	25	21	6.25	–	–	–	–
U.G. Dowe	4	3	2	8	5*	8.00	–	–	3	–
P.J.L. Dujon	81	115	11	3322	139	31.94	5	16	267	5
R.M. Edwards	5	8	1	65	22	9.28	–	–	–	–
W. Ferguson	8	10	3	200	75	28.57	–	2	11	–
M.P. Fernandes	2	4	0	49	22	12.25	–	–	–	–
T.M. Findlay	10	16	3	212	44*	16.30	–	–	19	2
M.L.C. Foster	14	24	5	580	125	30.52	1	1	3	–
G.N. Francis	10	18	4	81	19*	5.78	–	–	7	–
M.C. Frederick	1	2	0	30	30	15.00	–	–	–	–
R.C. Fredericks	59	109	7	4334	169	42.49	8	26	62	–

APPENDIX VII: TEST CAREER BATTING AVERAGES

Name	M	I	NO	Runs	HS	Ave	100	50	Ct	St
R.L. Fuller	1	1	0	1	1	1.00	–	–	–	–
H.A. Furlonge	3	5	0	99	64	19.80	–	1	–	–
A.G. Ganteaume	1	1	0	112	112	112.00	1	–	–	–
J. Garner	58	68	14	672	60	12.44	–	1	42	–
B.B.M. Gaskin	2	3	0	17	10	5.66	–	–	1	–
G.L. Gibbs	1	2	0	12	12	6.00	–	–	1	–
L.R. Gibbs	79	109	39	488	25	6.97	–	–	52	–
O.D. Gibson	1	2	0	43	29	21.50	–	–	–	–
R. Gilchrist	13	14	3	60	12	5.45	–	–	4	–
G. Gladstone	1	1	1	12	12*	–	–	–	–	–
J.D.C. Goddard	27	39	11	859	83*	30.67	–	4	22	–
H.A. Gomes	60	91	11	3171	143	39.63	9	13	18	–
G.E. Gomez	29	46	5	1243	101	30.31	1	8	18	–
G.C. Grant	12	21	5	413	71*	25.81	–	3	10	–
R.S. Grant	7	11	1	220	77	22.00	–	1	13	–
A.H. Gray	5	8	2	48	12*	8.00	–	–	6	–
A.E. Greenidge	6	10	0	222	69	22.20	–	2	5	–
C.G. Greenidge	108	185	16	7558	226	44.72	19	34	96	–
G.A. Greenidge	5	9	2	209	50	29.85	–	1	3	–
M.G. Grell	1	2	0	34	21	17.00	–	–	1	–
A.F.G. Griffith	1	2	0	14	13	7.00	–	–	–	–
C.C. Griffith	28	42	10	530	54	16.56	–	1	16	–
H.C. Griffith	13	23	5	91	18	5.05	–	–	4	–
S.C. Guillen	5	6	2	104	54	26.00	–	1	13	3
W.W. Hall	48	66	14	818	50*	15.73	–	2	11	–
R.A. Harper	25	32	3	535	74	18.44	–	3	36	–
D.L. Haynes	116	202	25	7487	184	42.29	18	39	65	–
G.A. Headley	22	40	4	2190	270*	60.83	10	5	14	–
R.G.A. Headley	2	4	0	62	42	15.50	–	–	2	–
J.L. Hendriks	20	32	8	447	64	18.62	–	2	42	5
E.L.G. Hoad	4	8	0	98	36	12.25	–	–	1	–
R.I.C. Holder	8	13	2	321	91	29.18	–	2	7	–
V.A. Holder	40	59	11	682	42	14.20	–	–	16	–
M.A. Holding	60	76	10	910	73	13.78	–	6	22	–
D.A.J. Holford	24	39	5	768	105*	22.58	1	3	18	–
J.K. Holt Jnr	17	31	2	1066	166	36.75	2	5	8	–
C.L. Hooper	68	114	11	3531	178*	34.28	8	16	76	–
A.B. Howard	1	0	–	–	–	–	–	–	–	–
C.C. Hunte	44	78	6	3245	260	45.06	8	13	16	–
E.A.C. Hunte	3	6	1	166	58	33.20	–	2	5	–
L.G. Hylton	6	8	2	70	19	11.66	–	–	1	–
H.H.H. Johnson	3	4	0	38	22	9.50	–	–	–	–
T.F. Johnson	1	1	1	9	9*	–	–	–	1	–

APPENDIX VII: TEST CAREER BATTING AVERAGES

Name	M	I	NO	Runs	HS	Ave	100	50	Ct	St
C.E.L. Jones	4	7	0	63	19	9.00	–	–	3	–
P.E. Jones	9	11	2	47	10*	5.22	–	–	4	–
B.D. Julien	24	34	6	866	121	30.92	2	3	14	–
R.R. Jumadeen	12	14	10	84	56	21.00	–	1	4	–
A.I. Kallicharran	66	109	10	4399	187	44.43	12	21	51	–
R.B. Kanhai	79	137	6	6227	256	47.53	15	28	50	–
E.S.M. Kentish	2	2	1	1	1*	1.00	–	–	1	–
C.L. King	9	16	3	418	100*	32.15	1	2	5	–
F.M. King	14	17	3	116	21	8.28	–	–	5	–
L.A. King	2	4	0	41	20	10.25	–	–	2	–
C.B. Lambert	1	2	0	53	39	26.50	–	–	2	–
B.C. Lara	48	82	2	4133	375	51.66	10	20	62	–
P.D. Lashley	4	7	0	159	49	22.71	–	–	4	–
R.A. Legall	4	5	0	50	23	10.00	–	–	8	1
D.M. Lewis	3	5	2	259	88	86.33	–	3	8	–
R.N. Lewis	1	2	0	4	4	2.00	–	–	–	–
C.H. Lloyd	110	175	14	7515	242*	46.67	19	39	90	–
A.L. Logie	52	78	9	2470	130	35.79	2	16	57	–
E.D.A. St J. McMorris	13	21	0	564	125	26.85	1	3	5	–
C.A. McWatt	6	9	2	202	54	28.85	–	2	9	1
I.S. Madray	2	3	0	3	2	1.00	–	–	2	–
M.D. Marshall	81	107	11	1810	92	18.85	–	10	25	–
N.E. Marshall	1	2	0	8	8	4.00	–	–	–	–
R.E. Marshall	4	7	0	143	30	20.42	–	–	1	–
F.R. Martin	9	18	1	486	123*	28.58	1	–	2	–
E.A. Martindale	10	14	3	58	22	5.27	–	–	5	–
E.H. Mattis	4	5	0	145	71	29.00	–	1	3	–
I.L. Mendonca	2	2	0	81	78	40.50	–	1	8	2
C.A. Merry	2	4	0	34	13	8.50	–	–	1	–
R. Miller	1	1	0	23	23	23.00	–	–	–	–
E.A. Moseley	2	4	0	35	26	8.75	–	–	1	–
G.H. Mudie	1	1	0	5	5	5.00	–	–	–	–
D.A. Murray	19	31	3	601	84	21.46	–	3	57	5
D.L. Murray	62	96	9	1993	91	22.90	–	11	181	8
J.R. Murray	28	37	4	848	101*	25.69	1	3	92	3
R. Nanan	1	2	0	16	8	8.00	–	–	2	–
J.M. Neblett	1	2	1	16	11*	16.00	–	–	–	–
J.M. Noriega	4	5	2	11	9	3.66	–	–	2	–
R.K. Nunes	4	8	0	245	92	30.62	–	2	2	–
S.M. Nurse	29	54	1	2523	258	47.60	6	10	21	–
A.L. Padmore	2	2	1	8	8*	8.00	–	–	–	–
B.H. Pairaudeau	13	21	0	454	115	21.61	1	3	6	–

Name	M	I	NO	Runs	HS	Ave	100	50	Ct	St
D.R. Parry	12	20	3	381	65	22.41	–	3	4	–
C.C. Passailaigue	1	2	1	46	44	46.00	–	–	3	–
B.P. Patterson	28	38	16	145	21*	6.59	–	–	5	–
T.R.O. Payne	1	1	0	5	5	5.00	–	–	5	–
N. Phillip	9	15	5	297	47	29.70	–	–	5	–
L.R. Pierre	1	0	–	–	–	–	–	–	–	–
A.F. Rae	15	24	2	1016	109	46.18	4	4	10	–
S. Ramadhin	43	58	14	361	44	8.20	–	–	9	–
F.L. Reifer	2	4	0	48	29	12.00	–	–	3	–
I.V.A. Richards	121	182	12	8540	291	50.23	24	45	122	–
R.B. Richardson	86	146	12	5949	194	44.39	16	27	90	–
K.R. Rickards	2	3	0	104	67	34.66	–	1	–	–
C.A. Roach	16	32	1	952	209	30.70	2	6	5	–
A.M.E. Roberts	47	62	11	762	68	14.94	–	3	9	–
A.T. Roberts	1	2	0	28	28	14.00	–	–	–	–
W.V. Rodriguez	5	7	0	96	50	13.71	–	1	3	–
F.A. Rose	9	11	2	95	34	10.55	–	–	1	–
L.G. Rowe	30	49	2	2047	302	43.55	7	7	17	–
E.L. St Hill	2	4	0	18	12	4.50	–	–	–	–
W.H. St Hill	3	6	0	117	38	19.50	–	–	1	–
R.G. Samuels	6	12	2	372	125	37.20	1	1	8	–
R.O. Scarlett	3	4	1	54	29*	18.00	–	–	2	–
A.P.H. Scott	1	1	0	5	5	5.00	–	–	–	–
O.C. Scott	8	13	3	171	35	17.10	–	–	–	–
B.J. Sealey	1	2	0	41	29	20.50	–	–	–	–
J.E.D. Sealy	11	19	2	478	92	28.11	–	3	6	1
J.N. Shepherd	5	8	0	77	32	9.62	–	–	4	–
G.C. Shillingford	7	8	1	57	25	8.14	–	–	2	–
I.T. Shillingford	4	7	0	218	120	31.14	1	–	1	–
S. Shivnarine	8	14	1	379	63	29.15	–	4	6	–
P.V. Simmons	26	47	2	1002	110	22.26	1	4	26	–
C.K. Singh	2	3	0	11	11	3.66	–	–	2	–
J.A. Small	3	6	0	79	52	13.16	–	1	3	–
M.A. Small	2	1	1	3	3*	–	–	–	–	–
C.W. Smith	5	10	1	222	55	24.66	–	1	4	1
O.G. Smith	26	42	0	1331	168	31.69	4	6	9	–
G. St A. Sobers	93	160	21	8032	365*	57.78	26	30	109	–
J.S. Solomon	27	46	7	1326	100*	34.00	1	9	13	–
S.C. Stayers	4	4	1	58	35*	19.33	–	–	–	–
J.B. Stollmeyer	32	56	5	2159	160	42.33	4	12	20	–
V.H. Stollmeyer	1	1	0	96	96	96.00	–	1	–	–
J. Taylor	3	5	3	4	4*	2.00	–	–	–	–
P.I.C. Thompson	2	3	1	17	10*	8.50	–	–	–	–

Name	M	I	NO	Runs	HS	Ave	100	50	Ct	St
J. Trim	4	5	1	21	12	5.25	–	–	2	–
A.L. Valentine	36	51	21	141	14	4.70	–	–	13	–
V.A. Valentine	2	4	1	35	19*	11.66	–	–	–	–
C.L. Walcott	44	74	7	3798	220	56.68	15	14	53	11
L.A. Walcott	1	2	1	40	24	40.00	–	–	–	–
P.A. Wallace	1	2	0	13	8	6.50	–	–	1	–
CA Walsh	96	128	39	785	30*	8.82	–	–	19	–
C.D. Watson	7	6	1	12	5	2.40	–	–	1	–
E. deC. Weekes	48	81	5	4455	207	58.61	15	19	49	–
K.H. Weekes	2	3	0	173	137	57.66	1	–	–	–
A.W. White	2	4	1	71	57*	23.66	–	1	1	–
C.V. Wight	2	4	1	67	23	22.33	–	–	–	–
G.L. Wight	1	1	0	21	21	21.00	–	–	–	–
C.A. Wiles	1	2	0	2	2	1.00	–	–	–	–
E.T. Willett	5	8	3	74	26	14.80	–	–	–	–
A.B. Williams	7	12	0	469	111	39.08	2	1	5	–
D. Williams	6	12	1	144	48	13.09	–	–	21	2
E.A.V. Williams	4	6	0	113	72	18.83	–	1	2	–
S.C. Williams	22	37	2	859	128	24.54	1	2	20	–
K.L. Wishart	1	2	0	52	52	26.00	–	1	–	–
F.M.M. Worrell	51	87	9	3860	261	49.48	9	22	43	–

Compiled by J. McDonald and published on the Internet at www-usa.cricket.org/

Appendix VIII

Test Career Bowling Averages for West Indian Players

Based on all matches up to and including Test # 1396: West Indies vs England at Kingston, First Test, 29 January 1998

Name	Balls	M	Runs	W	Ave	Best	5	10	SR
E.E. Achong	918	34	378	8	47.25	2–64	–	–	114.7
J.C. Adams	1233	34	654	15	43.60	5–17	1	–	82.2
F.C.M. Alexander	0	–	–	–	–	–	–	–	–
Imtiaz Ali	204	10	89	2	44.50	2–37	–	–	102.0
Inshan Ali	3718	137	1621	34	47.67	5–59	1	–	109.3
D.W. Allan	0	–	–	–	–	–	–	–	–
I.B.A. Allen	282	4	180	5	36.00	2–69	–	–	56.4
C.E.L. Ambrose	16748	710	6705	307	21.84	8–45	18	3	54.5
K.L.T. Arthurton	473	14	183	1	183.00	1–17	–	–	473.0
N.S. Asgarali	0	–	–	–	–	–	–	–	–
D. St E. Atkinson	5201	311	1647	47	35.04	7–53	3	–	110.6
E. St E. Atkinson	1634	77	589	25	23.56	5–42	1	–	65.3
R.A. Austin	6	0	5	0	–	–	–	–	–
S.F.A.F. Bacchus	6	0	3	0	–	–	–	–	–
L. Baichan	0	–	–	–	–	–	–	–	–
E.A.E. Baptiste	1362	60	563	16	35.18	3–31	–	–	85.1
A.G. Barrett	1612	83	603	13	46.38	3–43	–	–	124.0
I. Barrow	0	–	–	–	–	–	–	–	–
E.L. Bartlett	0	–	–	–	–	–	–	–	–
K.C.G. Benjamin	4754	144	2619	89	29.42	6–66	4	1	53.4
W.K.M. Benjamin	3694	136	1648	61	27.01	4–46	–	–	60.5
C.A. Best	30	0	21	0	–	–	–	–	–
N. Betancourt	0	–	–	–	–	–	–	–	–
A.P. Binns	0	–	–	–	–	–	–	–	–
L.S. Birkett	126	1	71	1	71.00	1–16	–	–	126.0
I.R. Bishop	8113	281	3748	158	23.72	6–40	6	–	51.3
K.D. Boyce	3501	99	1801	60	30.01	6–77	2	1	58.3
C.O. Browne	0	–	–	–	–	–	–	–	–

Name	Balls	M	Runs	W	Ave	Best	5	10	SR
C.R. Browne	840	38	288	6	48.00	2–72	–	–	140.0
B.F. Butcher	256	15	90	5	18.00	5–34	1	–	51.2
L.S. Butler	240	7	151	2	75.50	2–151	–	–	120.0
C.G. Butts	1554	70	595	10	59.50	4–73	–	–	155.4
M.R. Bynoe	30	4	5	1	5.00	1–5	–	–	30.0
G.S. Camacho	18	1	12	0	–	–	–	–	–
F.J. Cameron	786	34	278	3	92.66	2–74	–	–	262.0
J.H. Cameron	232	6	88	3	29.33	3–66	–	–	77.3
S.L. Campbell	0	–	–	–	–	–	–	–	–
G.M. Carew	18	2	2	0	–	–	–	–	–
M.C. Carew	1174	46	437	8	54.62	1–11	–	–	146.7
G. Challenor	0	–	–	–	–	–	–	–	–
S. Chanderpaul	1068	32	524	5	104.80	1–2	–	–	213.6
H.S. Chang	0	–	–	–	–	–	–	–	–
C.M. Christiani	0	–	–	–	–	–	–	–	–
R.J. Christiani	234	1	108	3	36.00	3–52	–	–	78.0
C.B. Clarke	456	2	261	6	43.50	3–59	–	–	76.0
S.T. Clarke	2477	81	1169	42	27.83	5–126	1	–	58.9
L.N. Constantine	3583	125	1746	58	30.10	5–75	2	–	61.7
C.E.H. Croft	6165	211	2913	125	23.30	8–29	3	–	49.3
C.E. Cuffy	512	14	306	7	43.71	3–80	–	–	73.1
A.C. Cummins	618	11	342	8	42.75	4–54	–	–	77.2
O.C. DaCosta	372	13	175	3	58.33	1–14	–	–	124.0
W.W. Daniel	1754	60	910	36	25.27	5–39	1	–	48.7
B.A. Davis	0	–	–	–	–	–	–	–	–
C.A. Davis	894	32	330	2	165.00	1–27	–	–	447.0
W.W. Davis	2773	53	1472	45	32.71	4–19	–	–	61.6
F.I. deCaires	12	0	9	0	–	–	–	–	–
C.C. Depeiza	30	0	15	0	–	–	–	–	–
D.T. Dewdney	1641	65	807	21	38.42	5–21	1	–	78.1
R. Dhanraj	1087	32	595	8	74.37	2–49	–	–	135.8
M.V. Dillon	502	15	259	9	28.77	5–111	1	–	55.7
U.G. Dowe	1014	30	534	12	44.50	4–69	–	–	84.5
P.J.L. Dujon	0	–	–	–	–	–	–	–	–
R.M. Edwards	1311	25	626	18	34.77	5–84	1	–	72.8
W. Ferguson	2568	83	1165	34	34.26	6–92	3	1	75.5
M.P. Fernandes	0	–	–	–	–	–	–	–	–
T.M. Findlay	0	–	–	–	–	–	–	–	–
M.L.C. Foster	1776	106	600	9	66.66	2–41	–	–	197.3
G.N. Francis	1619	54	763	23	33.17	4–40	–	–	70.3
M.C. Frederick	0	–	–	–	–	–	–	–	–
R.C. Fredericks	1187	41	548	7	78.28	1–12	–	–	169.5
R.L. Fuller	48	2	12	0	–	–	–	–	–
H.A. Furlonge	0	–	–	–	–	–	–	–	–

Name	Balls	M	Runs	W	Ave	Best	5	10	SR
A.G. Ganteaume	0	–	–	–	–	–	–	–	–
J. Garner	13175	576	5433	259	20.97	6–56	7	–	50.8
B.B.M. Gaskin	474	24	158	2	79.00	1–15	–	–	237.0
G.L. Gibbs	24	1	7	0	–	–	–	–	–
L.R. Gibbs	27115	1313	8989	309	29.09	8–38	18	2	87.7
O.D. Gibson	204	3	132	2	66.00	2–81	–	–	102.0
R. Gilchrist	3227	124	1521	57	26.68	6–55	1	–	56.6
G. Gladstone	300	5	189	1	189.00	1–139	–	–	300.0
J.D.C. Goddard	2931	148	1050	33	31.81	5–31	1	–	88.8
H.A. Gomes	2401	79	930	15	62.00	2–20	–	–	160.0
G.E. Gomez	5236	289	1590	58	27.41	7–55	1	1	90.2
G.C. Grant	24	0	18	0	–	–	–	–	–
R.S. Grant	986	32	353	11	32.09	3–68	–	–	89.6
A.H. Gray	888	37	377	22	17.13	4–39	–	–	40.3
A.E. Greenidge	0	–	–	–	–	–	–	–	–
C.G. Greenidge	26	3	4	0	–	–	–	–	–
G.A. Greenidge	156	4	75	0	–	–	–	–	–
M.G. Grell	30	1	17	0	–	–	–	–	–
A.F.G. Griffith	0	–	–	–	–	–	–	–	–
C.C. Griffith	5631	177	2683	94	28.54	6–36	5	–	59.9
H.C. Griffith	2663	89	1243	44	28.25	6–103	2	–	60.5
S.C. Guillen	0	–	–	–	–	–	–	–	–
W.W. Hall	10421	312	5066	192	26.38	7–69	9	1	54.2
R.A. Harper	3615	183	1291	46	28.06	6–57	1	–	78.5
D.L. Haynes	18	0	8	1	8.00	1–2	–	–	18.0
G.A. Headley	398	7	230	0	–	–	–	–	–
R.G.A. Headley	0	–	–	–	–	–	–	–	–
J.L. Hendriks	0	–	–	–	–	–	–	–	–
E.L.G. Hoad	0	–	–	–	–	–	–	–	–
R.I.C. Holder	0	–	–	–	–	–	–	–	–
V.A. Holder	9095	367	3627	109	33.27	6–28	3	–	83.4
M.A. Holding	12680	458	5898	249	23.68	8–92	13	2	50.9
D.A.J. Holford	4816	164	2009	51	39.39	5–23	1	–	94.4
J.K. Holt Jnr	30	2	20	1	20.00	1–20	–	–	30.0
C.L. Hooper	8056	289	3492	65	53.72	5–26	3	–	123.9
A.B. Howard	372	16	140	2	70.00	2–140	–	–	186.0
C.C. Hunte	270	11	110	2	55.00	1–17	–	–	135.0
E.A.C. Hunte	0	–	–	–	–	–	–	–	–
L.G. Hylton	965	31	418	16	26.12	4–27	–	–	60.3
H.H.H. Johnson	789	37	238	13	18.30	5–41	2	1	60.6
T.F. Johnson	240	3	129	3	43.00	2–53	–	–	80.0
C.E.L. Jones	102	11	11	0	–	–	–	–	–
P.E. Jones	1842	64	751	25	30.04	5–85	1	–	73.6
B.D. Julien	4542	192	1868	50	37.36	5–57	1	–	90.8

APPENDIX VIII: TEST CAREER BOWLING AVERAGES

Name	Balls	M	Runs	W	Ave	Best	5	10	SR
R.R. Jumadeen	3140	140	1141	29	39.34	4–72	–	–	108.2
A.I. Kallicharran	406	14	158	4	39.50	2–16	–	–	101.5
R.B. Kanhai	183	8	85	0	–	–	–	–	–
E.S.M. Kentish	540	31	178	8	22.25	5–49	1	–	67.5
C.L. King	582	24	282	3	94.00	1–30	–	–	194.0
F.M. King	2869	140	1159	29	39.96	5–74	1	–	98.9
L.A. King	476	19	154	9	17.11	5–46	1	–	52.8
C.B. Lambert	4	0	4	1	4.00	1–4	–	–	4.0
B.C. Lara	60	1	28	0	–	–	–	–	–
P.D. Lashley	18	2	1	1	1.00	1–1	–	–	18.0
R.A. Legall	0	–	–	–	–	–	–	–	–
D.M. Lewis	0	–	–	–	–	–	–	–	–
R.N. Lewis	144	6	93	0	–	–	–	–	–
C.H. Lloyd	1716	75	622	10	62.20	2–13	–	–	171.6
A.L. Logie	7	1	4	0	–	–	–	–	–
E.D.A. McMorris	0	–	–	–	–	–	–	–	–
C.A. McWatt	24	2	16	1	16.00	1–16	–	–	24.0
I.S. Madray	210	6	108	0	–	–	–	–	–
M.D. Marshall	17584	613	7876	376	20.94	7–22	22	4	46.7
N.E. Marshall	279	22	62	2	31.00	1–22	–	–	139.5
R.E. Marshall	52	2	15	0	–	–	–	–	–
F.R. Martin	1346	27	619	8	77.37	3–91	–	–	168.2
E.A. Martindale	1605	40	804	37	21.72	5–22	–	–	43.3
E.H. Mattis	36	1	14	0	–	–	–	–	–
I.L. Mendonca	0	–	–	–	–	–	–	–	–
C.A. Merry	0	–	–	–	–	–	–	–	–
R. Miller	96	8	28	0	–	–	–	–	–
E.A. Moseley	522	13	261	6	43.50	2–70	–	–	87.0
G.H. Mudie	174	12	40	3	13.33	2–23	–	–	58.0
D.A. Murray	0	–	–	–	–	–	–	–	–
D.L. Murray	0	–	–	–	–	–	–	–	–
J.R. Murray	0	–	–	–	–	–	–	–	–
R. Nanan	216	7	91	4	22.75	2–37	–	–	54.0
J.M. Neblett	216	11	75	1	75.00	1–44	–	–	216.0
J.M. Noriega	1322	47	493	17	29.00	9–95	2	–	77.7
R.K. Nunes	0	–	–	–	–	–	–	–	–
S.M. Nurse	42	4	7	0	–	–	–	–	–
A.L. Padmore	474	23	135	1	135.00	1–36	–	–	474.0
B.H. Pairaudeau	6	0	3	0	–	–	–	–	–
D.R. Parry	1909	65	936	23	40.69	5–15	1	–	83.0
C.C. Passailaigue	12	0	15	0	–	–	–	–	–
B.P. Patterson	4829	109	2875	93	30.91	5–24	5	–	51.9
T.R.O. Payne	0	–	–	–	–	–	–	–	–
N. Phillip	1820	46	1042	28	37.21	4–48	–	–	65.0

Name	Balls	M	Runs	W	Ave	Best	5	10	SR
L.R. Pierre	42	0	28	0	–	–	–	–	–
A.F. Rae	0	–	–	–	–	–	–	–	–
S. Ramadhin	13939	813	4579	158	28.98	7–49	10	1	88.2
F.L. Reifer	0	–	–	–	–	–	–	–	–
I.V.A. Richards	5170	203	1964	32	61.37	2–17	–	–	161.5
R.B. Richardson	66	4	18	0	–	–	–	–	–
K.R. Rickards	0	–	–	–	–	–	–	–	–
C.A. Roach	222	5	103	2	51.50	1–18	–	–	111.0
A.M.E. Roberts	11135	382	5174	202	25.61	7–54	11	2	55.1
A.T. Roberts	0	–	–	–	–	–	–	–	–
W.V. Rodriguez	573	10	374	7	53.42	3–51	–	–	81.8
F.A. Rose	1351	40	682	26	26.23	6–100	–	–	51.9
L.G. Rowe	86	3	44	0	–	–	–	–	–
E.L. St Hill	558	29	221	3	73.66	2–110	–	–	186.0
W.H. St Hill	12	0	9	0	–	–	–	–	–
R.G. Samuels	0	–	–	–	–	–	–	–	–
R.O. Scarlett	804	53	209	2	104.50	1–46	–	–	402.0
A.P.H. Scott	264	9	140	0	–	–	–	–	–
O.C. Scott	1405	18	925	22	42.04	5–266	1	–	63.8
B.J. Sealey	30	1	10	1	10.00	1–10	–	–	30.0
J.E.D. Sealy	156	4	94	3	31.33	2–7	–	–	52.0
J.N. Shepherd	1445	70	479	19	25.21	5–104	1	–	76.0
G.C. Shillingford	1181	38	537	15	35.80	3–63	–	–	78.7
I.T. Shillingford	0	–	–	–	–	–	–	–	–
S. Shivnarine	336	10	167	1	167.00	1–13	–	–	336.0
P.V. Simmons	624	27	257	4	64.25	2–34	–	–	156.0
C.K. Singh	506	35	166	5	33.20	2–28	–	–	101.2
J.A. Small	366	11	184	3	61.33	2–67	–	–	122.0
M.A. Small	270	7	153	4	38.25	3–40	–	–	67.5
C.W. Smith	0	–	–	–	–	–	–	–	–
O.G. Smith	4431	229	1625	48	33.85	5–90	1	–	92.3
G. St A. Sobers	21599	974	7999	235	34.03	6–73	6	–	91.9
J.S. Solomon	702	39	268	4	67.00	1–20	–	–	175.5
S.C. Stayers	636	20	364	9	40.44	3–65	–	–	70.6
J.B. Stollmeyer	990	30	507	13	39.00	3–32	–	–	76.1
V.H. Stollmeyer	0	–	–	–	–	–	–	–	–
J. Taylor	672	33	273	10	27.30	5–109	1	–	67.2
P.I.C. Thompson	228	1	215	5	43.00	2–58	–	–	45.6
J. Trim	794	28	291	18	16.16	5–34	1	–	44.1
A.L. Valentine	12953	789	4215	139	30.32	8–104	8	2	93.1
V.A. Valentine	288	14	104	1	104.00	1–55	–	–	288.0
C.L. Walcott	1194	72	408	11	37.09	3–50	–	–	108.5
L.A. Walcott	48	1	32	1	32.00	1–17	–	–	48.0
P.A. Wallace	0	–	–	–	–	–	–	–	–

APPENDIX VIII: TEST CAREER BOWLING AVERAGES

Name	Balls	M	Runs	W	Ave	Best	5	10	SR
C.A. Walsh	20465	716	9104	353	25.79	7–37	15	2	57.9
C.D. Watson	1458	47	724	19	38.10	4–62	–	–	76.7
E. deC. Weekes	122	3	77	1	77.00	1–8	–	–	122.0
K.H. Weekes	0	–	–	–	–	–	–	–	–
A.W. White	491	27	152	3	50.66	2–34	–	–	163.6
C.V. Wight	30	1	6	0	–	–	–	–	–
G.L. Wight	0	–	–	–	–	–	–	–	–
C.A. Wiles	0	–	–	–	–	–	–	–	–
E.T. Willett	1326	78	482	11	43.81	3–33	–	–	120.5
A.B. Williams	0	–	–	–	–	–	–	–	–
D. Williams	0	–	–	–	–	–	–	–	–
E.A.V. Williams	796	46	241	9	26.77	3–51	–	–	88.4
S.C. Williams	18	0	19	0	–	–	–	–	–
K.L. Wishart	0	–	–	–	–	–	–	–	–
F.M.M. Worrell	7141	274	2672	69	38.72	7–70	2	–	103.4

Compiled by J. McDonald and published on the Internet at www-usa.cricket.org/

Bibliography

CRICKET AND SPORT MAGAZINES
Caribbean Cricket Quarterly
Cricket Digest
Cricketer
Cricketer Quarterly
Inside Edge
The Sportsman
Thirdman
West Indian Sportsman
West Indies Cricket Annual
Wisden Cricket Monthly
Wisden Cricketers' Almanack, 1929-1992

NEWSPAPERS
Advocate News (Barbados)
Barbados Mercury and Bridgetown Gazette (nineteenth century)
Caribbean Contact (Barbados)
Chronicle (Guyana)
Daily Gleaner (Jamaica)
Daily Nation (Barbados)
Daily Observer (Jamaica)
Daily Telegraph (England)
Dominica Star (Dominica)
Guardian (Trinidad and Tobago)
Independent (England)
Independent (Trinidad and Tobago)
Indian Express (India)
Manchester Guardian (England)
Observer (England)
Outlet (Antigua)
Sunday Express (Trinidad and Tobago)
Sunday Sun (Barbados)

Sunday Times (England)
The Times (Barbados – nineteenth century)
Voice (England)
Weekend Nation (Barbados)

BOOKS AND ARTICLES

Aberdeen, Sean. *Sir Garfield Sobers*. San Juan, Trinidad: Inprint Caribbean, 1987.

Adrien, Peter. "Moments in West Indies cricket". n.p., 1995.

Allison, Lincoln, ed. *The Politics of Sport*. London: Manchester University Press, 1986.

Altham, H.S., and E.W. Swanton. *A History of Cricket*. London: Allen and Unwin, 1948.

Anderson, Benedict. *Imagined Communities: Reflection on Origin and Spread of Nationalism*. London: Verso, 1983.

Archer, Robert, and Antoine Bouillon. *The South African Game: Sport and Racism*. London: Zed Books, 1983.

Arlott, John. *Cricket the Great Ones: Studies of the Eight Finest Batsmen of Cricket History*. London: Sportsman's Book Club, 1968.

Aspinall, Algernon E. *The British West Indies: Their History, Resources and Progress*. London: Pitman, 1912.

Bailey, Trevor. *Sir Gary*. Glasgow: Fontana-Collins, 1976.

Bailey, Jack. *Conflicts in Cricket*. London: Kingswood, 1989.

Bajnath, Hiralal. *West Indies Cricketers*. Port of Spain: Columbus Publishers, 1970.

Bannister, Jack. *Jack in the Box: A TV Commentator's Diary of England vs West Indies*. London: Queen Anne Press, 1992.

Bannister, Jack. *Brian Lara: The Story of a Record-Breaking Year*. London: Stanley Paul, 1994.

Barbados Cricket Association. *100 Years of Organised Cricket in Barbados*. Bridgetown: BCA, 1992.

Barker, J. *Summer Spectacular: The West Indies vs England 1963*. London: Collins, 1963.

Barker, John. *In the Main: West Indies vs MCC 1968*. London: Sportsman's Book Club, 1969.

Baxter, Peter, *England vs West Indies: Highlights since 1948*. London: BBC Books, 1991.

Beckford, George, "The dynamics of growth and the nature of metropolitan plantation enterprise". *Social and Economic Studies* 19, no. 4 (1970).

Beckles, Hilary McD. "The radical tradition in the culture of West Indies cricket". In *An Area of Conquest: Popular Democracy and West Indies Cricket Supremacy*, edited by H. Beckles, 42–54. Kingston: Ian Randle Publishers, 1994.

Beckles, Hilary McD., ed. *An Area of Conquest: Popular Democracy and West Indies Cricket Supremacy*. Kingston: Ian Randle Publishers, 1994.

Beckles, Hilary McD., and Brian Stoddart, eds. *Liberation Cricket: West Indies Cricket Culture*. London: Manchester University Press; Kingston: Ian Randle Publishers, 1995.

Beecher, Eric. *The Cricket Revolution*. London: Newspress, 1978.

Bell, Carl. *A Complete Statistical History of Shell Shield Cricket*. Kingston: Management Research and Computing Services, 1988.

Bell, Gordon. *Sir Garfield Sobers*. Middlesex: Nelson, 1978.

Benaud, Richie. *A Tale of Two Tests*. London: Hodder and Stoughton, 1962.

Benaud, Richie. *Willow Patterns*. London: Sportsman's Book Club, 1970.

Berry, Scyld. *Cricket Wallah, with England in India, 1981–82*. London: Hodder and Stoughton, 1982.

Best, Lloyd. "Outline of a model of pure plantation economy". *Social and Economic Studies* 17, no. 3, 1968.

Birbalsingh, Frank, and Clem Seecharan. *Indo-West Indian Cricket*. London: Hansib, 1988.

Birbalsingh, Frank. *The Rise of West Indian Cricket: From Colony to Nation*. St John's: Hansib, 1996.

Birley, Derek. *Sport and the Making of England*. London: Manchester University Press, 1993.

Bose, Mihir. *A History of Indian Cricket*. London: André Deutsch, 1990.

Botham, Ian. *My Autobiography*. London: Collins Willow, 1994.

Boycott, Geoff. *In the Fast Lane: West Indies Tour of 1981*. London: Arthur Baker, 1981.

Bradman, Don. *Farewell to Cricket*. London: Hodder and Stoughton, 1950.

Brathwaite, Edward. *The Arrivants: A New World Trilogy*. Oxford: Oxford University Press, 1981.

Burrowes, S. *George Headley*. London: Nelson, 1971.

Burton, Richard. "Cricket, carnival, and street culture in the Caribbean". In *Liberation Cricket: West Indies Cricket Culture*, edited by H. Beckles and B. Stoddart. London: Manchester University Press; Kingston: Ian Randle Publishers, 1995.

Butcher, Roland. *Rising to the Challenge*. London: Pelham, 1989.

Callinicos, Luli. *Gold and Workers, 1886–1924*. Johannesburg: Ravan Press, 1980.

Cameron, D.J. *Caribbean Crusade: The New Zealand Cricketers in the West Indies, 1972*. Newton Abbot: Devon Readers Union, 1974.

Caple, Canynge. *England vs The West Indies, 1895–1957*. Littleburg: Worcester Press, 1957.

Cardus, Neville. *English Cricket*. London: Collins, 1945.

Cashman, Richard, and M. McKernan, eds. *Sport: Money, Morality and the Media*. Brisbane: University of Queensland Press, 1981.

Chandler, Joan. *Television and National Sport: the USA and Britain*. Chicago: University of Illinois Press, 1988.

Chester, Revd Grenville John. *Transatlantic Sketches, 1869*. Reprint, Bridgetown: National Cultural Foundation, 1990.

Clarke, John, and Brian Scovell. *Everything That's Cricket: the West Indies Tour of 1966*. London: Stanley Paul, 1966.

Constantine, Learie. *Cricket and I*. London: Allan, 1933.

Constantine, Learie. *Cricket in the Sun*. London: Allan, 1947.

Constantine , Learie. *Cricketers' Carnival*. London: Stanley Paul, 1948.

Constantine, Learie. *Cricket Crackers*. London; New York: Stanley Paul, 1949.

Constantine, Learie. *The Young Cricketer's Companion: the Theory and Practice of Joyful Cricket*. London: Sportsman's Book Club, 1966.

Constantine, Learie, and Denzil Batchelor. *The Changing Face of Cricket*. London: Eyre and Spottiswoode, 1966.

Cotter, Gerry. *England vs West Indies: a History of Test Cricket and Other Matches*. Swindon: Crowood, 1991.

Coward, Mike. *Caribbean Odyssey*. London: Simon and Schuster, 1991.

Cozier, Tony. *The West Indies: Fifty Years of Test Cricket*. Newton Abbot: Devon Readers Union, 1978.

Cozier, Tony. *Supercat's Summer: the Inside Story of How the Windies Decimated Australian Cricket*. Melbourne: ACCA Sporting Publications, 1995.

Cummings, Christine. "The ideology of West Indies cricket". *Arena Review* 14, no. 1 (1990).

Dale, Harold. *Cricket Crusaders*. London: Laurie, 1952.

Dalrymple, Henderson. *50 Great West Indian Test Cricketers*. London: Hansib, 1983.

Goodwin, Clayton. *Caribbean Cricketers from the Pioneers to Packer*. London: Harrap, 1980.

Davie, Michael, and Simon Davie. *The Faber Book of Cricket*. London: Faber, 1987.

Davies, John. "Politics, sport and education in South Africa". *African Affairs* 85, no. 340 (1986).

Devonish, Hubert. "African and Indian consciousness at play: a study in West Indies cricket and nationalism". In *Liberation Cricket: West Indies Cricket Culture*, edited by H. Beckles and B. Stoddart. London: Manchester University Press; Kingston: Ian Randle Publishers, 1995.

Dobbs, Brian. *The Edwardians at Play, Sport 1890–1914*. London: Pelham, 1973.

D'Oliveira, Basil. *The D'Oliveira Affair*. London: Collins, 1969.

D'Oliveira, Basil. *Time to Declare: an Autobiography*. London: W.H. Allen, 1982.

Eagar, Patrick. *West Indian Summer: The Test Series of 1988*. London: Hodder and Stoughton, 1988.

Eastmond, Harold. *The Eastmond Book of Test Cricket Records, 1877–1955*. Barbados: Coles Printery, 1995.

Edmonds, Frances. *Another Bloody Tour: England in the West Indies, 1986*. London: Kingswood Press, 1986.

Ehimani, Kishore. *West Indies '76: India's Caribbean Adventure*. Calcutta: Nachiketa Publications, 1976.

Evans, Richard. *The Ultimate Test*. London: Partridge, 1990.

Eytle, Ernest. *Frank Worrell*. London: Hodder and Stoughton, 1963.

Fanon, Frantz. *The Wretched of the Earth*. London: Penguin, 1967.

Figueroa, John J. *West Indies in England: the Great Post-War Tours*. London: Kingswood Press, 1991.

Frewin, L. *The Poetry of Cricket*. London: MacDonald, 1965.

Frindall, Bill. *The Wisden Book of Test Cricket, 1876–1978*. London: Book Club Association, 1979

Garner, Joel. *'Big Bird' Flying High: an Autobiography*. London: A. Barker, 1988.

Gavaskar, Sunil. *Sunny Days: an Autobiography*. Calcutta: Rupa, 1984.

Gibbes, Michael. *Testing Time: The West Indies vs England 1974: an Account of the MCC Tour of the Caribbean*. San Fernando: Unique Services, 1975.

Gilchrist, Roy. *Hit Me For Six*. London: Stanley Paul, 1963.

Giuseppi, Undine. *Sir Frank Worrell*. London: Nelson, 1969.

Giuseppi, Undine. *A Look at Learie Constantine*. London: Nelson, 1974.

Gooch, Graham. *Testing Times*. London: Robson Books, 1992.

Goodwin, Clayton, *West Indians at the Wicket*. London: Macmillan, 1986.

Grace, John. *Wasim and Waqar: Imran's Inheritors*. London: Boxtree, 1992.

Grant, Jack. *Jack Grant's Story*. London: Lutterworth, 1980

Greenidge, Gordon. *Gordon Greenidge: the Man in the Middle*. Newton Abbott: David and Charles, 1980.

Griffith, Charles. *Chucked Around*. London: Pelham Books, 1970.

Grimshaw, Anna, ed. *C.L.R. James: Cricket*. London: Allison and Busby, 1986.

Guha, Ramachandra. *Wickets in the East: an Anecdotal History* Delhi: Oxford University Press, 1992.

Guha, Ramachandra. *Spin and Other Turns: Indian Cricket's Coming of Age*. New Delhi: Penguin, 1994.

Hain, Peter. *Don't Play with Apartheid*. London: Allen and Unwin, 1971.

Hall, Ken, Joe Farier, and Arnold Thomas. "The anti-apartheid campaign in the Caribbean: the case of sport". *Caribbean Journal of African Studies*, no. 1 (1978).

Hall, Stuart. "Cultural studies: two paradigms". In *Culture, Ideology and Social Process: A Reader*, edited by T. Bennett. London: Open University Press, 1981.

Hamilton, Bruce. *Cricket in Barbados*. Bridgetown: Advocate, 1947.

Hammond, Dave. *Foul Play: a Class Analysis of Sport*. London: Ubique Books, 1993.

Hargreaves, John. *Sport, Power and Culture*. Cambridge: Polity Press, 1986.

Harragin, Horace. *Sixty Years of Cricket: Australia vs. the West Indies*. Port of Spain: Paria Publishers, 1991.

Harris, Bruce. *West Indies Cricket Challenge*. London: Stanley Paul, 1957.

Harte, Chris. *A History of Australian Cricket*. London: André Deutsch, 1993.

Hector, Tim. "The roots of islands' cricket: acceptance at last after years of frustration". *The West Indies Cricket Annual, 1977*.

Hector, Tim. "West Indian nationalism, integration, and cricket politics". In *An*

Area of Conquest: Popular Democracy and West Indies Cricket Supremacy, edited by H. Beckles, 113–26. Kingston: Ian Randle Publishers, 1994.

Holding, Michael. *Whispering Death: the Life and Times of Michael Holding*. Kingston: West Indies Publishers, 1993.

Holt, Richard. *Sport and the British: a Modern History*. Oxford: Clarendon Press, 1989.

Howat, Gerald. *Plum Warner*. London: Unwin Hyman, 1987.

Howat, Gerald. *Learie Constantine*. London: Allen and Unwin, 1975.

Hunte, Conrad. *Coping with Black Agony*. Bridgetown: Cedar Press, 1977.

Hunte, Conrad. *Playing to Win*. London: Hodder and Stoughton, 1971.

James, C.L.R. *The Case for West Indian Self-Government*. London: Hogarth, 1933.

James, C.L.R. *Beyond a Boundary*. London: Hutchinson, 1963.

James, C.L.R. *The Black Jacobins: Toussaint L'Ouverture and the San Domingue Revolution*. New York, Vintage, 1963.

James, C.L.R. "The Caribbean confrontation begins". *Race Today* 2 (1970).

James, C.L.R. *The Future in the Present*. London: Allison and Busby, 1977.

James, C.L.R. *At the Rendezvous of Victory*. London: Allison and Busby, 1984.

James, C.L.R. *Spheres of Existence*. London: Allison and Busby, 1984.

James, C.L.R. *Cricket*. London: Allison and Busby, 1989.

John, Errol. *Moon on a Rainbow Shawl*. London: Faber and Faber, 1958.

Jones, Brunell. *Cricket Confusion: the 1978 West Indies vs Australia Series*. Curepe: Trinidad, Sports News Services, 1978.

Kanhai, Rohan. *Blasting for Runs*. London: Souvenir, 1966.

Keating, Frank. *Another Bloody Day in Paradise*. London: Deutsch, 1981.

Kidd, Bruce. "The campaign against sport in South Africa". *International Journal* 43, no. 4 (1988).

Landsberg, Pat. *The Kangaroo Conquers*. London: Museum Press, 1955.

Lapchick, Richard. "South Africa: sport and apartheid politics". *Annals* 445, 1979.

Lara, Brian, *Beating the Field*. London: Partridge, 1995.

Lawrence, Bridgette. *Diamond Jubilee of West Indian Test Cricket, 1928–1988*. London: Hansib, 1988.

Lawrence, Bridgette. *100 Great West Indian Test Cricketers: from Challenor to Richards*. London: Hansib, 1988.

Lawrence, Bridgette. *Master Class: the Biography of George Headley*. Leicester: Polar, 1995.

Lawrence, Bridgette, and Ray Goble. *The Complete Record of West Indian Cricketers*. London: A.C.L. and Polar, 1991.

Lazarus, Neil. "Cricket and national culture in the writing of C.L.R. James". In *Liberation Cricket: West Indies Cricket Culture*, edited by H. Beckles and B. Stoddart. London: Manchester University Press; Kingston: Ian Randle Publishers, 1995.

Lemmon, David. *Great One-day Cricket Matches*. London: Unwin Paperbacks, 1984.

Lewis, Tony. *Double-Century: the Story of MCC and Cricket*. London: Hodder and Stoughton, 1987.

Lloyd, Clive. *Living for Cricket*. London: Stanley Paul, 1980.

Lloyd, W. "The game in the Leewards and Windwards". *The West Indies Cricket Annual, 1977*.

Lowenthal, David. *West Indian Societies*. Oxford: Oxford University Press, 1972.

Mandle, W.F. "Cricket and Australian nationalism in the nineteenth century". *Journal of the Royal Australian Historical Society* 59, no. 4 (1973).

Mangan, J.A., ed. *Pleasure, Profit and Proselytism: British Culture and Sport at Home and Abroad*. London: Frank Cass, 1989.

Manley, Michael. *A History of West Indies Cricket*. London: André Deutsch, 1988.

Manley, Michael. "Cricket and West Indian society". In *An Area of Conquest: Popular Democracy and West Indies Cricket Supremacy*, edited by H. Beckles, 142–51. Kingston: Ian Randle Publishers, 1994.

Manning, Frank. "Celebrating cricket: the symbolic construction of Caribbean politics". In *Liberation Cricket: West Indies Cricket Culture*, edited by H. Beckles and B. Stoddart. London: Manchester University Press; Kingston: Ian Randle Publishers, 1995.

Marqusee, Mike. *Anyone But England: Cricket and the National Malaise*. London: Verso, 1994.

Marqusee, Mike. *War Minus the Shooting: a Journey Through South Asia During Cricket's World Cup*. London: Heinemann, 1996.

Marshall, Roy. *Test Outcast*. London: Pelham Books, 1970.

Marshall, Malcolm, *Marshall Arts: The Autobiography of Malcolm Marshall*. London: Queen Anne Press, 1987.

Marshall, Tony. "The management of West Indies cricket". In *An Area of Conquest: Popular Democracy and West Indies Cricket Supremacy*, edited by H. Beckles, 127–41. Kingston: Ian Randle Publishers, 1994.

Marshall, Trevor. "Ethnicity, class, and the democratization of West Indies cricket". In *An Area of Conquest: Popular Democracy and West Indies Cricket Supremacy*, edited by H. Beckles, 15–29. Kingston: Ian Randle Publishers, 1994.

Marshall, Woodville, K. "The Worrell-Sobers revolution". In *An Area of Conquest: Popular Democracy and West Indies Cricket Supremacy*, edited by H. Beckles, 30–41. Kingston: Ian Randle Publishers, 1994.

Martin-Jenkins, Christopher. *Testing Time: MCC in the West Indies*. London: Macdonald and Jane, 1974.

Martin-Jenkins, Christopher. *The Spirit of Cricket: a Personal Anthology*. London: Faber, 1994.

Mazrui, Ali. *Cultural Forces in World Politics*. London: James Currey, 1990.

McDonald, H.G. *The History of Kingston Cricket Club*. Kingston: Gleaner, 1938.

McDonald, Trevor. *Viv Richards*. London: Sphere Books, 1984.

McDonald, Trevor. *Clive Lloyd: The Authorised Biography*. London: Granada, 1985.

McLellan, Alistair. *The Enemy Within: the Impact of Overseas Players on English Cricket*. London: Blandford, 1994.

Meyer, Michael, ed. *Summer Days: Writers on Cricket*. London: Oxford University Press, 1983.

Miller, Keith. *Cricket from the Grandstand*. London: Sportsman's Book Club, 1960.

Mills, Gladstone. *Grist for the Mills: Reflections on a Life*. Kingston, Ian Randle Publishers, 1994.

Mosey, Don. *The Wisden Book of Captains on Tour: Test Cricket, 1946–1989*. London: Stanley Paul, 1990.

Moyes, Alban. *With the West Indies in Australia, 1960–61: a Critical Story of the Tour*. London: Heinemann, 1961.

Naipaul, V.S. *The Middle Passage*. London: Penguin, 1962.

Narinesingh, Clifford. *Gavaskar: Portrait of a Hero*. Port of Spain: Royards Publishers, 1995.

Nicole, Christopher. *West Indian Cricket: the Story of Cricket in the West Indies*. London: Sportsman's Book Club, 1960.

Patterson, Orlando. "The ritual of cricket". In *Liberation Cricket: West Indies Cricket Culture*, edited by H. Beckles and B. Stoddart. London: Manchester University Press; Kingston: Ian Randle Publishers, 1995.

Pearce, F.L., and T.L. Roxburgh. *The Jamaica Cricket Annual*. Kingston: DeSouza, 1897.

Pilgrim, Torrey. *Sir Frank Worrell Pictorial*. New York: Innovation Services, 1992.

Pollard, Jack. *The Complete Illustrated History of Australian Cricket*. New York: Viking, 1992.

Proctor, Mike. *South Africa: the Years of Isolation and Return to International Cricket*. London: Queen Anne Press, 1994.

Queen's Park Cricket Club. *The Queen's Park Cricket Club Diamond Jubilee, 1896–1956*. Port of Spain: QPCC, 1956.

Rajan, Sunder. *India vs West Indies, 1974–1975*. Bombay: Jaico Publisher, 1975.

Richards, Jimmy. *Red Stripe Statistics of West Indies Cricket, 1865–1989*. Kingston: Heinemann, 1990.

Richards, Viv. *Viv Richards*. London: W.H. Allen, 1982.

Richards, Viv. *Hitting Across the Line*. London: Headline Books, 1991.

Roberts, E.L. *Test Cavalcade, 1877–1947*. London: Arnold, 1948.

Rodney, Walter. *Groundings with My Brothers*. London: Bogle L'Ouverture, 1970.

Roebuck, Peter. *Tangled Up In White*. London: Hodder and Stoughton, 1992.

Rohlehr, Gordon. "Music, literature, and West Indies cricket values". In *An Area of Conquest: Popular Democracy and West Indies Cricket Supremacy*, edited by H. Beckles, 55–102. Kingston: Ian Randle Publishers, 1994.

Ross, Alan. *The Cricketer's Companion*. London: Bibliographic Books, 1986.

Ross, Alan. *Through the Caribbean: England in the West Indies, 1960*. London: Pavilion Library, 1986.

Ross, Alan. *West Indies at Lord's*. London: Constable, 1986.

Ross, Gordon. *A History of West Indies Cricket*. London: A. Barker, 1976.

Rundell, Michael. *The Dictionary of Cricket*. London: George Allen and Unwin, 1985.

Said, Edward. *Culture and Imperialism*. London: Chatto and Windus, 1993.

Sandiford, Keith. "Cricket and the Barbadian society". *Canadian Journal of History* (December 1986).

Sandiford, Keith. *Cricket and the Victorians*. London: Scolar Press, 1994.

Sandiford, Keith. "Imperialism, colonial education and the origins of West Indian cricket". In *An Area of Conquest: Popular Democracy and West Indies Cricket Supremacy*, edited by H. Beckles, 1–14. Kingston: Ian Randle Publishers, 1994.

Sandiford, Keith, and Brian Stoddart. "The elite schools and cricket in Barbados: a study in colonial continuity". In *Liberation Cricket: West Indies Cricket Culture*, edited by H. Beckles and B. Stoddart. London: Manchester University Press; Kingston: Ian Randle Publishers, 1995.

Sanyal, Saradindu. *India-West Indies Test Cricket, 1948–1971*. Delhi: Macmillan, 1974.

Savidge, Michélle. *Real Quick: a Celebration of the West Indies Pace Quartets*. London: Blandford, 1995.

Scott, Neville, and Nick Cook. *England Test Cricket: the Years of Indecision*. London: Kingswood, 1992.

Searle, Chris. "Race before cricket: cricket, empire and the White Rose". *Race and Class* 31 (1990).

Soares, Dave. "A history of the Melbourne Cricket Club, 1892–1962". MA thesis, Department of History, University of the West Indies, Mona, Jamaica, 1987.

Sobers, Garfield. *Cricket Crusade*. London: Pelham Books, 1966.

Sobers, Garfield. *Bonaventure and the Flashing Blade*. London: Pelham, 1967.

Sobers, Garfield. *Gary Sobers' Most Memorable Matches*. London: Stanley Paul, 1984.

Sobers, Garfield. *Sobers: Twenty Years at the Top*. London: Macmillan, 1988.

Sobers, Garfield. *Sobers: the Changing Face of Cricket*. London: Ebury Press, 1996.

Soomer, June. "Cricket and the origins of Federation Organization". In *An Area of Conquest: Popular Democracy and West Indies Cricket Supremacy*, edited by H. Beckles, 103–12. Kingston: Ian Randle Publishers, 1994.

Spivak, Gayatri. *Nationalist Thought and the Colonial World*. London: Zed Books, 1986.

St John, Bruce. "Cricket". *Bumbatuk* (Bridgetown) 1 (1982).

St Pierre, Maurice. "West Indies cricket: a cultural contradiction?" *Arena Review* 14, no. 1 (1990).

St Pierre, Maurice. "West Indian cricket – Part 1: a socio-historical appraisal". In *Liberation Cricket: West Indies Cricket Culture*, edited by H. Beckles and B. Stoddart. London: Manchester University Press; Kingston: Ian Randle Publishers, 1995.

St Pierre, Maurice. "West Indian cricket – Part 2: "An aspect of creolization". In *Liberation Cricket: West Indies Cricket Culture*, edited by H. Beckles and

B. Stoddart. London: Manchester University Press; Kingston: Ian Randle Publishers, 1995.

Steen, Rob. *Desmond Haynes: Lion of Barbados*. London: Witherby, 1993.

Stoddart, Brian. "Caribbean cricket: the role of sport in emerging small-nation politics". *International Journal* 43, no. 3 (1981).

Stoddart, Brian. "Cricket and colonialism in the English-speaking Caribbean to 1914: towards a cultural analysis". In *Liberation Cricket: West Indies Cricket Culture*, edited by H. Beckles and B. Stoddart. London: Manchester University Press; Kingston: Ian Randle Publishers, 1995.

Stoddart, Brian. "Cricket, social formation, and cultural continuity in Barbados: a preliminary ethnohistory". In *Liberation Cricket: West Indies Cricket Culture*, edited by H. Beckles and B. Stoddart. London: Manchester University Press; Kingston: Ian Randle Publishers, 1995.

Stollmeyer, Jeffrey. *Everything Under the Sun*. London: Stanley Paul, 1983.

Surin, Keith. "C.L.R. James' material aesthetic of cricket". In *Liberation Cricket: West Indies Cricket Culture*, edited by H. Beckles and B. Stoddart. London: Manchester University Press; Kingston: Ian Randle Publishers, 1995.

Swanton, E.W. *West Indian Adventure: with Hutton's MC Team, 1953–54*. London: Museum Press, 1954.

Swanton, E.W. *The Test Matches of 1956*. London: Daily Telegraph, 1956.

Swanton, E.W. *West Indies Revisited: the MCC Tour of 1959/60*. London: Heinemann, 1960.

Swanton, E.W., and George Plumtree, eds. *Barclays World of Cricket: the Game from A–Z*. London: Willow Books, 1986.

Tennant, Ivo. *Frank Worrell: a Biography*. Cambridge: Lutterworth, 1989.

Thompson, L. O'Brien. "How cricket is West Indian cricket? Class, racial and colour conflict". In *Liberation Cricket: West Indies Cricket Culture*, edited by H. Beckles and B. Stoddart. London: Manchester University Press; Kingston: Ian Randle Publishers, 1995.

Tiffin, Helen. "Cricket, literature, and the politics of decolonisation: the case of C.L.R. James". In *Liberation Cricket: West Indies Cricket Culture*, edited by H. Beckles and B. Stoddart. London: Manchester University Press; Kingston: Ian Randle Publishers, 1995.

Tresidder, Phil. *Captains on a See-Saw: the West Indies Tour of Australia, 1968–69*. London: Souvenir Press, 1969.

Walcott, Clyde. *Island Cricketers*. London: Hodder and Stoughton, 1958.

Wallerstein, Immanuel. *The Politics of the World Economy*. Cambridge: Cambridge University Press, 1984.

Wallerstein, Immanuel. "The national and the universal: can there be such a thing as world culture". In *Culture, Globalization and the World Economy*, edited by A.D King. London: Macmillan, 1991.

Wanderers Cricket Club (Barbados) Centenary, 1877–1977. Barbados: WCC, 1977.

Warner, Pelham Francis. *Cricket Between Two Wars*. London: Chatto and Windus, 1942.

Warner, Pelham Francis. *Lord's 1787–1945*. London: Harrap, 1946.

Warner, Pelham Francis. *Long Innings: the Autobiography of Sir Pelham Warner*. London: Harrap, 1951.

Waugh, Steve. *The West Indies Tour Diary, 1995*. Sydney: Harper Sports, 1995.

West Indian Commission. *Time for Action: Report of the West Indian Commission*. Barbados: West Indian Commission, 1992.

Wheeler, Paul. *Bodyline: the Novel*. London: Faber, 1983.

White, Noel. *George 'Atlas' Headley*. Kingston: Institute of Jamaica, 1974.

Whitington, R. *Fours Galore: the West Indians and Their Tour of Australia, 1968–69*. Melbourne: Cassell, 1969.

Wilde, Simon. *Letting Rip: the Fast Bowling Threat from Lillee to Waqar*. London: Witherby, 1994.

Williams, Raymond. *Culture and Society, 1780–1958*. London: Chatto and Windus, 1958.

Wolstenholme, Gerry. *The West Indies Tour of England, 1906*. Blackpool: Nelson, 1992.

Wooldridge, Ian. *Cricket Lovely Cricket*. London: Robert Hale, 1963.

Worrell, Frank. *Cricket Punch*. London: Stanley Paul, 1959.

Wright, Graeme. *Betrayal: the Struggle for Cricket's Soul*. London: Witherby, 1993.

Wyatt, George. *The Tour of the West Indies Cricketers, August and September, 1886*. Demerara: Argosy Press, 1887.

Yelvington, Kevin. "Ethnicity 'not out': the Indian cricket tour of the West Indies and the 1976 elections in Trinidad and Tobago". In *Liberation Cricket: West Indies Cricket Culture*, edited by H. Beckles and B. Stoddart. London: Manchester University Press; Kingston: Ian Randle Publishers, 1995.

Index

Photographs are indicated by bold page numbers

73, 76, 82, 94, 123, 157, 160, 173, 174,
181, 183, 196
Tyldesley, Ernest, 45, 47

Underwood, Derek, 87
University of the West Indies (UWI), xi, xii,
77, 81, 168
UWI Vice Chancellor's XI game, xii, 97

Valentine, Alf, 109
Valentine, V.A., **139**
Vere and Clarendon Cricket Club, 7, 10
"Viv Richards", 111

Walcott, Clyde, 93, 103, 151; as cricket
administrator, 185–187, 192–193
Walcott, Frank, 154
Wanderers Cricket Club, 8, 10, 17, 42, 46
Warner, Aucher, 37
Warner, R.S., 27
Warner, Sir Pelham 'Plum', 24, 27, 35, 39,
44, 45, 47, 48; early years, 35–37; social
agenda, 39–42, 51–57; working to inte-
grate black players, 25–27
Weekes, Everton D., 93, **137**, **142**
Weight, C.V., **138**
West India Committee, 5, 16
West Indian Commission, 81, 82
West Indianization. *See* West Indianness.
West Indianness, 1, 15–16, 18
West Indies Cricket Board (WICB), 15, 77,
80, 81, 93, 94, 95, 96, 129, 145, 146, 151,
155, 156, 158, 159, 160, 161, 162, 168
West Indies Cricket Board of Control
(WICBC). *See* West Indies Cricket
Board (WICB).
West Indies cricket culture, x, xiv–xix, 1–5,
15–18, 35–36, 39–41, 69–72, 86–94,
101–103, 117, 145–147, 168–169,
177–178, 187–193, 198–200; Cable and
Wireless as sponsors, 191; drug testing,
193; West Indies vs South Africa in
Barbados, 165–168; emergence of black
players, 25–27; first tour to England,
1906, 28–29; gender bias, 117; importance of the crowd, 116; introduction of
cricket, 1–2, 8, 10; lectures on cricket,
xi, 173–179, 190; tension between paradigms, 94–97; the importance of the
crowd, 108–115; values in the élite
schools, 36–37; West Indies vs South
Africa Test, 80–81. *See also* Sobers,
Gary, 'Sobers Affair', *and* Cummins,

Andy: 'Andy Cummins Affair'.
West Indies Federation, 76
West Indies touring teams: 61; 1886 West
Indies tour of North America, 19–21;
first tour (to England), 27; record book,
for England 1928 tour, **138**; souvenir
programme 1950, 140; team photograph 1957, 140; to Australia 1930–31,
50–51, 66, 67; to Australia 1960–61, 82;
to Australia 1975–76, 85; to England
1900, 43, 54; to England 1906, 28, 39,
43, 46, 54; to England 1923, 44, 46, 47;
to England 1928, 33, 47, 61, 63, **138**;
tour results 1906, 31; 1929–30, 49; to
England 1933, 51, 52–54, 64, 65, 67,
139, ; to England 1939, 55,, 62, 64, 65,
68; to England 1950, 108; to England
1957, 138, 141, **142**; to England 1976,
85; to England 1984, 84
Whispering Death, 96
Wiles, C.A., 47, **139**
Williams, Grace, 131
Willis, Bob, 86
Windward Islands, 10
Windwards Cricket Club, 8
Wisden, 27, 38
Wolstenholme, Gerry, 31
Women's cricket, **143**, **144**; and apartheid,
159; World Cup, 159
Women's cricket: batting averages for
JWCA 1968 season, 124; bowling aver-
ages for JWCA 1968 season, 125; first
West Indies women's cricket team 1976,
130; first women's Test match, 121;
media treatment, 131–133; 1979 Test
team, **144**; organizations, 121–124, 127,
132; regional expansion of, 126–131,
191; World Cup, 125, 126, 130, 132
Wood, S., 25, 27
Woods, J., 39, 41–42
Workers' Voice, 155
World Cup (men's), 82, 96, 165
"World Cup", 111
Worrell, Frank, 44, 52, 79, 83, 86, 93, 94,
136, **137**, **142**, 149, 151, 152, 153, 169,
174, 178, 187, 188; fight for his leadership of the West Indies team , xvii,
75–78, 177
Worrell–Sobers axis, 183
Wyatt, George, 19–21, 22, 23

Young America Cricket Club, 20